Contents

Preface 5

PART – 1

Introduction, Key Concepts, and Strategy Development

Chapter – 1   What is Strategy? 11
Chapter – 2   Strategy Management – Key Concepts You
                Should Know 15
Chapter – 3   Strategy Development..43

PART – 2

Strategy Execution Using Balanced Scorecard

Chapter – 4   What is Strategy Execution, and Why is it
                Important? 59
Chapter – 5   Problems with Traditional Strategy Execution 61
Chapter – 6   Introducing Balanced Scorecard...................................67
Chapter – 7   Strategy Maps 79
Chapter – 8   Strategic Objectives and Strategic Themes 87
Chapter – 9   Performance Measures..91
Chapter – 10   Strategic Initiatives 101
Chapter – 11   Implementing Balanced Scorecard................................107

PART – 3

Balanced Scorecards for Corporate and Support Functions

Chapter – 12   Evolution of Corporates..117
Chapter – 13   Alignment and Cascading of Strategy...........................121
Chapter – 14   Corporate Scorecard..127

Chapter – 15   HR Function Scorecard.. 135
Chapter – 16   IT Function Scorecard... 141
Chapter – 17   Finance Function Scorecard... 145
Chapter – 18   Procurement Function Scorecard 149
Chapter – 19   Implementing and Evaluating the
                Balanced Scorecard... 155

PART – 4
Balanced Scorecard for Nonprofit Organizations and the Triple Bottom Line

Chapter – 20   Balanced Scorecard for Nonprofit Organizations.......167
Chapter – 21   Incorporating the Triple Bottomline and CSR
                in the Balanced Scorecard 173

PART – 5
Case Study

Chapter – 22   Implementing a Strategy Map and Balanced
                Scorecard in a Commercial Organization 185

PART – 6
Appendices

Appendix – A... 197
Appendix – B... 233
Appendix – C... 245
Appendix – D: Commonly Used KPIs.. 257
Selected Bibliography 267

MASTERING STRATEGIC EXCELLENCE

Your Success Guide to Growth and Profitability Using

Balanced Scorecard

Gopal Sharma

Preface

This is my first book! For some reason, I always wanted to write a book. If I look back at my life, it appears to be running on a perfectly written script. I was good in studies and wanted to become an engineer or a doctor (those days, these were the only two professions available in the science stream. By the time I completed engineering, I wanted to travel the world and do my MBA. By the time I graduated, I had my passport ready. Within six months after graduation, I got an employment opportunity to work in the Middle East (Abu Dhabi). Among the finalists, I was the only candidate who had a passport and I landed the job. For next 20 years I worked in facility management and engineering construction field. I worked on some of the most prestigious projects in the UAE. I got an opportunity to do my MBA in the year 1998 and completed in 2000. It took 4 years to transit from engineering/project management role to management role. A chance opportunity landed me a role in strategy function within my employer organization. During 2004–05 I bought all the books written my Kaplan and Norton and implemented first Balanced Scorecard in my organization. To gain further knowledge, I attended 5-days Kaplan & Norton BSC Bootcamp in Dubai and within a year, I left my full-time job. For the next 15 years, I worked as an independent consultant implementing Balanced Scorecards in dozens of organizations across Middle East and India. During this period, I also got an opportunity to assess more than 15 organizations (for both MBNQA and EFQM Business Excellence frameworks) across different industries in UAE and India.

This book is based my real experience of implementing Balanced Scorecard and I have written this book as a practitioner and not as an academician. This book is not about the theory of strategy and evolution of Balanced Scorecard. It is about strategy and its execution in the real world.

Why this book should interest you?

Poor performance is failing organizations and businesses worldwide, especially due to the reasons that are manageable. Research has proved again and again that having a clearly articulated mission, vision, and long-term strategy; and implementing the same diligently, help an organization in long-term sustenance and delivering superior performance. Most of the organizations either do not have these critical elements or they do not know the purpose and how to link them to long-term strategy and daily activities. Our experience shows that the focus is mostly on year-on-year business planning rather than long-term strategy planning.

Implementing a streamlined process for strategy management can help any organization in developing long-term strategy and align its daily activities to the organization's strategic objectives.

Major Benefits of Implementing Balanced Scorecard

The Balanced Scorecard helps aligning and integrating your actions, resources, internal processes and customer value proposition to achieve planned financial objectives. The major benefits of implementing Balanced Scorecard framework can be under three main categories:

1. Developing and aligning your organization's Mission, Vision and strategy helps you in staying focused on your long-term strategy and achieving your vision and financial outcomes.
2. Balanced Scorecard describes the strategy by linking tangible and intangible assets in value creating activities, the focus shifts to enablers and resolve matter or concern proactively.
3. Since Balanced Scorecard combines traditional financial measures and other non-financial measures, consolidated

performance data are available for periodic review to enable you to take proactive actions beforehand to address gaps in performance.

4. Balanced Scorecard instils a sense of accountability and responsibility (being process owners and measure owners) among employees and management towards organization's performance.

5. Balanced Scorecard helps aligning all initiatives and action plans to organizations' long-terms strategy.

PART – 1

Introduction, Key Concepts, and Strategy Development

Chapter – 1

What is Strategy?

The Origin of Strategy

The word *Strategy* is derived from the ancient Athenian word *strategos.* Strategos was a compound of *stratos,* which meant an encamped army spread out over the ground. The emergence of the term coincided with the increased complexity in war units and military decision-making and reflected on the overall game plan for winning the war.

A similar parallel can be drawn in the business environment. But it is not possible to provide a simple definition. Some of the elements of strategy-making are universal. However, other elements are heavily dependent on the nature of the firm, its constituencies, its structure, and its culture.

The Six Dimensions of Strategy[1]

If a strategy provides a sense of unity, direction, and purpose, as well as facilitates the necessary changes induced by a firm's environment; the following six critical dimensions must be included in any unified definition of the concept of strategy.

- Strategy as a coherent, unifying, and integrative pattern of decisions
- Strategy as a means of establishing an organization's purpose in terms of its long-term objectives
- Strategy as a definition of a firm's competitive domain

---

1   Wahl, M.; Prause, G. 2013. Toward understanding resources, competencies, and capabilities: a business model generation approach, Entrepreneurship and Sustainability Issues 1(2): 67–80. http://dx.doi.org/10.9770/jesi.2013.1.2(1)

- Strategy as a response to external opportunities and threats and to internal strengths and weaknesses as a means of achieving a competitive advantage
- Strategy as a logical system of differentiating managerial tasks at corporate, business, and functional levels
- Strategy as a definition of the economic and noneconomic contribution the firm intends to make to its stakeholders

To me, the simple definition of strategy would be:

"A strategy is an integrated set of choices that position a firm in an industry to earn superior returns over the long run."

Bain & Company has done 30 surveys over the past 30 years (up to 2023) regarding the usage of management tools and the satisfaction derived from using those tools (exhibit 1.1). According to a survey done in 2023, valuable tools like mission and vision statements were used by 88% of respondents in 1993 but only 28% in 2023. Similarly, the usage of a Balanced Scorecard for strategy execution—a key concept that is covered in detail in later chapters, both from a design and an implementation perspective—has reduced from a peak of around 60% in 2006 to only 18% in 2023. Interestingly, those who are using these two tools have reported consistently higher levels of satisfaction (above 4 out of 5) with an upward trend over the years. *Strategic Planning* has been one of the most widely used tools, with the highest satisfaction score. However, just 45% of the respondents were satisfied with the strategy planning process, and only 23% said that the major decisions were made within its confines (exhibit 1.1).

It means that the usage of mission, vision, strategy planning, and the Balanced Scorecard is reduced, but not because these tools have become irrelevant or ineffective. The question then arises: *Why organizations have abandoned these important tools even though they were delivering their intended outcomes? Is it because these tools were too cumbersome or time-consuming?* Since these tools are useful for organizations' long-term survival and are not quick fixes, organizations need to be patient and persistent in their implementation and usage.

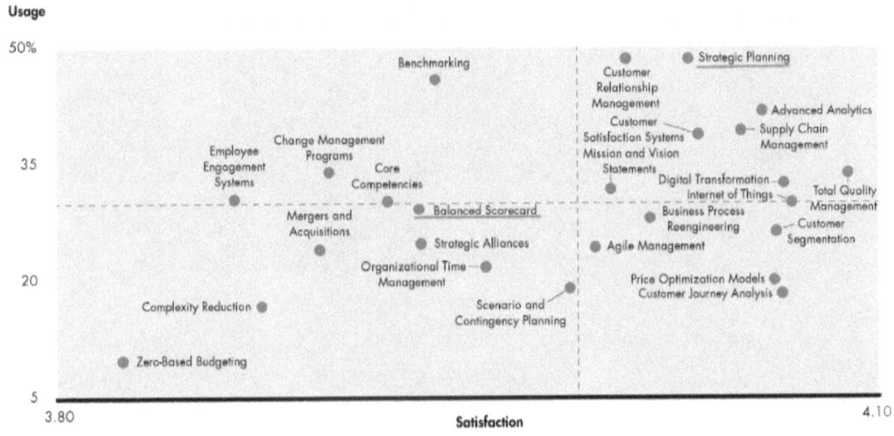

Source: Bain Management Tools & Trends survey, 2017

Exhibit 1.1

Evaluation of Good Business Strategy

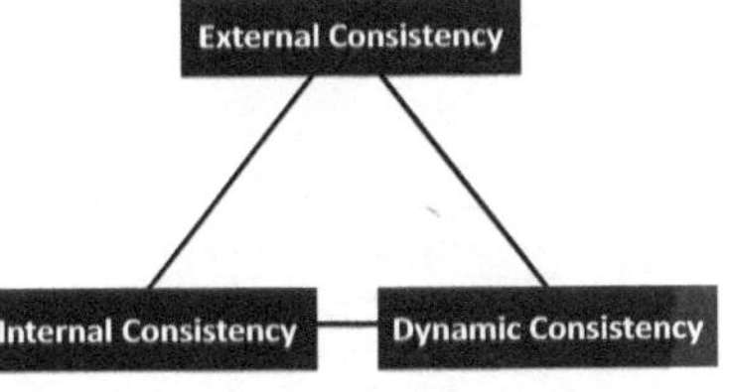

Without a process of evaluation, strategies can neither be formulated nor adjusted to changing circumstances. Of the many tests that could be used for evaluating business strategy, most would fit into one of these broad criteria:

- External Consistency: The strategy should be able to address the challenges and opportunities offered by the external environment.
- Internal Consistency: The strategy should be able to provide coherence to organizational actions based on the organization's strengths, weaknesses, resources, and infrastructure.
- Dynamic Consistency: The leadership team should be able to change/manage the strategy based on changes in the external and/or internal environment.

Apart from passing the above three tests, a strategy must help the business create and/or maintain a competitive advantage in the selected area of business. Moreover, it should be feasible to implement/execute the chosen strategy with the available/planned resources.

Strategy Management – Key Concepts You Should Know

This chapter covers some of the contemporary management models and concepts, and explains how each of them is used in developing and implementing business strategies. Management models are useful tools for problem-solving, analysis, clarification, supporting decision-making, and improving the effectiveness and efficiency of organizations, teams, and individual managers.

Each of the models is introduced with a description, a pictorial representation (wherever possible), and how and when to use it. It is worth mentioning here that not all models apply to all situations, and one should avoid biases and preferences and use the models based on applicability and appropriateness.

The selection of the models is based on our experience in using various models and may not be exhaustive.

Mission, Vision, and Values

Mission, Vision, and Values together define an organization's purpose, long-term aspirations, and culture. And they also answer the following questions:

Mission – Why do we exist? According to Jim Collins, *The mission is an organization's fundamental reason for*

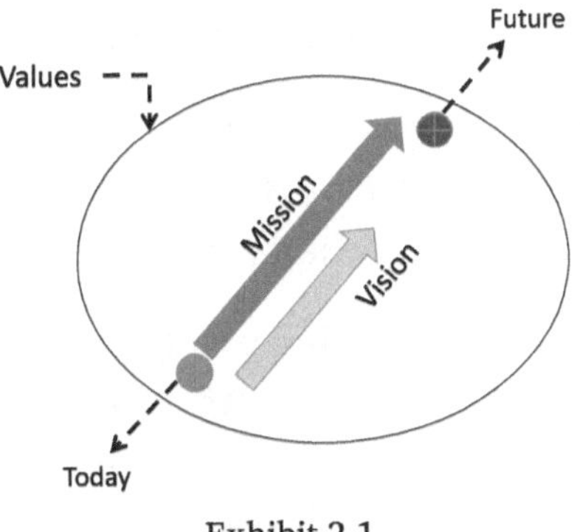

Exhibit 2.1

existence, which goes beyond just making money. It acts as a company's compass. The mission statement links the two dimensions: an inside-out description of what the company does and the market side of who buys it and why. Change in your mission statement is evolutionary rather than revolutionary. For example: *Nike's mission statement is: "To bring inspiration and innovation to every athlete* in the world."*

**If you have a body, you are an athlete. – Nike*

Vision – Where are we going? An elaborate vision statement has three elements: Mission, core values, and a big, huge, but achievable goal (BHAG – Big Hairy Audacious Goal). Since mission and values are defined separately by most organizations, vision often includes a big and audacious goal with a timeframe to achieve that goal. It answers the question, *'What will our business look like in 3 to 10 years from now?'*; and is often worded in engaging language that reaches out and grabs people's attention. Example: *We will put a man on the moon before the end of the decade. – John F. Kennedy, 1961*

Values – What we will and/or will not do to get there? According to Jim Collins, *'It does not matter what core values you have. It matters that you have core values, that you preserve them over time, that you are passionately committed to them, and that you align your behaviours, organizational practices, structures, and strategies with those core values.'* A Value statement explains, *'what you stand for and what you believe in.'* Values guide every decision that is made in the organization and greatly impact an organization's code of conduct. Examples of values include customer-centricity, integrity, collaboration, respect, etc.

Apart from Mission, Vision, and Values, many organizations also have a *Purpose Statement.* A purpose statement combines important elements of mission, vision, and values into a single engaging statement.

In my consulting practice, I have often found that people are confused between mission and vision, and often consider that a vision has a larger scope than a mission. As exhibit 2.1 shows, the mission continues to be the same in the future, unless and until the business (the reason for existence) is completely changed. Whereas, vision is an audacious but achievable goal, for example, becoming number one on certain parameters or becoming the most preferred organization for its customers within a timeframe. The mission is the path, and the vision is the endpoint. A vision statement declares, at the highest organizational level, ambitious targets for the strategy, including a clear measure of success and a specific time horizon to achieve the same.

BHAGs – Big Hairy Audacious Goals

BHAGs (pronounced bee-hags, short for Big Hairy Audacious Goals) are bold missions often used by highly visionary organizations. The term was first coined by Jim Collins and Jerry Porras in their book, 'Built to Last' (exhibit 2.2). All businesses have a goal. But there is a big difference between merely having a goal and committing to a huge, audacious challenge or objective. A true BHAG unifies the whole organization towards a common objective and creates a powerful team spirit. BHAGs can be applied to stimulate progress at any level of an organization, not just at the corporate level. The following key points should be kept in mind while considering BHAGs for your own organization:

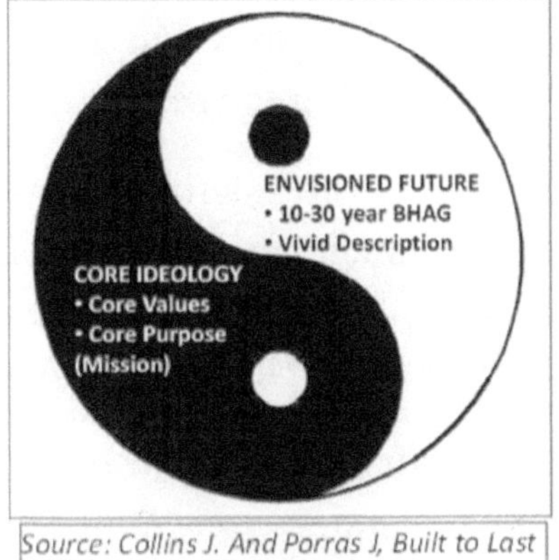

Source: Collins J. And Porras J, Built to Last

Exhibit-2.2

- A BHAG is a goal, not a statement. It should be clear and concise, requiring no explanation.
- A BHAG should fall well outside the comfort zone and should require extraordinary effort and focus. In that sense, a BHAG is not really a sure bet.
- BHAG should be consistent with an organization's core ideology.
- BHAG should be long-term and should have the potential to make a huge impact on the organization's fortunes in the future.

- It is required to have follow-on BHAGs to avoid stagnation after achieving the current BHAG.
- BHAG should have a clear finish line.

Macroenvironment (PESTEL) Analysis

A business should be able to relate to its broad environment and survive the challenges it faces. Broadly speaking, the environment can be classified as macro and micro environment.

Macroenvironment is the set of conditions that exist in the economy, rather than a particular sector, region, or industry. PESTEL Framework is used to analyze these macroenvironmental factors affecting the whole economy in general.

Whereas, the microenvironment includes factors or elements in a firm's immediate environment that affect its performance, decision-making, and strategic choices. Porter's Five Forces analysis is used to analyze these factors in the context of the industry.

In exhibit 2.3 below, the outer circle represents the macroenvironment, and the inner circle represents the industry in which the business operates.

PESTEL is the acronym for Political, Economic, Social, Technological, Environmental, and Legal factors. It is a framework used to analyze and monitor macroenvironmental factors in which an organization operates. PESTEL analysis is especially useful when starting a business in a new geography. However, the analysis is done at regular intervals to find out if

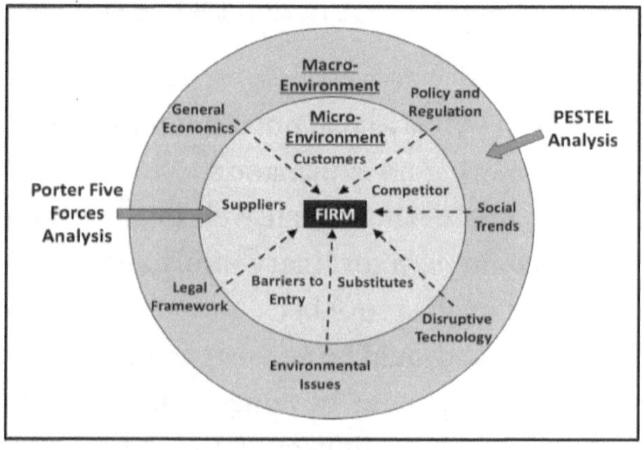

Exhibit-2.3

there are any changes in any of the elements that may have detrimental effects on business operations.

Political Factors: These include factors related to government policies that impact businesses and could affect organizations' decisions. These include tax policy, foreign trade policy, incentive schemes, labour laws, environmental laws, trade restrictions, tariffs and duties, etc.

Economic Factors: Economic factors include economic progress, availability of credit, interest rates, exchange rates, working hours, minimum wage, inflation, cost of living, unemployment rates, the extent of disposable income (purchasing power), etc.

Social Factors: These include demographic characteristics, customs, norms, and preferences of the population. Also included are age, income distribution, health, safety awareness, population growth rate, career preferences, etc.

Technological Factors: These factors refer to awareness and adoption of the latest technologies, incentives for upgrading, R&D facilities, level of innovation, automation, etc.

Environmental Factors: With the adoption of ESG (Environmental, Social, and Governance) requirements by most countries, environmental factors have got the required focus lately. These factors include environmental and ecological factors such as businesses' impact on climate, local weather, pollution, carbon footprint, recycling, availability of natural resources, impact on native population, etc.

Legal Factors: Legal factors cover specific laws related to consumer protection, employment, antitrust, copyright, data protection, patents, discrimination, public health, and safety. There is often an overlap between political and legal factors.

It is important to carry out thorough research on how each of these factors will impact the business. There are probably many more factors that could influence certain businesses. Moreover, the importance of each of the factors will vary from one industry to another, and country to country.

Microenvironment (Porter's Five Forces) Analysis

The essence of formulating a competitive strategy is to beat competitors within the same industry. Industry structure has a strong influence on determining the rules of the game and the potential strategies available to the players within the industry. The underlying economic structure determines the competition in an industry. According to Michael Porter, an academician known for his theories on economics, business strategy, and social causes, there are five key forces or structural features of the industry that determine the strength of the competitive forces and, hence, profitability. In exhibit 2.3, the inner circle represents the microenvironment or industry in which the business operates. The five key forces that act within the industry include the threat of new entrants, rivalry among existing competitors, pressure from substitute products, the bargaining power of buyers, and the bargaining power of suppliers.

Threat of New Entrants: The threat of new entrants in an industry depends on the *barriers to entry* that are present, coupled with the reaction of existing players. If the entry barriers are high, the threat of entry is low. Barriers to entry include economies of scale, product differentiation, capital requirements, switching costs, access to distribution channels, and cost disadvantages independent of scale and government policy.

Rivalry Among Existing Competitors: Rivalry leads to price competition, advertising battles, increased customer service, warranties, etc. Price competition is very bad for the entire industry and leaves it worse off from the standpoint of profitability. Intense rivalry is the result of several interacting structural factors, such as numerous or equally balanced competitors, slow industry growth, high fixed or storage costs, lack of differentiation, switching costs, capacity augmented in large increments, diverse competitors, high strategic stakes, and high exit barriers.

Pressure From Substitute Products: All firms in an industry compete with industries producing substitute products. Substitute products can perform the same function as the products of the industry. For example, sugar producers are confronted with high fructose corn syrup and other artificial sweeteners. Substitutes not only limit profits in normal times, but they also reduce the higher profits in the boom period.

Bargaining Power of Buyers: Buyers force down prices, bargain for higher quality or more services, and play competition against each other, thus reducing industry profitability. A buyer group is powerful if:

- it purchases large volumes relative to the seller's sales,
- the product it purchases represents a significant fraction of the buyer's costs or purchases,
- the product it purchases is standard or undifferentiated, and a buyer can always find alternative suppliers,
- it faces few switching costs,
- buyer poses a credible threat of backward integration,
- the product is unimportant to the quality of the buyers' product or service, and
- the buyer has full information.

Bargaining Power of Suppliers: Suppliers can exert bargaining power by threatening to raise prices or reduce the quality of goods or services. A supplier group is powerful if:

- it is dominated by a few companies and is more concentrated than the industry it sells to,
- it is not obliged to contend with other substitute products for sale to the industry,
- the industry is not an important customer of the supplier group,
- the supplier's product is an important input to the buyer's business,
- the supplier's products are differentiated or it has built up switching costs, and,
- the suppliers pose a credible threat to forward integration.

Once the structural forces and their underlying causes are identified, the firm will be able to identify its strengths and weaknesses relative to the industry. An effective competitive strategy includes both offensive and defensive actions to create a defendable position against the five competitive forces.

SWOT (Strengths, Weaknesses, Opportunities, and Threats) Analysis

SWOT is a business framework that helps identify and assess a wide variety of factors that may have a major impact on a business's ability to perform in the chosen market and ultimately deliver actual results. These factors may either be internal to the organization or external. Favourable and unfavourable internal factors are called the strengths and weaknesses of an organization. Similarly, favourable and unfavourable factors in the external environment are termed opportunities and threats, respectively.

Any organization undertaking strategic planning must assess its strengths and weaknesses at some point. Strengths and weaknesses are identified during the internal analysis. These are the skills, capabilities, and assets (or lack thereof) that are intrinsic to the organization and help it perform in the marketplace relative to the competition.

Opportunities and threats, however, are external factors. They are not created by the organization but emerge due to changes in the marketplace and the activities of the competition. Exhibit 2.4 shows some of the elements that are analyzed under strengths, weaknesses, opportunities, and threats.

Strengths and weaknesses are identified and measured with the help of internal or external audits or benchmarking with competitors. Strengths come from resources and capabilities that are valuable, rare, and hard to imitate. These may include the brand image, patents, exclusive access to unique resources, financial strength, unique know-how, and unique systems and processes developed over a long period of time.

Strengths	Weaknesses
• Recent Successes • Annual Review Findings • Core Competences • Distinctive Competences • Capability Audits (+ve) • Customer Feedback (+ve) • Projects Win Analysis • Competitors Analysis	• Recent Failures • Annual Review Findings • Structural weaknesses • Processes Audits (-ve) • Capability Gaps • Customer Complaints • Projects Lost Analysis • Competitors Analysis
Opportunities	Threats
• Deliberate Strategies • Market/Industry Analysis • Adjacent Industries • Competitors Weaknesses • Possibility of Partnering, Collaboration • Statutory Regulations • Country's PEST Analysis • Competitors Analysis	• Competitors Strategies • Industry Trends • Buying Powers of Customers & Suppliers • Statutory Regulations • New Entrants • Competitors Analysis • Country's PESTEL Analysis

Exhibit-2.4

Opportunities and threats occur because of changes in the external environment. Outputs from PESTEL and Porter's Five Forces analyses are very useful for identifying opportunities and threats.

Opportunities include benefits from technological advancements, favourable demographic changes, an increase in customers' purchasing power, favourable economic environments, etc. Threats may come from unfavourable changes in the regulations, higher costs of capital, increased competition, new entrants in the industry, etc.

It is worth noting that SWOT analysis is termed as a situational analysis, since it shows the status of various internal and external factors at a particular point in time and may change in the future. For this reason, SWOT analysis is done regularly (at least once a year) by most organizations as part of their annual business or strategy planning. Moreover, although SWOT analysis appears deceptively simple, it is far more complex than it looks at first sight.

TOWS Matrix

A SWOT analysis helps an organization identify its current internal and external situation in terms of Strengths, Weaknesses, Opportunities, and

TOWS Matrix: Development of Strategic Alternatives / Initiatives						
		OPPORTUNITY			THREAT	
		O1			T1	
		O2			T2	
		O3			T3	
		O4			T4	
		O5			T5	
		SO Strategies / Initiatives	Comb	ST Strategies / Initiatives		Comb
STRENGTH	S1	SO1		ST1		
	S2	SO2	Use interal STRENGTHS to exploit external OPPORTUNITIES	ST2	Use internal STRENGTHS to minimize the impact of external THREATS	
	S3	SO3		ST3		
	S4	SO4		ST4		
	S5	SO5		ST5		
		WO Strategies / Initiatives	Comb	WT Strategies / Initiatives		Comb
WEAKNESS	W1	WO1				
	W2	WO2	Overcome internal WEAKNESSES to exploit external OPPORTUNITIES	Avoid as far as possible to preserve resources and assets		
	W3	WO3				
	W4	WO4				
	W5	WO5				

Exhibit-2.5

Threats; but it does not help us decide on what strategic actions to take. By mapping internal strengths and weaknesses against the opportunities and threats in the external environment, an organization can come up with four sets of strategies to address the current situation (exhibit 2.5):

The four possible sets of strategies are:

SO Strategies: This is the best position for an organization. A business may have some existing strengths that it can use to take advantage of the current opportunities offered by the market. Alternatively, it can also work on developing totally new capabilities to encash current opportunities. For example, an organization that has a large cash reserve (strength) and a huge, expanding market with sustained demand for its products (opportunity) can expand its manufacturing capabilities to take advantage of the expanding market.

WO Strategies: In this scenario, the organization has more weaknesses (vulnerabilities) than strengths, but its environment provides enough opportunities to incentivize the organization to work on its weaknesses to gain from the opportunities. The organization may also look at acquiring know-how for the weak areas and/or outsource those activities where it has weaknesses. For example, if the same organization is weak in manufacturing, it can outsource manufacturing to a third party and focus on marketing and distribution of its products (one of the company's strengths).

ST Strategies: In this situation, the organization should work on its strengths to address the threats. Threats could include a new entrant in the industry, a price war, new legislation, etc. Price war happens when big players fend off smaller ones by reducing prices and running aggressive and expensive promotions. A company with inherent strengths could become more cost-efficient and lower the price to beat the competition or drive out new entrants. For example, if the same organization enjoys the highest market share with relatively higher margins (strength) and there is a new entrant in the market (threat), it can reduce its products' price temporarily to oust the new entrant.

WT Strategies: An organization with inherent weaknesses operating in a hostile environment with many threats is most vulnerable. There are not many choices in this scenario, as the organization does not have any significant strengths to ward off the threats. The company can only adopt defensive strategies to protect itself from losses. WT strategies cannot be relied on to create success.

Strategic Challenges

The term 'Strategic Challenges' refers to those pressures/obstacles that exert a decisive influence on an organization's likelihood of future success. If the challenge is not important in the real sense, it is not strategic. These are frequently driven by an organization's future competitive position relative to other providers of similar products or services. These may include:

- *Business Related:* Globalization, entry of new competitors, rising customer expectations, mergers and acquisitions, new partnerships, etc.

- *Operations Related:* Increasing costs, rapid technological changes, demand patterns, suppliers' capacity/capability, capacity constraints, etc.
- *Human Resource Challenges:* Recruitment and retention of capable workforce, succession planning, rapid skill upgrading, etc.
- *Sustainability:* Competitors' activities, substitute products, natural disasters, ageing plants and equipment, man-made disasters, etc.

The strategic challenges can be derived from the weaknesses and threats in view of the available opportunities.

Strategic Advantages

The term 'strategic advantages' refers to those marketplace benefits that exert a decisive influence on an organization's likelihood of future success. These advantages are frequently sources of an organization's current and future competitive success relative to other providers of similar products. Strategic Advantages generally arise from:

- *Core Competencies:* These focus on building unique internal capabilities
- ***Strategically Important External Resources:*** These are shaped and leveraged through key external relationships and partnerships
- ***Access to new or Proprietary Technology:*** Through constant research and innovation
- ***Specific Talent Pool:*** These include unique skill-sets & human resources
- ***Knowledge:*** Know-how, intellectual property, designs, processes, information, etc.

Strategic advantages generally come from the company's strengths and help organizations make use of opportunities and deal with threats in the external environment.

Resources, Capabilities, and Competencies

Resources are a business's assets, capabilities are the ability to exploit its resources, and competency is the cross-functional integration and coordination of capabilities[2]. Understanding internal sources of competitive advantage has become critically important for any organization due to increased competition. Let us look at each one of them in more detail.

Resources: The activities and processes of the organization utilize certain assets. These assets are called resources. These resources can be created within the organization. They form internal resources and are organization-specific. Certain resources could be procured externally from the suppliers available in the resource markets. They form external resources. Resources could also be categorized as specific and non-specific. Specific resources are those resources that could be utilized for specific or specialized purposes and are significant to the organization in adding value to its products and services. Non-specific resources are less specific and less significant in adding value to the products and services.

As evident from exhibit 2.6, it is easy to acquire the resources in a short period of time, but it takes sustained effort over a long period of time to develop competencies.

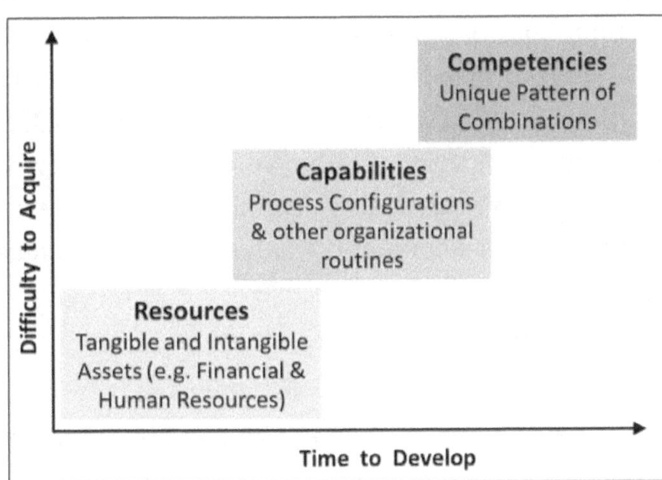

Exhibit-2.6

---

2   Wahl, M.; Prause, G. 2013. Toward understanding resources, competencies, and capabilities: business model generation approach, Entrepreneurship and Sustainability Issues 1(2): 67–80

Resources can also be categorized as tangible and intangible. Tangible resources are generally physical assets and include offices, factories, human resources, equipment, machinery, raw materials, finished products, etc. Intellectual properties, patents, copyrights, and technological resources are called intangible resources. Reputation and goodwill that an organization has acquired over time in the marketplace are also intangible resources.

Capabilities: A capability is the ability to execute a repeatable pattern of actions that are necessary in order to create value for the customer. Capabilities refer to a firm's capacity to deploy resources by incorporating organizational processes and are generated by a firm to provide enhanced productivity of its resources as well as strategic flexibility and protection for its final product or service. Moreover, in contrast to resources, capabilities are based on developing, carrying, and exchanging information through the firm's human capital.

Competencies: For any organization to survive in an industry, competencies are a must. Competency is the cross-functional integration and coordination of capabilities. Competencies are not useful to an organization when they stand alone. Competencies allow an organization to have the ability to compete with other organizations in the marketplace. For example, an information technology (IT) company competing in the software industry should possess the competencies to write programs and design tools and combine them to provide it with a competitive advantage in the industry.

Core Competencies

The term 'core competencies' refers to the organization's areas of greatest expertise. Core competencies are a collection of competencies that cross divisional boundaries. Core competencies are widespread throughout the corporation and are something the corporation does exceedingly well. Core competencies are those strategically important capabilities that provide an advantage in the marketplace or service environment. Core competencies are typically challenging for competitors and partners to imitate, and they provide a sustainable competitive advantage. Distinctive competencies are core competencies that are superior to those of the competition. Exhibit 2.7 lists the core competencies of some of the well-known businesses worldwide.

Core Competencies are like Organizational DNA and have all of the following attributes:

- Greatest Expertise
- Uniqueness
- Should be hard to imitate
- Sustainable
- Should make a substantial contribution to stakeholders' value
- Should open doors to other business opportunities

Organization	What they do?	Core Competency
Ikea	Understand customer requirements.	Operational Excellence.
	Develop the product, develop the source for manufacturing and supply the products to customer.	Supply Chain Management.
Toyota	Understand market requirements.	Manufacturing efficiency.
	Develop the 4-wheelers, manufacture them and supply to customer.	Superior product quality
Starbucks	Marketing and selling variety of coffee for every occasion, every taste.	Relationship with farmers. Marketing.
Bose	Bose is a research company dedicated to developing breakthrough technologies and quality products that enrich people's lives.	Excellence. Innovation.
Nike	Producer of Sports related products	Brand management Design/Development

Exhibit-2.7

Value Chain and Generic Strategies

The concept of a value chain was introduced by Michael Porter in 1985, and its significance and relevance to strategic management and marketing have not diminished even today.

A value chain is defined as a set of consequent activities

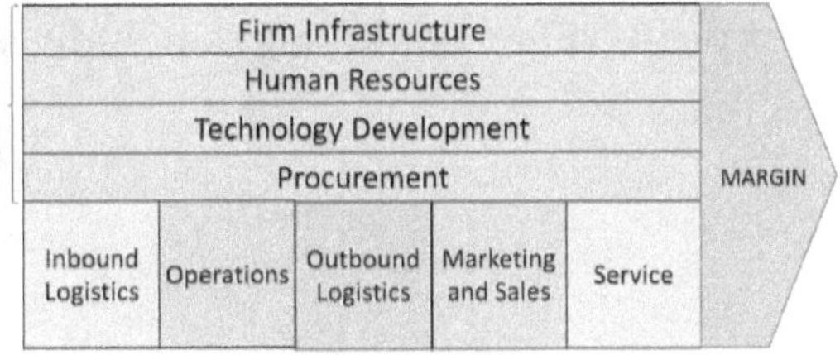

Exhibit-2.8

that organizations perform to achieve their primary objective of profit maximization. Value chain analysis highlights the base where organizations can create value for their customers and identifies the sources of competitive advantage for businesses. The framework divides all activities carried out by businesses into two categories: primary activities and support activities. Primary activities are a set of activities that directly contribute to the creation of value. Support activities include those functions and activities that are required to support the primary activities. It is worth noting that the relevance of value chain analysis applies to all industries and businesses. Exhibit 2.8 shows a generic value chain along with the primary support activities for an organization.

Primary activities include procurement, inbound logistics, operations (transforming raw materials into finished products and/or delivering services as per customers' requirements), outbound logistics (warehousing, distribution), and marketing and sales of products or services.

Use of Value Chain Analysis

Value Chain Analysis can be applied to any type of business, regardless of the industry or size of the business. The framework can be used for:

- Identifying organizational, tactical, and strategic issues related to business
- Identifying potential sources of competitive advantages
- Developing and implementing various strategies based on the sources of competitive advantage.

A typical value chain may include various activities, as shown in exhibit 2.9:

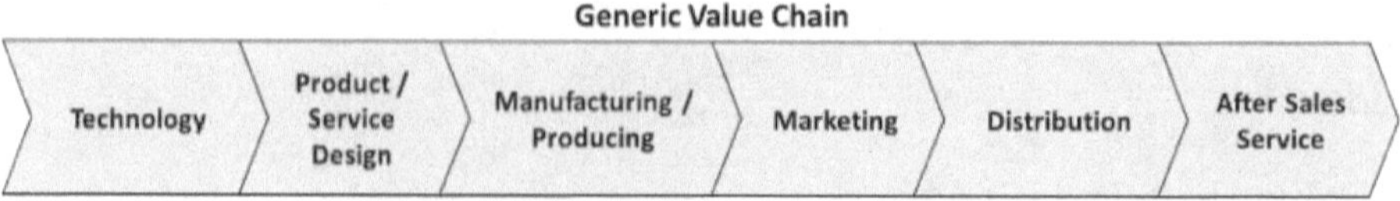

Exhibit-2.9

Further analysis in terms of resources (tangible and intangible assets), capabilities (systems, processes, interlinks, and configurations), and competencies (unique combination of resources and capabilities) can lead to different strategies that an organization can use to differentiate itself from the competition.

Based on a company's focus on specific components of the value chain, it can follow any one of the three generic strategies. These were first described by Michel Porter in 1985 in his book, 'Competitive Advantage: Creating and Sustaining Superior Performance'. These three generic strategies (exhibit 2.10) are:

Cost Leadership Strategy: This strategy involves being the leader in terms of the overall cost of the industry or market through a set of functional policies aimed at reducing costs. This may include large and efficient facilities affording economies of scale, vigorous pursuit of cost reduction from experience, and tight control over costs and overheads. Businesses can follow one of two tactics to earn reasonable profits: high sales volume with a lower-than-normal profit margin or reasonable sales with normal profits. Lower costs relative to competitors become the overall theme running throughout the organization and all areas of operations.

Product Differentiation Strategy: The second generic strategy focuses on differentiating its product or service to make it unique across the industry. Companies that adopt this strategy focus on the technology, quality, design, features, brand image, etc., of their products/services. Differentiation, if achieved, allows companies to have above-average profits by defending their position to cope with the competition. By providing unique features, the company can create brand loyalty that results in lower sensitivity to price. A product differentiation strategy helps in addressing the five industry forces that a company must deal with. Differentiation reduces the threat of substitutes through unique product features/services, reduces the bargaining power of buyers, raises the barriers for new entrants, and wards off competition by offering unique products. However, differentiation may not lead to a high market share since not all customers will be willing or able to pay the required higher price.

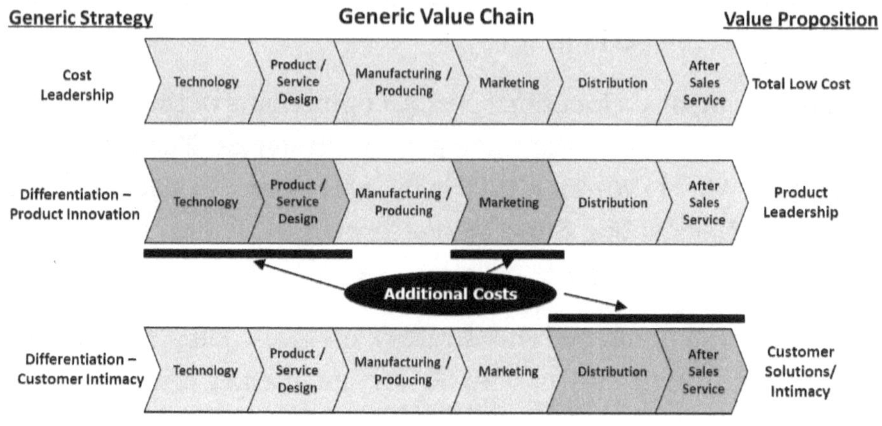

Exhibit-2.10

Customer Intimacy (focus) strategy: Companies adopting this strategy focus on a particular buyer group. It could be a particular segment of the product line, geography, or a sub-segment of the overall market. This strategy focuses on serving a particular segment very well, assuming that the firm will be able to serve its narrow strategic target more effectively and efficiently. As an outcome, the firm can serve its target customers at a lower cost or achieve differentiation by meeting the needs of the focused target segment better. Such a firm may also potentially earn above-average profits due to its high differentiation, low-cost position, or both.

Although some of the requirements for adopting the above strategies are common, implementing them successfully requires different resources and skills. Implementing these strategies may also require different leadership styles, corporate cultures, and work environments. It will be very difficult for a firm to adapt to multiple strategies within the same business unit. Firms that cater to multiple customer segments adopt different marketing strategies, branding, pricing, and positioning. Some firms are not able to develop any of the three strategies explained above and are 'stuck in the middle'. Such firms are bound to have low profitability.

Such businesses will lose high-volume customers who are looking for low prices and, at the same time, are not able to cater to customers looking for better-quality products and are willing to pay a higher price. It usually takes time and sustained effort to come out of such a position.

Customer Value Proposition

A Customer Value Proposition (CVP) is a statement that an organization uses to convince a potential customer to purchase its products or services over others. Its purpose is to convince customers that this company's product or service provides better value than competitors' products or services. The value proposition describes the unique mix of product, price, service, relationship, and image offered to a customer.

CVP has three main components:

- How a company uniquely meets targeted customers' needs with its products or services
- How a company's product or service is different from similar products or services offered by its competitors
- How a company is able to maintain its competitive advantage for a longer period of time

The customer value proposition is at the heart of the strategy, and it influences the internal processes of an organization and marketing and sales strategies in the marketplace. According to Treacy and Wiersema, three differentiation strategies are used by organizations:

- *Product Leadership:* Best products to fulfil customer needs. Making products highly innovative and desirable. Apple and Sony use differentiation strategies to provide uniquely designed products with innovative features.
- *Customer Intimacy:* Superior knowledge of customers and their needs. Knowing exactly what customers need and expect, and creating unique products and services to meet those expectations. An example of customer intimacy would be Starbucks.

- ***Operational Excellence:*** Combination of competitive pricing, customer-perceived quality, lead time, and on-time delivery. McDonald's provides competitively priced meals at very reasonable prices within a few minutes.

Product/Service Attributes				Relationship		Image
Price	Quality	Time	Selection/ Functiona- ity	Service	Relation- ship	Brand
Operational Excellence Strategy						
√	√	√	√	X	X	√
Customer Intimacy Strategy						
X	X	X	X	√	√	√
Product Leadership Strategy						
X	√	√	√	X	X	√

Exhibit-2.11

Brand image is important for all organizations irrespective of the strategy they choose. However, competitive price, customer-perceived quality, on-time delivery, lead time, and wider selection/functionality are crucial for organizations following an operational excellence strategy. Organizations that follow the customer intimacy strategy will emphasize their relationship with customers, the completeness of the solution offered, and providing excellent service to their customers while maintaining threshold levels in other attributes.

As the name suggests, product leadership strategy requires an organization to focus on product quality, features/functionalities, performance of their product or service, and on-time delivery, while maintaining price, service, and relationship at threshold levels.

Successful organizations excel at one of these three dimensions of value while maintaining 'threshold standards' on the other two. Targeted customers are those who place the highest importance on the attributes of the value proposition offered by the organization, as shown in exhibit 2.11.

It is important to remember that an organization's chosen value proposition has a direct impact on the organization's value chain. For example, if an organization adopts 'product leadership' as its core strategy, it needs to excel in processes related to innovation, new product development, product design, and its features. Apple is one of the best examples of a product leadership strategy.

Boston Consulting Group (BCG) (Growth-Share) Matrix

BCG matrix was popularized by Bruce Henderson in the 1970s while working with BCG. However, it is still one of the most widely used matrices by organizations to manage portfolios of products, investments, and research and development in a disciplined and systematic manner. According to Bruce Henderson, *"A company should have a portfolio of products with different growth rates and different market shares (The Product Portfolio, 1970)."* A company may be able to build a market leadership position in a high-growth market.

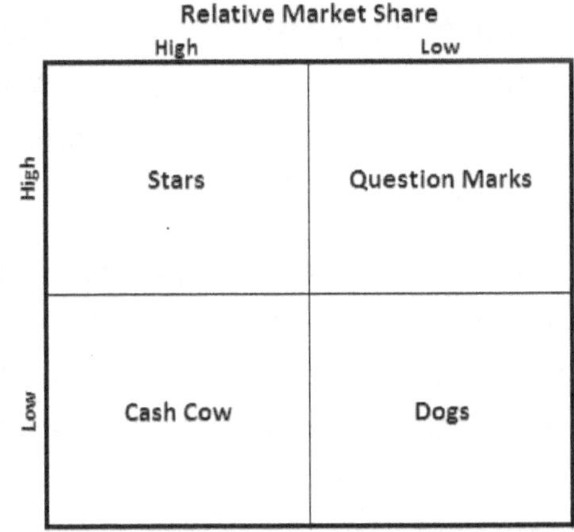

Exhibit-2.12

The matrix has the Relative Market Share on the X-axis and Market Growth Rate on the Y-axis (exhibit 2.12). Putting these drivers in a matrix result in four quadrants, each with a specific strategic imperative:

Cash Cows: They are low-growth and high-market-share products. The products are well-established in the market and require little investment to hold their market share. The 'Cash Cows' should be milked for cash to reinvest in high-growth and high-share 'stars' with high future potential.

Stars: Stars are high-growth and high-share businesses or products. They are well-established in their target markets. Since market growth rates are high in such markets, some investment is required to maintain the market position and ward off competitors and new entrants.

Question Marks: Question Marks are low-share businesses or products in high-growth markets. Depending on the chances of their becoming 'stars,' the 'question marks' should be phased out or invested in.

Dogs: Dogs are low market-growth and low market-share businesses or products. They are essentially worthless and unlikely to ever generate cash. These should be phased out, liquidated, divested, or repositioned.

BCG matrix is a useful tool for analyzing how profitable the industry is and what strategy needs to be pursued. However, it is less effective if someone is planning on entering an entirely new industry or if the company's revenues are growing at a different rate than its market share. In such scenarios, a more customized approach needs to be adopted.

Moreover, due to the rapid pace and unpredictable nature of changes in today's marketplace, successful companies need to explore new products, markets, and business models more frequently to continuously renew their advantage through disciplined experimentation.

Strategic Risk Management

What is Business Risk?

Business risk is defined as an exposure of the organization or business to a factor or factors that may adversely affect the achievement of its objectives.

Strategic Risk Management is the process of identifying, evaluating, quantifying, and mitigating any risk that affects or is inherent to a company's business strategy, strategic objectives, and strategy execution. Types of risks may include legal and regulatory risks, risks from competition, technological changes, shifts in consumer demand and preferences, etc. Several management frameworks and tools (discussed earlier) are aimed at identifying these risks and include

PESTEL analysis, SWOT analysis, Porter's Five Forces analysis, the BCG Matrix, etc. Identifying strategic risks enables an organization to develop effective risk mitigation strategies to effectively address the root causes and mitigate the identified risks. Broadly speaking, most of the risks fall into four categories: Hazard Risks, Financial Risks, Strategic Risks, and Operational Risks.

Any risk or uncertainty has two dimensions: a) *Probability* or *likelihood* of occurrence of the risk event, and b) the *impact* it is going to have on the planned outcome. Using a simple scale of 1 to 5 for both dimensions (likelihood and impact) and multiplying them, we get a minimum score of 1, for a risk with remote probability and negligible impact; and a maximum score of 25, for a risk of very high likelihood and extreme catastrophic impact (exhibit 2.13).

Using such heatmaps offers the following benefits:

- A common understanding of all risks across the organization.
- A holistic view of risks that can be shared across the organization to make strategic decisions.
- Improved management of risks and governance of the risk management process.
- Greater integration of risk management actions across the whole organization.

Potential Impact		Likelihood				
		Remote	Unlikely	Possible	Likely	Very Likely
	Extreme	5	10	15	20	25
	High	4	8	12	16	20
	Medium	3	6	9	12	15
	Low	2	4	6	8	10
	Negligible	1	2	3	4	5

Exhibit-2.13

Risk Management Strategies:

An organization can adopt five possible approaches to manage the identified risks:

- Avoidance: As far as possible, an organization should take appropriate preventive actions to avoid risk completely.

- Acceptance: At times, based on the likelihood and severity of the potential risk, retaining the risk or a portion of the risk may be cost-effective.
- Spreading: It is possible to spread the risk of loss of property or person. For example, storing raw materials or finished products in two smaller, separate locations instead of one large warehouse will reduce losses in the event of a natural calamity or fire.
- Loss Prevention and Reduction: Installing fire detection and protection systems in buildings can greatly reduce the probability and impact of any fire incident.
- Transfer: Sometimes risks can be transferred to others, usually by contract. The purchase of insurance is one such option, where the insurer takes on the risk of the insured for a fee.

Key Performance Indicators or Performance Measures

Key Performance Indicators (KPIs) are a set of measures that focus on the most important aspects of an organization's performance that are *critical* for its current and future success. From a strategy perspective, KPIs help us know the answers to the two most important questions:

- Are we *doing things right*? The 'How' of strategy, or Business Planning, is concerned with inputs and processes.
- Are we doing the *right thing*? The 'What' of strategy, or Strategic Planning, is concerned with outputs and outcomes.

Well-designed KPIs may help the decision-makers of an organization in:

- establishing baseline performance.
- setting performance standards and targets to motivate continual improvement.
- showing *trends* to demonstrate that improvements are being made over time.
- measuring and reporting performance over a period.

- determining if the basic business operations are functioning properly and are sustainable.
- comparing performance across geographies, business units, and departments.
- benchmarking performance against regional and international norms and peers.
- evaluating if the underlying assumptions or hypotheses of the strategy are valid or need changing.

Characteristics of Great KPIs

- *Relevance:* KPIs should align with the specific organization's vision, strategy, and objectives and have an impact on one or more critical success factors or perspectives.
- *Strategic Value:* KPIs should focus on organization-wide strategic value rather than non-critical or local business outcomes.
- *Appropriateness:* KPIs should be appropriate for the organization, considering its operational performance.
- *Realistic:* KPIs should be realistic and fit within the organization's constraints and overall strategy.
- *Specific:* KPIs should be clear and focused to avoid any misinterpretation.
- *Measurable:* KPIs should be quantifiable or qualifiable, allowing for measurement.
- *Attainable:* KPIs should be achievable, reasonable, observable, and credible under expected conditions.
- *Timeliness:* KPIs should be measured frequently and achievable within the given time frame.
- *Limited Dark Side:* KPIs should instigate appropriate actions and desired behaviour without negative consequences.

Criteria for Selecting KPIs:

- *Validity* – Does the KPI measure what it is supposed to measure?
- *Reliability* – Does the KPI provide a consistent measure?

- *Acceptability* – Are the KPIs acceptable?
- *Feasibility* – Is it possible to collect the data, and is it worth the resources?
- *Sensitivity* – Are small changes reflected in the results?
- *Specificity* – Does the KPI capture changes that occur in the performance for which the measure is intended?
- *Relevance* – What useful decisions can be made from the KPI?

Lead and Lag Measures

Lead Measures are also called *in-process* measures or *efficiency* measures. Efficiency is a measure of the optimum use of resources for transforming inputs into outputs. These resources include manpower, machine, material, time, money, environment, and measurement. Good in-process measures:

- are proactive
- are important to customers
- help determine whether to intervene in a process
- help determine where to intervene in a process
- are effective in motivating process teams towards a goal
- are effective in predicting later performance (results)

Lag Measures are *Result* measures, also referred to as *outcome* measures or *effectiveness* measures. Effectiveness measures the extent of the achievement of the desired result in terms of quality and quantity. Good outcome measures:

- are important to customers (internal or external)
- focuses on output performance
- can drive upstream actions to improve the results

A 'balance' of lead and lag indicators is required to ensure that the right activities are in place to ensure the right outcome.

The table below summarizes the key differences between the lead and lag measures:

Lead Measures:	Lag Measures:
■ Also called as in-process or efficiency measures	■ Also known as effectiveness, outcome or result measures
■ Are predictive of a lag measure or result	■ It's ultimate goal or objective you are trying to accomplish
■ Are influenceable, i.e. some actions may be taken to influence the final outcome	■ Nothing more can be done once you accomplish a lag indicator
■ Lead indicators are always more difficult to determine than lag indicators.	■ Essential for charting progress but useless when attempting to influence the future.
■ Often require some kind of investment to implement	■ Traditionally we tend to settle for lag indicators
■ Provides an early warning for achieving relevant lag indicator	

How to Develop Meaningful Measures

Three different models can be adopted to get most of the measures:

- *The Logic Model:* Exploring the relationships among four types of performance measures: inputs, processes, outputs, and outcomes.
- *Process Flow:* Flowcharting processes help identify the activities (and measures) that matter most to produce good outcomes.
- *Causal Analysis:* Identifying the causes and effects of good performance, and identifying input and process measures that are leading indicators of future results.

Chapter – 3

Strategy Development

In the last 10–15 years, the business environment has evolved more than it has in the last 50 years. The rate of change is so high that sometimes one wonders if it makes sense to have a business strategy at all! But then, think about not having a strategy or plan at all. Will you be able to achieve anything, if you have not figured out what you want to achieve and by when you want to achieve it? The answer is obvious. For this reason, the need for planning, executing, and tracking progress will always be there as long as humans exist with the desire to succeed and corporations exist with the intention of being successful.

The business world has changed in several ways. Some of them are:

- The world has become flatter and smaller than ever
- Startups have changed the game
- Shift to service-based industries
- Direct-to-Customer (D2C) businesses have exploded
- Apps and Mobile Adoption
- Work-from-home phenomenon
- The speed of digital transformation
- Outsourcing
- Crowd-funding

All these changes imply that the organizational strategy needs to be planned for and executed in a flatter world with frequent disruptions (in both external and internal environments). Some of the key implications include:

- The whole world is your customer.
- Your costs and efficiency will need to be globally competitive.
- Your products will have to be competitive in multiple segments.
- Your revenue drivers will include organic and inorganic cross-border growth.
- Crisis management and contingency planning will be critical for business success.
- Staying proactive and agile is key to business sustenance.
- Digital transformation and e-commerce are critical to business.
- Moving from value to shareholders to social value.

In this changed world, planning has become more critical than ever. Otherwise, a business will be struggling with crisis after crisis without any preparedness or contingency planning.

Has Strategy Lost Its Significance?

On the contrary, it has more to do with relevance and making strategies work. To execute a strategy, we must have a strategy in the first place. And what is the use of having a strategy if it can't be executed? So, we need a strategy that is relevant to the circumstances and can be successfully executed.

This chapter is about developing a relevant and appropriate strategy, one that can be successfully implemented.

A few management ideas, frameworks, and models have been discussed in detail in the previous chapters. These are going to be used in this section. For this reason, only references will be made to these frameworks and models, along with the methodology for using them. You can always revisit the previous chapter to review it.

Strategy Development Process

The overall strategy development/planning process is shown in exhibit 3.1.

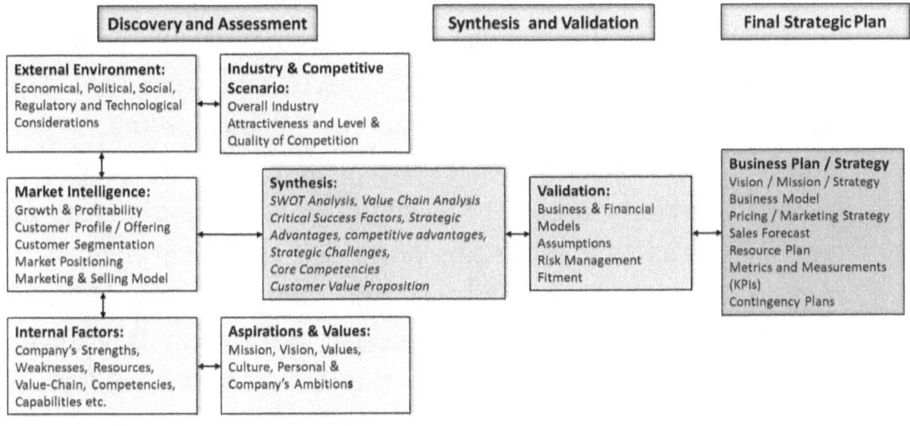

Exhibit-3.1

Strategy development involves gathering and analyzing the information collected from the external environment and internal assessment, and synthesizing this information for meaningful inferences:

- ***External Environment:*** External environment includes the general business environment and industry-specific factors that have an impact on the business we are in or plan to start. For analyzing the general business environment, we use the PESTEL (Political, Economic, Social, Technological, Environmental, and Legal) framework (Page 18). For the evaluation of industry-specific factors, we use Porter's Five Forces Framework (page 20). Apart from these, we also collect market intelligence with regard to customers, including segmentation, growth and profitability of each segment, market positioning, channel partners, and marketing/selling models. Historical data on market size, competitors' performance, and the company's share are also collected and analyzed. Market growth projections may be collected from various reports from research institutions, trade journals, and other relevant sources. Scanning the external environment provides us with information regarding available opportunities, potential threats, and competitive intelligence. A strong external assessment involves reading everything available about the market and gathering as much information as possible. It is also a good idea to meet important customers, suppliers, competitors, industry experts, and regulators. This will help in validating the information collected online.

- *Internal Assessment:* Internal assessment involves identifying an organization's strengths and weaknesses, analyzing its internal value chain and value-creating processes, and the availability of required resources, capabilities, and competencies. Although the required information for internal assessment is available within the organization; most of the time, it is not available in the right format or may not be reliable. Sometimes, it may be possible that the required information is not accessible to you or is hidden from you purposely (due to office politics or fear). A comprehensive internal assessment requires all financial, customer, product, process, channel, IT, Human Resources (HR), and other organizational data from within the organization.

  Internal assessment typically starts with a critical review of performance during the previous planning cycle. We look at what went well and what could have been better during that period and identify key learnings and opportunities for improvement. We also look at the expectations of the key stakeholders, including shareholders/owners, channel partners, suppliers, employees, institutions, and society at large.

- At this stage, we also revisit and/or articulate the organization's mission, vision, and values (Page 15); assess culture; and articulate goals and objectives based on inputs from all employees. Inputs from the leadership team may be sought at this stage, especially with regard to future aspirations and long-term strategy.

- *Synthesis:* After collecting the relevant information from the external environment and internal assessment, we do the synthesis. Based on the external assessment, we articulate opportunities and threats, and internal analysis provides us with the organization's strengths and weaknesses. The collected information is used for developing a SWOT matrix and, subsequently, a TOWS matrix (Page 22-25). The available information is used for identifying and articulating strategic advantages, strategic challenges, and critical success factors and developing the initial set of strategies based on the TOWS matrix. As part of the internal analysis, we also identify the organization's core competencies and, based on that customer value proposition is developed.

- ***Developing a Strategic Business Plan:*** The final step involves putting all the information and data into a logical flow. Depending on the size of the organization, a business plan will have around 120 to 150 pages, and the whole planning cycle could be completed in 10 to 12 weeks. At the minimum, the business plan will include:

  a. Financial Plan/Strategy: In terms of overall financial objectives such as revenue, gross margin, net profit etc., along with other supporting strategies such as revenue strategy, profit strategy, credit strategy, risk strategy, and cost strategy.

  b. Customer and Product Strategy: This will include product/service strategy, brand strategy, customer relationship strategy, and warranty policy.

  c. Operational Strategy: This includes manufacturing/outsourcing strategy, procurement strategy, marketing and sales strategy, channel strategy, delivery strategy, and innovation strategy.

  d. Support Functions Strategy: This primarily includes strategies related to support functions, i.e., HR strategy; IT strategy; environment, health and safety strategy; etc.

Balanced Scorecard (BSC) Development Teams

The Balanced Scorecard development process requires the formation and operation of at least three teams: the Core Team, the Leadership Team, and the Measurement Team. In smaller organizations, an individual could be a member of more than one team. However, the role should be clearly defined for the membership of each team.

Core Team: The core team is the most important component of the Balanced Scorecard initiative. This team collects and analyses the initial data that will be used to drive the process and begins constructing some initial ideas about the scorecard by drawing models, themes, and linkages to the desired strategic outcomes. The core team also conducts interviews with members of the leadership team, collects data, validates assumptions, enhances models, and presents them to the leadership team.

Leadership Team: The leadership team provides the leadership, endorsement, and vision of the project. Their support helps encourage other participants, from whom input and support will be needed during the process. The leadership team owns the Balanced Scorecard and takes final decisions regarding strategic themes, objectives, measures, targets, and initiatives based on the recommendations of the core team.

Measurement (Analytics) Team: The measurement team enables data integration into the Balanced Scorecard process. These teams generally come from various functional areas and Strategic Business Units (SBU). Their job is to recommend measures to the core team and provide data to populate the scorecard.

Leadership Team	Core Team	Analytics Team
Role: • Champion process & make strategy decisions • Participate in workshops & provide oversight • Provide resources to the core & analytics teams **Membership:** • Leader of the organization & direct reports • Functional leaders as required **Time Required:** • Half day kick off meeting • 90 minutes interviews • 3 days of workshops over 6-8 weeks • Pre-work assignment completion	**Role:** • Lead the execution of the strategy development process • Create pre-work materials • Facilitate workshops • Direct work of the analytics teams **Membership:** • 4 to 5 mid level managers • Broad base of experience from across the organization **Time Required:** • Team Leader: 50% to 100% of time over period • Team Member: 20% to 50% of time over period	**Role:** • Collect data as directed by the core team • Analyze data & develop into analysis • Identify cause & effect **Membership:** • 2 to 3 managers with facility in analytical methods. **Time Required:** • Varies depending upon level & depth of analysis required

Exhibit-3.2

Any changes in the Balanced Scorecard can only be recommended by the core team to the leadership team, and changes can be implemented only after approval from the leadership team. Details of these teams are briefly presented in exhibit 3.2.

Typical Strategy Planning Schedule

A typical planning schedule is given in exhibit 3.3 and has four phases:

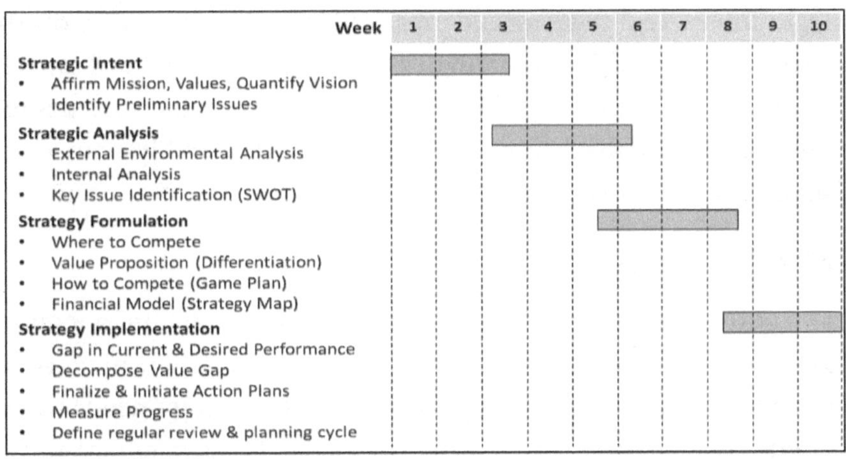

Exhibit-3.3

Phase I: Setting Strategic Intent

Before an organization develops its strategy, senior leaders have the responsibility to set the overall direction of the organization. An organization's Mission, Vision, and Values provide overall guidance at the highest level to all the key stakeholders (the board of directors, shareholders, business partners, customers, and employees). It is also important to quantify the vision and set the timeframe for achieving it. Without quantification, it would be difficult to measure progress towards the vision. A quantified vision helps in deciding the scope and requirements of the strategy development process and the timeframe to achieve the vision. Apart from vision, organizations may also choose to develop a strategic destination statement, vividly describing the vision in more detail. It may also include the organization's BHAGs, a term coined by Jim Collins in his book, Good to Great. The value gap can be defined in many different financial terms: shareholders' value, revenue growth, profit, ROI, etc. The timeframe for achieving the vision and planning horizon will depend on the industry in which a business operates. These, in turn, depend on how fast the technology, products and services, and organizations themselves, are changing. For example, large industries such as steel, petroleum, and paper are considered slow, while personal computers, toys, and games are considered fast.

Strategic intent is discussed and finalized in an interactive workshop attended by the Core Team, Analytics Team, and Leadership Team. The core team leads the meeting and presents the prework; the analytics team provides support for the data and analysis; and the leadership team reviews and approves the information and the final outcomes of the meeting.

Phase II: Strategic Analysis

Organizations do not live in a vacuum; they exist in a complex ecosystem that includes both internal and external environments. The environment changes constantly, and business strategy needs to keep pace with the changes in the environment. Though environmental scanning can become time-consuming, it is a critical step in the formulation of a strategy. The internal environment includes all internal factors, such as physical resources, financial resources, human capital, technology, business processes, management capability, organizational culture, brand equity, innovation capacity, etc.

The external environment includes both macro and micro environments. The macroenvironment includes the general economic environment in which an organization operates, along with economic, societal, political, regulatory, technological, and geo-specific factors. The PESTEL Framework is used for carrying out the analysis of the macroenvironment.

The microenvironment includes industry-specific factors, market segments, customers, competitors, suppliers, and partners. This analysis is done using Porter's Five Forces Framework (page no. 20) and includes the following factors: Barriers to Entry, Bargaining Power of Suppliers,

Bargaining Power of Customers, Threats of Substitutes and Rivalry, and Competition among existing players. The analysis is done from the standpoint of firms within the industry and looks for the forces that have the most impact. Subsequently, an analysis of the Internal Value Chain is carried out. The value chain, initially developed by McKinsey and then advanced by Porter, represents the sequence and configuration of the business activities that deliver value to the customer. Value Chain enables us to both formulate and conduct detailed cost analyses. The generic value chain is given in exhibit 3.4. While doing the internal analysis, the organization also needs to identify its resources (tangible and intangible), capabilities, and core competencies.

Generic Value Chain

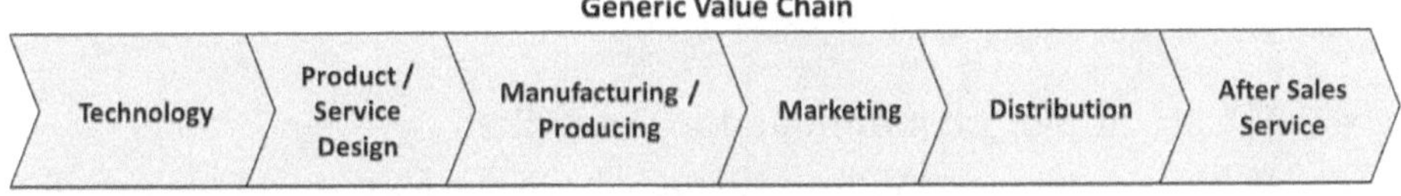

Exhibit-3.4

The next step, after collecting all the relevant information, is to synthesize the information gathered during the environmental scan and evaluate the key issues that may have detrimental effects on the organization. Both qualitative and quantitative analyses are used to gain insight. Key activities include:

- Classifying, collating, integrating, analyzing, and documenting all the information to make sense of it.
- Identifying, evaluating, and assessing risks to develop risk management strategies during the next step.
- Developing scenarios based on projections (both optimistic and pessimistic) for the future to define plausible business outcomes.
- Identifying key issues and strategies to address these issues. Pinpointing the critical few strategic issues enables more effective and efficient strategy development.
- Using various tools such as PESTEL analysis, Porter's five forces analysis, basic SWOT analysis, competitor SWOT analysis, etc., to analyze the current state of the external environment and competitors.

The final step is to communicate the insights synthesized during the previous steps to the leadership team and the core team to validate and/or correlate with the vision, destination, and strategy formulation. It is possible that the results of the scan may change some of the original assumptions associated with the initial direction setting.

Phase III: Strategy Formulation

As per the definition, strategy is about making choices. If that is the case, then the question is: *'What choices must be made by our organization to formulate a coherent business-level strategy?'*

As per Kaplan and Norton, there are five choices that need to be made to develop a strategy:

- What will our economic model look like?
- Which customers will we serve, where, and what will we provide them?
- How can our organization serve these customers?
- What skills do we need to have in our organization?
- What is the portfolio of initiatives and their timing that we need to execute?

These choices must be viewed as an integrated, mutually reinforced set.

Once an organization defines its economic model (how revenue and profit will be created), it must decide how it will create unique value for its targeted customers to earn those profits. And this is called Value Proposition. Value Proposition is the heart of the strategy, and it describes a unique mix of product, price, service, relationship, and image offered to the targeted customers to meet their specific needs. Management researchers Brian Tracy and Fred Wiersema organized customer value propositions into three broad categories (exhibit 3.5).

- ***Cost Leadership or Operational Excellence:*** Companies that follow 'Cost Leadership or Operational Excellence' strategies deliver a combination of price, quality, and ease of purchase that no one else can match. Toyota and McDonald's follow this strategy.

- ***Product Leadership:*** 'Product Leadership' companies provide the most innovative products that incorporate new technologies and features, making their products highly desirable. Apple, Sony, and Tesla are companies that are at the forefront of providing innovative products with industry-leading features.

- ***Customer Intimacy:*** 'Customer Intimacy' value proposition requires a business to build long-term relationships with their customers and provide personal/customized service tailored to produce results for them. Many of the services or consulting organizations follow this strategy and build long-term relationships with their customers.

Both Product Leadership and Customer Intimacy are differentiation strategies that create differentiation in terms of product and service delivery, respectively. In recent years, one more strategy option, 'System Lock-in', has been added as an option. System Lock-in helps the company retain its customers by increasing switching costs. The generic strategy selected by the organization needs to be consistent with the value proposition selected for the targeted customer segments to be served and the strategy formulation technique used.

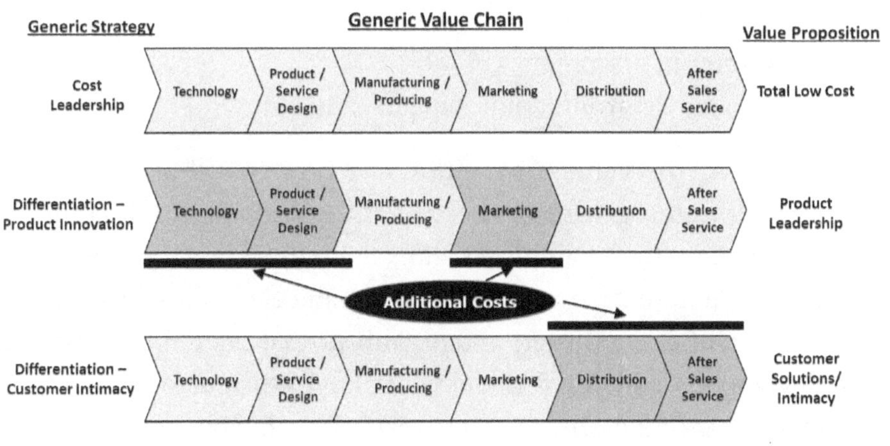

Exhibit-3.5

Strategy Formulation techniques need to be applied based on the strategy and the value proposition or propositions intended. Some of the common strategy formulation techniques are given in exhibit 3.6. There are many others.

Value Proposition	Generic Strategy	Strategy Formulation Technique
Low Total Cost	Cost Leadership	Activity Based Costing (ABC)
Product Leadership	Differentiation	Open Innovation, Profit from the Core
Customer Solution (Intimacy)	Differentiation	Experience Co-creation, Blue Ocean, Judo Strategy
System Lock-in	System Lock-in	Switching Costs, Barriers to Exit

Exhibit-3.6

Once an organization finalizes the economic model, broad generic strategy, strategy formulation techniques, and targeted customers, it needs to organize and align its internal processes to the value proposition (strategy) to make sure that it delivers value to the targeted customers as planned. These processes typically fall into one of four categories:

- Innovation, R&D, Product Development, etc.
- Operations, including procurement, manufacturing, logistics, supplier relations, etc.
- Customer management
- Social and Environmental Aspects, and Safety

After finalizing the value proposition and how it will be delivered to the customers, an organization needs to take stock of the situation and identify the gaps in the required skills and capabilities for successful strategy implementation and current capabilities. This leads to the identification of new skill sets and organizational capabilities that need to be developed or acquired to deliver value to the customers. Actions may include training the existing resources, hiring new resources, revamping existing processes, and/or implementing new processes. All these actions and new initiatives with timelines for implementation become part of the strategy execution plan.

The meeting for strategy formulation is conducted in a typical workshop format. The purpose of the workshop is to review the results of all analyses, formulate strategies, create a draft strategy map, and schedule the next step for the Balanced Scorecard. The meeting is attended by the core team, analytics team, and leadership team. The core team leads the meeting and presents the draft documents of the strategy, and the leadership team reviews and approves the strategy and strategy map. The key outputs of the meeting include a finalized value proposition, a decomposed value gap, a formulated strategy, an approved strategy map, and finalized key strategic initiatives.

Phase IV: Strategy Implementation and Reporting

Once the detailed strategic plan is developed, it needs to be executed brilliantly to achieve the intended outcomes. Strategy execution will be covered in detail in the subsequent chapters. Successful strategy execution requires ongoing support, monitoring, reporting, and possible course correction.

The key to successful strategy implementation and reporting is to identify those responsible for managing each part of the process:

Project Manager:

- Gathers updated data, produces reports, and disseminates them to the reporting team prior to the review meeting
- Heads Balanced Scorecard review meetings and reports production
- Manages logistics of review meetings
- Percolates Balanced Scorecard Review meeting

Objectives and Theme Owners:

- Analysis and commentary on owned Objectives and Themes
- Assigning Measure Owners to measures
- Validating measures and initiative data
- Review targets for measures and milestones for initiatives
- Present objective, measure, and initiative performance analysis at the meetings

Measure Owners:

- Provide performance analysis on owned measures
- Develop content and graphs
- Collect data and key assumptions
- Ensure consistency in the measurement approach is followed from period to period

Initiative Owners:

- Provide performance analysis on initiatives owned
- Identify issues or problems with initiatives
- Manage initiatives' milestones

PART – 2

Strategy Execution Using Balanced Scorecard

Chapter – 4

What is Strategy Execution, and Why is it Important?

Having a good strategy is not even half the battle; the real challenge is executing your strategy. A great strategy or innovative product may give you initial success, but if your organization does not have solid execution capabilities, success in the marketplace will not last long. According to one survey by Fortune, '*Less than 10% of strategies effectively formulated are effectively executed.*' And another survey revealed that '*In 70% of cases, failure occurred because of bad execution and not a bad strategy*'. Most of the time, the gap between strategy planning and strategy execution is the main reason for not getting the planned results.

What is Strategy Execution?

Strategy execution is translating an organization's strategic initiatives into action. Execution is a systematic process of rigorously discussing the 'hows' and the 'whats', questioning, following through, and ensuring accountability. Execution is the single biggest obstacle to success and is often not addressed or tackled at the leadership level. Execution is not just about tactics. It is a discipline and a system. It must be built into a company's strategy, its goals, and its culture. And the leadership team must be deeply engaged in it. This responsibility cannot be delegated.

Execution is a specific set of behaviours and techniques that companies need to master in order to have a competitive advantage. It is a discipline on its own and is the most critical for success. Execution must be part of an organization's strategy and goals. It is the missing link between aspirations and results. Moreover, execution must be a core element of the organization's culture.

The heart of execution lies in the three core processes: the people process, the strategy process, and the operation process. The processes are tightly linked with one another and cannot be compartmentalized among staff. And the leader of the business and his or her leadership team are deeply engaged in all three. They are the owners of the processes, not the strategic planning team, HR team, or finance team. Leading the execution department is not about micromanagement. Rather, it is about active involvement in doing the things leaders should be doing in the first place.

Why is Strategy Execution Important?

As noted above, most of the strategies fail not because they are wrong or incorrect; they fail because of incorrect execution. Failed strategies can deprive organizations of the profits that they were supposed to make. This can also deprive customers of innovative technology, products, or services. Most importantly, failed strategies result in the waste of critical resources, human effort, and investments.

According to a survey done in 2006, organizations with a formal strategy execution process outperform organizations without one (The Execution Premium, Kaplan & Norton).

Recent surveys also reveal that 60% of the time, organizations fail to achieve the planned strategic outcomes due to the bad execution of the strategies. Strategic execution requires a systemwide approach that consistently drives organizations to do the right things in the right way.

Chapter – 5

Problems with Traditional Strategy Execution

According to an article published by the Harvard Business Review in June 2022, 60%–90% of strategic plans never fully launch. The cause of the derailment varies widely, but execution consistently bears the blame. While that can be, and perhaps often is, a fair diagnosis, it is not the whole story. The strategy design itself sometimes can be the real problem[3]. Another survey reveals that 70% of the time, execution is the main reason for not achieving strategic outcomes.

If, in 70% of the cases, failures occur due to bad execution of the strategy and not because of the strategy, there must be a problem with the traditional method of strategy execution. A lot of research is done on this subject, and if you search on the internet, you will be able to find at least 50–60 different reasons that could potentially lead to failure in strategy execution. If we do further analysis and try to group them under different headings, we get six main reasons.

Why Does Strategy Fail?

There could be many reasons for a strategy's failure. The important ones are discussed below:

Intangible factors are not given enough importance

Any organization has both tangible and intangible assets. The tangible assets of an organization include cash, receivables, inventory, land,

---

3   4 Common Reasons Strategies Fail by Andrea Belk Olson, Harward Business Review, June 2022

plant, equipment, etc. The book value of an organization is based on the current value of its net physical assets. Intangible assets include the organization's patents, technologies, high-quality and responsive operating processes, IT and databases, employees' capabilities, the organization's culture, customer databases and relationships, etc. These intangible assets help an organization satisfy customer requirements. Market capitalization (based on the current share price) is the organization's future value, which includes both tangible and

intangible assets and reflects the organization's future potential to make profits.

Brookings Institute Study (almost two decades ago) highlighted that the book value of tangible assets as a percentage of the market value of industrial organizations was rapidly declining; from 62% in 1982 to 10% in 2001 (exhibit 5.1).

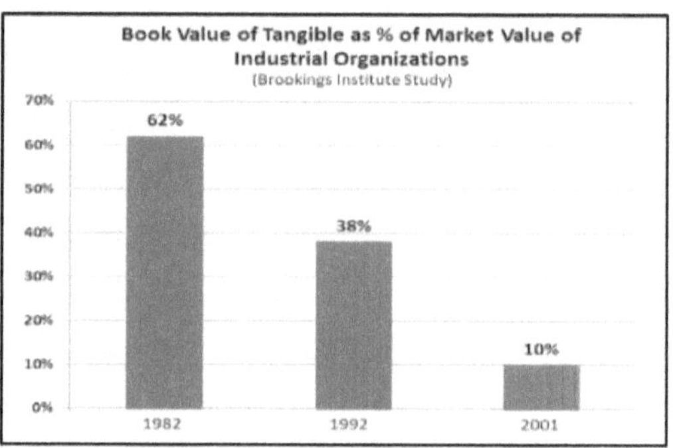

Exhibit-5.1

Exhibit 5.2 shows Apple's price-to-book value ratio since 2010, which has been continuously going up over the years and was close to 40 in 2022. This means that the tangible assets represented only 2.5% of the total value. The remaining 97.5% of the value is created by intangible factors, as the company earned its reputation, built products with superior features and qualities, and started enjoying a loyal customer base.

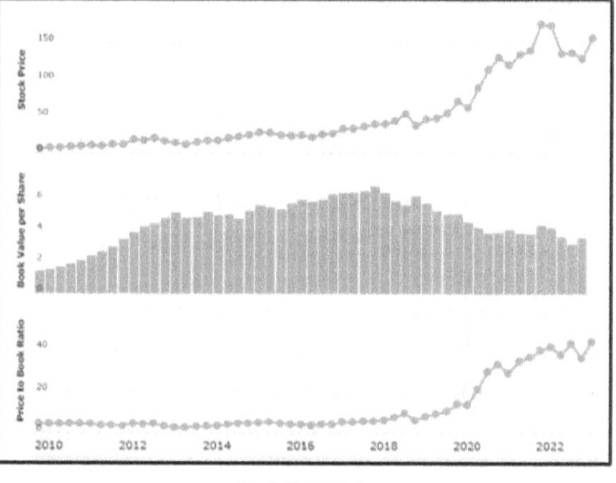

Exhibit-5.2

Based on a study by J. Low & T. Siesfield, titled Measures That Matter, the top ten non-financial variables considered by financial analysts include:

- Execution of corporate strategy
- Management credibility
- Quality of corporate strategy
- Innovation
- Ability to attract and retain talented people
- Market share
- Management expertise
- Alignment of compensation with shareholders' interests
- Research leadership
- Quality of major business processes

As one can see, the successful execution of the corporate strategy appears at the top of the list.

In the traditional system of strategy execution, these intangible assets are not given due importance and are looked at in isolation. As we will see later, the Balanced Scorecard provides a comprehensive causal map (that includes both tangible and intangible assets) showing how value is created by an organization using both kinds of assets.

Lack of Communication Across the Organization

Since the traditional strategy planning process involves only executives and the leadership team, communication becomes a tedious task. Understanding and communicating the strategy is left to the line managers and individuals. Without frequent and elaborate communication, most of the employees will not be able to understand and assimilate the strategy and what their role is in executing it. A strategy needs to be repeatedly discussed in all departmental and review meetings so that its execution becomes part of the culture. Moreover, for successful strategy execution, a consistent and comprehensive communique is required to avoid any ambiguity and confusion.

Strategy is treated like an event and not as a system

Most organizations treat strategy planning as an annual event, which is mostly held at a remote location and involves a few executives and outside guests. The group typically spends a few days and comes up with several strategic objectives and an action agenda. The problem is that only a handful of people are involved in the whole process, and it becomes nearly impossible to get a buy-in from the rest of the employees. Moreover, since these people were not involved in the planning process, they will not be able to understand the logic and reasons for the actions they are supposed to take.

Many a time, executives feel that strategy is too complex for employees of the organization to understand. For this reason, strategic objectives and related action plans remain with the executive, leading to a disconnect between actions and strategy.

Disconnect Between Strategy and Budget

When strategy planning is done in isolation and the budgeting team is not part of the planning group, it will very likely lead to a disconnect between budget and strategy. The budgeting team will need to have inputs from the marketing and operational teams to arrive at the budget. The disconnect between strategy and budget may lead to a situation where resources are not allocated to important strategic initiatives, leading to failure in achieving strategic objectives or performance targets.

Disconnect Between Strategy and Actions

In the traditional strategic planning process, executives meet and outline several strategic objectives. These objectives are then rolled out or emailed to the rest of the company.

The people who are responsible for executing these strategies do not realize how they impact their jobs and are unable to connect specific actions to outcomes and objectives. This absence of linkage between strategy and strategic actions reduces the effectiveness of strategic execution.

Lack of Clarity Regarding Measurement and Outcomes

Most companies use some form of KPIs or Objectives and Key Results (OKRs) as measurement tools for performance. Since only high-level executives are involved in strategy execution, there is a danger of these KPIs having a disconnect from the strategic outcomes. In order to maximize the effectiveness of strategic execution, strategy measurement systems need to be directly or indirectly linked to the everyday activities of all employees. Very often, it is found that the line of sight is completely missing between what is being measured at the shopfloor level and the organizational (strategy) level.

Barriers to Strategy Implementation

According to one survey by CFO Magazine, the key barriers to strategy implementation include:

Vision Barrier: Only 5% of the staff members understand the strategy

People Barrier: Only 25% of the managers have incentives linked to strategy

Resource Barrier: 60% of organizations do not link budget to strategy

Management Barrier: 85% of top management teams spend less than 10 hours/month discussing the strategy.

It is obvious that *'If the strategy cannot be holistically described, then it cannot be effectively communicated, AND if it cannot be effectively communicated, then it cannot be understood, AND if it cannot be understood, then it cannot be executed.'*

Balanced Scorecard is a tool developed by Robert Kaplan and David Norton in the 1990s that can be used effectively for strategy execution. Many large and small organizations in India are using Balanced

Scorecards to manage their strategies. These include Tata Motors, Tata Steel, TCS, INFOSYS, Mahindra Group, etc. According to various research reports, more than 30% of the large organizations in India use a Balanced Scorecard for the implementation of their strategies. However, the quality of implementation is the cause of concern. Many organizations use OKRs and KPIs that may not be logically linked to the corporate strategy.

Chapter – 6

Introducing Balanced Scorecard

The origin of the Balanced Scorecard can be traced back to the late 1980s when Analog Devices in the US was using a 'Corporate Scorecard'. In 1990, the Nolan Norton Institute, the research arm of KPMG, sponsored a one-year multi-company study on 'Measuring Performance in the Organization of the Future'. David Norton, CEO of Nolan Norton, served as study leader, and Robert Kaplan, an academic consultant. The discussions led to the expansion of the 'Corporate Scorecard' (used by Analog Devices) to what they labelled a 'Balanced Scorecard'. Based on this study, the findings of the study group were published in the Harvard Business Review (HBR) in Jan-Feb 1992 titled, 'Balanced Scorecard: Measures that Drive Performance'. Before publishing their first book, 'Balanced Scorecard: Translating Strategy into Action', the duo published two more articles in HBR: 'Putting the Balanced Scorecard to Work (September–October 1993) and 'Using the Balanced Scorecard as a Strategic Management System' (January–February 1996). Since then, the Balanced Scorecard has evolved from an improved *measurement system* to a *Core Management System.*

What is a Balanced Scorecard?

At the highest conceptual level, the Balanced Scorecard is a *framework* that helps organizations *translate strategy* into *operational objectives* that drive both *behaviour* and *performance*. In simple language, Balanced Scorecard is a framework that combines traditional financial measures with long-term competitive capabilities, customer relationships, and intangible assets such as customers, suppliers, employees, processes, technology, and innovation. The Balanced Scorecard complements financial measures of past performance with measures of the drivers of future performance. It is a simple and intuitive framework that consistently shows the relationships among various elements of the strategy and takes into consideration customers as well as other intangible assets in a simple cause-and-effect relationship that is easily understood by all members of the organization.

The Balanced Scorecard is a performance management system that:

- *Aligns* Vision and Mission with customer requirements and day-to-day work
- *Translates* needs into strategy
- *Describes* a strategy by linking tangible and intangible assets in value-creating activities
- *Manages* and evaluates strategy
- *Focuses* on customers'/stakeholders' needs
- *Monitors* operation improvement efficiency
- *Builds* organizational capacity
- *Increases* organizational alignment and accountability
- *Communicates* progress to all employees
- *Helps* in executing and managing strategy
- *Helps achieve the required balance and linkage between strategy and operations.*

Basic Design of the Balanced Scorecard

Since the Balanced Scorecard combines traditional financial measures with other non-financial measures (customer results, internal business processes, and learning & growth), these four perspectives provide the framework of the Balanced Scorecard (exhibit 6.1).

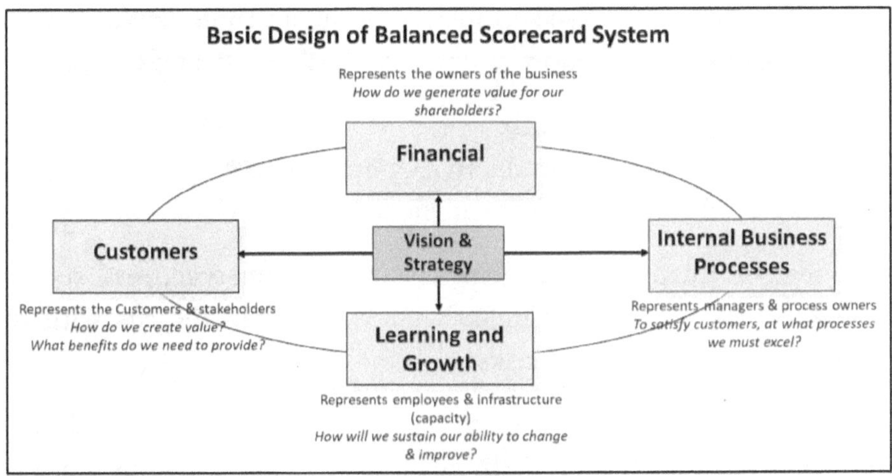

Exhibit-6.1

The Four Perspectives

The architecture of a Balanced Scorecard follows a top-down approach:

Financial Perspective: The financial perspective defines the strategy from the shareholders' perspective. Objectives can differ considerably at each stage of the business lifecycle—Growth, Sustain, and Harvest.

Growth – The overall financial objective for growth-stage businesses will be percentage growth rates in revenues and sales growth rates in targeted markets, customer groups, and regions.

Sustain – Most business units in the sustain stage will use profitability as a financial objective. Measures will include return on investment, return on capital employed, economic value added, etc.

Harvest – Some business units may reach a mature phase of their life cycle, and the company may want to harvest the investments made in the two earlier stages. The overall financial objectives for such businesses would be operating cash flow and a reduction in working capital requirements.

For each of the above three strategies, there are three corresponding financial themes that support or drive the business strategy:

- Revenue growth and mix
- Cost reduction and productivity improvement
- Asset utilization and investment strategy

An effective financial management strategy must address returns as well as risk. A business must balance expected returns with the management and control of risks.

Customer Perspective: The customer perspective identifies and defines the target customers and their needs through a value proposition customized for each customer group. Customers are never homogeneous and have different preferences. During strategy formulation processes, customers are researched to reveal different segments and their preferences regarding price, quality, functionality, service, image, reputation, relationship, etc. The customer strategy is then defined by the customers and market segments that it chooses to serve. Customer objectives are then identified for each of the segments.

Core measures for customer outcomes are generic across all kinds of industries. These include market share, customer acquisition, customer satisfaction, customer retention, and customer profitability.

Apart from core measures, an organization must also articulate a Customer Value Proposition for each of the customer groups. The value proposition helps us understand the drivers of the core measurement. The three main value propositions include Product Leadership, Customer Intimacy (Relationship), and Operational Excellence (image and reputation). For more discussion on the value proposition, please refer to Chapter 2 (page 33).

Internal Perspective: The internal perspective defines the activities needed to create the desired customer value proposition and differentiation for achieving customer and shareholder objectives. Most companies today have multiple measurements for cross-functional and integrated business processes. The objectives and measures for internal perspective are derived from explicit strategies to meet shareholder and targeted customer expectations.

The generic value chain provides a template that organizations can customize when preparing their internal business process perspective. This model comprises three principal value processes: Innovation, Operation, and After-Sales Service. Depending on the company's focus on specific components of the value chain, the company can adopt any one of the following three generic strategies:

- Cost Leadership Strategy
- Product Differentiation Strategy
- Customer Intimacy Strategy

For further details, please refer to Chapter 2.

Measures for this perspective will vary widely depending on the industry an organization operates in and the nature of its products or services. Innovation-related measures include the percentage of sales from new products, the number of new products introduced, the time required to develop new products, manufacturing capabilities, etc. Operational measures will include industry-specific measures right from the receipt of a customer order to the delivery of the product or service to the customer. Measures for post-sale service will include measures related to warranty and repair activities, managing defects and returns, processing of payments, etc. Quality-related measures will include yield, defect rate, rework, waste, scrap, returns, and process improvement.

Learning & Growth Perspective: This perspective defines the organization's infrastructure to execute internal business processes; skills, capabilities, and knowledge of the employees; technology; work environment; etc. Objectives in the first three perspectives (financial, customer, and internal business process) define where the organization must excel to achieve breakthrough performance. The objectives in the learning & growth perspective provide the infrastructure and capabilities to achieve the ambitious objectives in the other three perspectives.

There are three principal categories for the learning & growth perspective: Employee capabilities and work environment; information systems capabilities; and organizational infrastructure.

Employee capabilities include training and development, employee satisfaction/engagement, employee productivity, and employee retention. Organizations need to invest in their employees' capabilities to remain competitive in today's dynamic business landscape. This involves providing regular training, skill development programs, and opportunities for personal growth. A company's culture plays a crucial role in shaping its employees' mindsets and behavior. A culture that encourages innovation, collaboration, and a growth mindset can drive individuals to expand their skill sets and adapt to new challenges. Measures for employees' motivation and empowerment include suggestions made and implemented by employees, employees' engagement scores, achievement of yearly objectives/targets by employees, absenteeism, level of alignment of individual goals to team goals, organizational goals, etc.

Information system capabilities include IT systems' capability and capacity, strategic information coverage ratio, level of technology adoption, employee reskilling, etc. In the digital age, information technology is the backbone of organizational efficiency and competitiveness. From streamlining operations to enabling data-driven decision-making, IT plays a pivotal role in sustaining businesses. Investing in IT infrastructure and capabilities allows organizations to harness the power of data analytics, automation, and emerging technologies. By aligning IT investments with strategic objectives, organizations can ensure that their technology infrastructure supports learning, innovation, and growth initiatives.

Robust organizational infrastructure is the foundation upon which all other perspectives of the Balanced Scorecard rest. Without the right processes, systems, and resources in place, it becomes challenging to foster employee capabilities, nurture a learning culture, or effectively utilize information technology. This infrastructure encompasses everything from well-defined workflows to efficient supply chains, all aimed at enabling the organization to function smoothly. Investments in organizational infrastructure can improve resource allocation, reduce waste, and enhance agility. When employees have the tools and systems they need to excel, and when the organization can adapt quickly to changing circumstances, the Learning & Growth perspective becomes a springboard for success in achieving broader strategic goals.

Balanced Scorecard Shows the Cause and Effect of Strategy

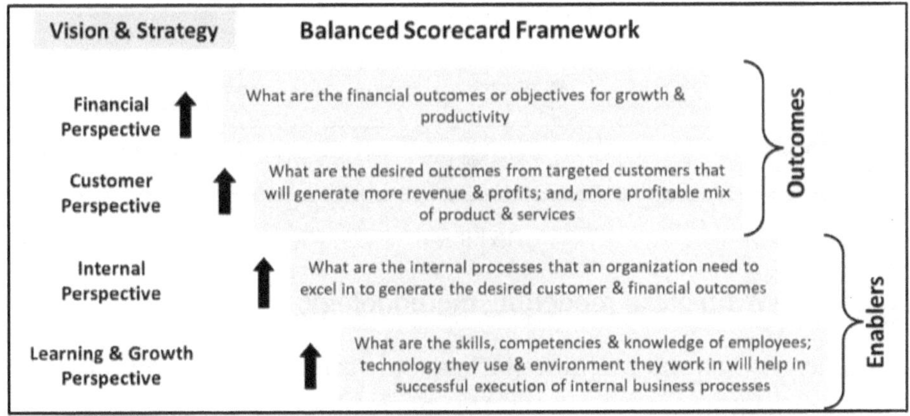

Exhibit-6.2

If we carefully look at the four perspectives, the top two perspectives are the outcomes, and the bottom two perspectives are the enablers (exhibit 6.2). The Balanced Scorecard shows the cause-and-effect relationships among the four perspectives (starting from the bottom): *'What skills, competencies, knowledge, technology, and environments do our people need to run the internal processes to produce and deliver what customers need to generate the financial results required by the shareholders.'* The use of cause-and-effect logic is the main differentiator between the Balanced Scorecard and other approaches to organizational measurement. Without the logical cause-and-effect linkages, you simply have a 'bucket of measures'.

The four perspectives capture the idea of 'Balance' in the Balanced Scorecard by focusing not only on the results of the company's efforts (e.g., financial results), but also on customer, internal, and learning & growth activities that drive financial success. In formulating goals from each perspective, the following management tools may be used:

Components of a Balanced Scorecard				
	What strategy must achieve & what is critical to its success	How success will be measured & tracked	Performance expectations	Key action programs required to achieve objectives
Perspective	**Objectives**	**Measure**	**Target**	**Initiatives**
Financial	Grow Revenue	Revenue Mix	$200 M – new geographies $100 M – new Products	Establish office in Dubai Establish New Product Line
Customer	Increase customer satisfaction	Customer satisfaction index	15	Managing complaints Regular visits
Internal	Assure timely project completion	Project schedule performance	90% in 2014	Improve key PM processes Training in PM skills
Learning and Growth	Improve skills	Av. Training hours	40 hours in 2014	Custom Training Knowledge Library

Exhibit-6.3

Financial – A financial modelling methodology

Customer – Customer segmentation and targeting, and the customer value proposition

Internal – A value chain of internal processes

Learning & Growth – Frameworks for measuring intangible asset values, infrastructure, tools, and technology.

The Balanced Scorecard functions as an integrating tool for multiple performance and organizational improvement programs/initiatives existing today. It does not exclude existing programs in the organization but seeks to use and integrate these existing programs within the Balanced Scorecard. For example, the financial perspective may include ROI and EVA to show profitability and growth; the Customer Perspective may include Customer Relationship Management (CRM) and Experience

Co-Creation (ECC); the Internal Perspective can include TQM/ISO/ABC/Six Sigma/Lean manufacturing; and the learning perspective may have change management and HR strategies. Exhibit 6.3 shows all the key components of the Balanced Scorecard in an integrated manner and includes objectives, measures, targets, and initiatives under four perspectives.

Developing a Balanced Scorecard

There are six steps in the Balanced Scorecard process. The development of a Balanced Scorecard typically takes 8–12 weeks depending on various factors, such as the level of support from the leadership team, organizational size/complexity, the availability of stakeholders' time, and the availability of the required data (exhibit 6.4).

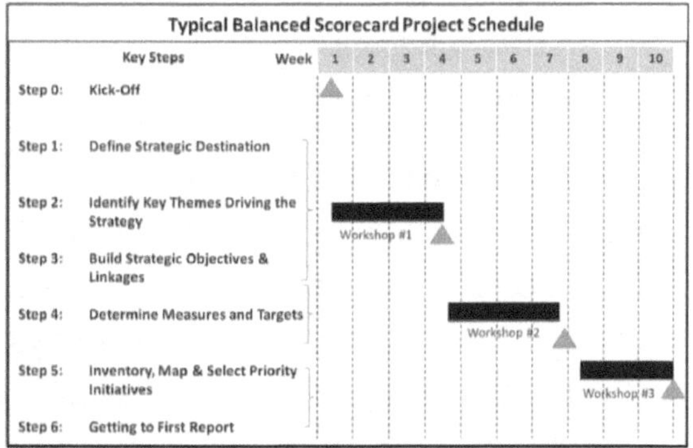

Exhibit-6.4

These six steps are completed in three workshops spread over 8-12 weeks.

Workshop #1: During the first workshop, the strategic destination is articulated and finalized. Key inputs for this exercise are interviews with senior executives, background strategic research, and the company's historical performance data. The main outputs of strategy mapping in steps 1–3 include:

- Statement of strategic destination (usually defined prior to the Balanced Scorecard process)
- Identification of strategic themes
- Linked objectives within each theme across four business perspectives
- A straw model strategy map to be presented in Workshop #1

These deliverables form an integrated set. They cannot function as 'stand-alone' elements within the Balanced Scorecard process.

Strategic destination guides all remaining activities in the development of the Balanced Scorecard. A good statement of strategic destination goes to the essence of the business, is agreed to, and supported by all key stakeholders, and does not contain 'fluff'. Some methods for clarifying/articulating a strategic destination are:

- past organization performance,
- expectations of shareholders,
- industry trends,
- competitive benchmarking.

Strategic Themes help focus the organization on arriving at its strategic destination. Each of these themes should have a direct impact on your financial objectives. These themes are the major thrusts with which the organization will accomplish its strategic destination. In most cases, strategic themes will emerge from an internal perspective. Common strategic themes include:

- Operational Management Processes (Best Total Cost)
- Customer Management Processes (Best Customer Relationship)
- Innovation Processes (Most Innovative Products)
- Regulatory and Societal Processes (Employer of Choice)

Workshop #2: This workshop is organized to determine and finalize measures and performance targets. Preliminary discussions with the concerned teams and individuals are held prior to the workshop. For some of the measures, the leadership team, business heads, and functional heads may be involved. It is critically important to have buy-in from the objective owners and employees who are going to deliver the performance.

Corporate Social Responsibility (CSR) is an emerging strategic theme that is used mainly by organizations that are regulated or that have a significant environmental impact.

Workshop #3: In the third workshop, initiatives, strategic projects, and budgets are finalized. Initiatives and strategic projects are executed to bridge the gaps between current performance and desired performance levels. It is important to assign an initiative owner for each of the strategic projects/initiatives. Each of the strategic initiatives and projects will also have timelines for completion with key milestones.

Chapter – 7

Strategy Maps

As we have learned in the previous chapter, a Balanced Scorecard allows us to have a more comprehensive performance measurement system. By adding measures from three perspectives (Customers, Internal Processes, and Learning & growth), the Balanced Scorecard allows us to measure the performance of processes, capabilities, resources, and customer outcomes that are critical to assess and predict the performance of an organization. Additionally, the Balanced Scorecard allows organizations to undergo remarkable transformation through alignment and focus.

Unlike financial management, strategy has no general definitions or framework. There are as many definitions of strategy as there are strategy gurus. A strategy must be at the centre of the management process for real transformation. It must be clearly understood by everyone in the organization since 'strategy cannot be executed if it cannot be understood, and it cannot be understood if it cannot be described[4]'.

Moreover, in today's knowledge economy, sustainable value is created by developing intangible assets, such as the skills and knowledge of the workforce, creating a conducive work environment, having IT infrastructure that links the firm to its customers and suppliers, and having a climate that encourages innovation, improvement, and problem-solving. Several factors prevent financial systems from measuring these intangible assets and linking them to value creation:

---

4   The Strategy Focused Organization by Robert S. Kaplan and David P. Norton

- Value is Indirect: Intangible assets (mentioned above) seldom have a direct impact on financial outcomes.

- Value is Contextual: The value of intangible assets depends on organizational context and strategy. The skills of a workforce in a manufacturing industry may not be useful in a service or IT industry.

- Value is Potential: Tangible assets can be valued based on historical costs. Intangible assets have potential value and need organizational processes to transform the potential value into products and services that have tangible value.

- Assets are Bundled: Intangible assets seldom have a value of their own and must be bundled with other assets to create value. The value of intangible assets arises from creating the entire set of assets (in a cause-and-effect relationship) along with the strategy that links them together.

What is a Strategy Map?

A Balanced Scorecard provides a framework to describe a strategy by linking intangible and tangible assets in value-creating activities. The linkage model called Strategy Map, is the pictorial view of the scorecard that describes how intangible assets get mobilized and combined with other assets, both tangible and intangible, to create a customer value proposition and achieve desired financial outcomes.

Financial Perspective:

The financial perspective answers the critical question: *'What will our Economic Model look like?'* Any good strategy balances the two contradictory forces: Long-Term vs. Short-Term. Organizations can make more money either by selling more (growth strategy) or spending less (productivity). Actions required for revenue growth generally take longer to create value since they involve capital expenditures for capacity expansion. On the other hand, actions for productivity enhancement require short-term initiatives (e.g., process improvement, training, re-orienting the production lines, Six Sigma initiatives, etc.). For this reason, the financial perspective of the strategy must have both long-term (growth) and short-term (productivity) dimensions. Hence, both themes are important for improving the financial performance of an organization. Refer (exhibit 7.1).

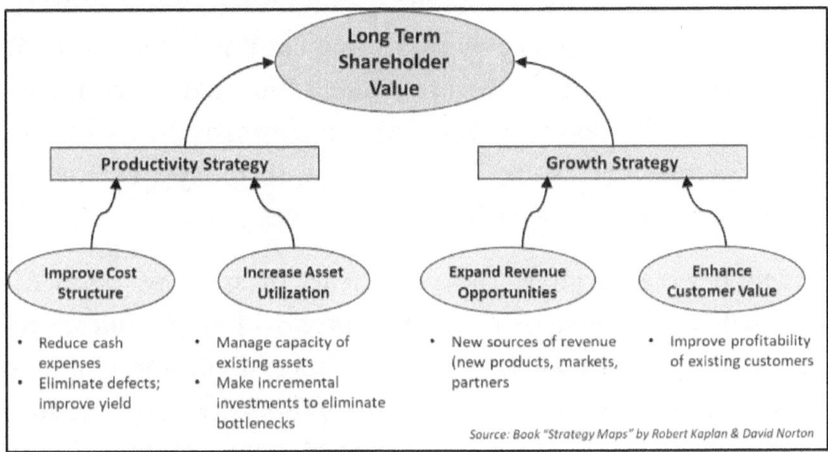

Exhibit-7.1

Customer Perspective

During the Industrial Era, strategies were product-driven. Since there were not many alternative products with different features, the underlying philosophy was, *'If we can manufacture it and it solves a problem, the customers will buy it'*. During this era, organizations succeeded through efficient operations management processes and product innovation. Building customer relationships was not a priority.

Exhibit-7.2

The new economy brought customers to centre stage. The evolution of computers, communication technologies, the internet, and free access to information has shifted the balance of power from producers to customers. Customers can find correct information about a company's product or service, including price, availability, delivery time, etc., on the internet including that of competitors. Moreover, the physical proximity of the company to its customers has also become irrelevant. In that sense, in today's economy, the 'Customer is King.'

The customer perspective, the very heart of strategy, defines how growth will be achieved. The value proposition provides specific details to attract new customers and/or increase the share of existing customers' businesses. A clear definition of this value proposition is the most important step in the development of a strategy map. From the customer perspective of the strategy map, organizations identify the targeted customer segments in which the business will compete and measure the business's performance for customers in these targeted segments. Measures will typically include several common and specific measures (depending on the industry) for customers in these targeted segments (exhibit 7.2).

Internal Process Perspective

The strategic objectives from the customer's perspective describe the strategy—the targeted customers and value proposition. And the financial perspective describes the economic outcomes (revenue, profit, and growth). Internal perspective answers the vital questions: How the organization will produce and deliver value to

Exhibit-7.3

customers and how it will improve its processes to reduce costs and improve productivity? It will typically include the processes related to (exhibit 7.3):

- Operations Management
- Customer Management
- Innovation Management
- Regulatory and Social Processes

While developing the internal perspective of their strategy map, companies need to identify the processes that are most critical for their strategies and/or value proposition. While companies give the highest importance to one of the four groups of internal processes, they still need to follow a 'balanced' strategy and address the requirements of all four clusters. However, it is very important to identify and excel at the critical few processes that are most important for delivering the chosen customer value proposition.

Operations Management: Operations management processes include day-to-day activities by which companies produce their existing products and services and deliver them to customers. For example, a manufacturing company will have processes for procuring raw materials from its suppliers, converting raw materials into finished goods, delivering finished goods to its customers, and managing risks to ensure that its customers are satisfied. In a service company, operating processes will produce and deliver services used by customers instead of products.

Customer Management: Processes related to customer management help a company build, expand, and deepen its relationships with its customers. These will include the selection of targeted customers, the acquisition of the targeted customers, customer retention, and customer loyalty (lock-in).

The customer selection process involves identifying the characteristics of the most desirable customer based on the company's value proposition. Depending on the product or service of the company, customers can be segmented based on lifestyle, income, age, family size, ethnicity, etc.

Customer acquisition involves generating leads, communicating with potential customers, choosing entry-level products/services, pricing the product/service, and closing the sale.

Customer retention is an outcome of excellent service and responsiveness to customers' requests.

Customer lock-in involves nurturing long-term relationships with existing customers, cross-selling multiple products and services, and becoming a trusted supplier or service provider.

Innovation: For an organization to have a sustained competitive advantage, it needs to continually innovate to create new products, services, and internal processes to deliver better products and services to its customers. Without innovations, other companies will be able to eventually imitate the products and services, leading to competition purely based on price. This will ultimately lead to the erosion of profits and market share. Managing innovation includes processes related to:

- Identifying opportunities for new products and services
- Managing research and development for new products/services
- Design and development of new products and services
- Making new products and services available in the market

Regulatory Compliance and Community Wellbeing: Companies need to comply with several international, national, and local regulations related to the environment, employees' health and safety, employment practices, social responsibilities, and reporting. Depending on the size of the company and the area in which it operates, most of the requirements are mandatory. However, many companies proactively seek to go beyond the mandatory requirements to build a reputation to attract and retain high-quality employees and to build a reputation as a responsible organization. Moreover, companies manage and report their regulatory and social performance along several critical dimensions, including the environment, health and safety, employment practices, and CSR.

Learning & Growth Perspective

The learning & growth perspective defines the competencies, skills, know-how, technology, environment, and work culture required to support critically important processes and activities.

This perspective serves as the bedrock upon which an organization can build and achieve exceptional performance in the other three perspectives. For more discussion on the learning & growth perspective, please refer to chapter 6.

In this way, the strategy map (exhibit 7.4) portrays an integrated and logical description of how the strategy will be executed to accomplish financial and customer objectives. The linkages in the strategy map clearly articulate and display cause-and-effect relationships to describe which improvements in the capabilities of intangible assets result in tangible customers and financial outcomes. Stand-alone measures are not very useful in this regard. Only clear linkages in the strategy maps provide the recipes for transformation and value creation.

The formulation of strategy is an art, and it will remain so. The description of strategy; however, should not be an art. If you can describe the strategy in a more disciplined way, you increase the likelihood of successful implementation[5].

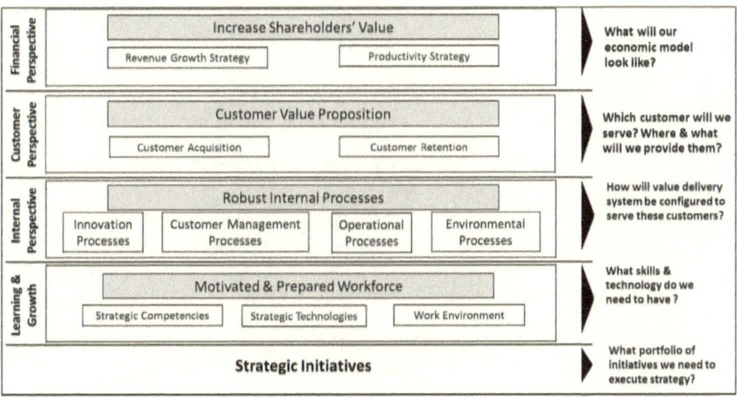

Exhibit-7.4

---

5   Chapter 3, The Strategy Focused Organization, by Robert S. Kaplan and David P. Norton 2000

Chapter – 8

Strategic Objectives and Strategic Themes

In this chapter, we will look at the strategic objectives and strategic themes. Strategic objectives are the building blocks of the strategy, and achieving these objectives is an indication of successful strategy execution. Strategic themes are high-level business strategies that comprise more than one strategic objective. Strategic themes are part of the overall business model.

Strategic Objectives

In the previous chapter, we looked at the strategy map, its four perspectives, and the strategic objectives under each of the four perspectives. We are quite clear by now that strategic objectives are the building blocks of a strategy. The strategic objective works as a linchpin and helps us define four critical elements of the strategy (exhibit 8.1).

Exhibit-8.1

Desired Results: What are we trying to accomplish? It links to the customers' requirements. A customer can be internal (within the organization) or the final customer (who finally uses the organization's product or service).

Objective Owners: Who is responsible and accountable for accomplishing this objective? Objectives are defined at the organizational/departmental level and cascaded to the individual level.

Strategic Initiatives or Projects: What strategic projects or initiatives must we accomplish to achieve the objectives? These are action plans to accomplish the desired performance level for a particular objective.

Performance Measures: How are we going to measure our performance, and how are we currently performing?

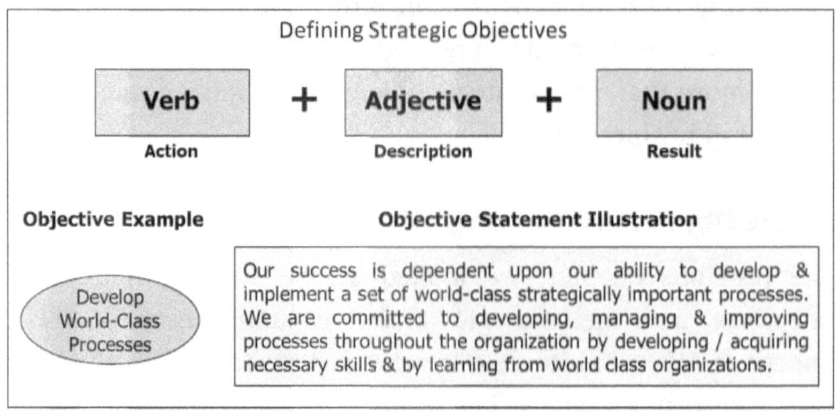

Exhibit-8.2

Defining and wording the strategy objective is no less than an art. If we use too few words, it may not be descriptive enough to be able to explain what we are trying to achieve. It also becomes very generic and loses its relevance to the specific goal we are trying to achieve. And if we use too many words, it becomes hard to keep it within the small bubble in the strategy map. And if we use smaller fonts, it becomes hard to read. It is important to strike a balance between long sentences and a very brief description of strategic objectives.

In articulating a strategic objective, a minimum of three words/components are used—a verb, an adjective, and a noun (exhibit 8.2). It calls for action to achieve superior results. There is one thing that should be kept in mind while creating good objectives. We need to be careful about the *intensity* of the objective and ensure that it reflects what we want to achieve. A good set of Balanced Scorecard objectives should 'tell a story' of the strategy and reflect systems/logical thinking.

In the example above, we want to 'Develop World-Class Processes', and consider the implications of this commitment. Developing world-class processes is not an easy task and it does not clarify which specific process needs improvement. Moreover, depending on the current level of performance, significant improvements may have to be made to the processes. Do we have the know-how and the resources to make that happen? More importantly, is it necessary? We should commit to objectives that are necessary, and feasible.

This also helps us in ensuring the feasibility of executing the strategy. Having big audacious goals and objectives in the strategy (that are almost impossible to achieve) may have an adverse impact on the morale of the employees.

It is a good practice to define strategic objectives at two levels of detail:

- Objective name/headline – A short four to six-word objective to be used in graphical representations like the strategy map.
- Objective definition/statement – Several sentences that define the objective with greater precision for use in the backup material.

Strategic Themes

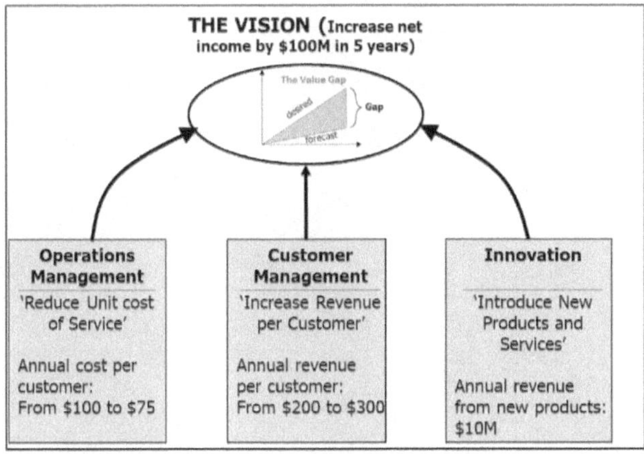

Exhibit-8.3

Strategic themes are the main, high-level business strategies that form the basis for the organization's business model. They often cut across the four perspectives of the Balanced Scorecard. Once you have agreed upon the vision for your organization, the same vision is systematically decomposed into three or four strategic themes. Too many themes dilute the focus and make it difficult to manage. If an organization can excel in areas defined by strategic themes, it should be able to achieve its vision. Strategic themes have a very broad scope compared to individual strategic objectives. They define the major thrust areas the organization must focus on to achieve the vision. A strategic theme is an area in which your organization must excel in order to achieve your vision. Examples of strategic themes could be operational excellence, product innovation, strategic outsourcing, etc.

Decomposing the high-level value gap (between the current performance level and the vision) into its actionable components leads to strategic themes that facilitate cross-functional teamwork and management (exhibit 8.3). Building themes helps us ensure that we have fully considered the strategies needed to achieve each strategic result. This, in turn, ensures that we achieve the vision we set for ourselves. Once all the themes are developed, they are combined to create a business strategy map that includes all the strategic objectives and strategic themes. Themes also ensure the structural integrity of the strategy. Another benefit of strategic themes is the opportunity to involve more people (their voices, their experiences, and their knowledge) in developing strategy through their inclusion on theme teams. This also helps in getting the buy-in of the people.

Chapter – 9

Performance Measures

What are Performance Measures or Indicators?

All organizations use various processes to achieve certain outputs and outcomes. To know how the processes are performing, organizations track various performance indicators that measure the performance and/or results. Having the right measures is as important as running the processes properly. Measures are also used for comparing results against standards, previous timeframes, or other similar organizations. Measures also show trends to demonstrate that improvements are being made over time. The most important measures are termed 'key measures'. The rest of the measures are simply called 'measures'. The measures are broadly divided into two categories: result indicators and performance indicators. Let us look at each one of them to know the difference and what purpose they serve.

The Difference Between Result Indicators and Performance Indicators

According to David Parmenter, the result and performance indicators are used interchangeably, though there is a big difference between the two. Let us look at each one of them.

Result Indicators are used to reflect the fact that these measures are the summation of more than one team's input. These help in looking at the combined teamwork but do not help in fixing a problem due to the inability to find the real cause of the performance or non-performance. Results are generally final outcomes. Result indicators are also called 'lag measures'.

Performance Indicators, on the other hand, are measures that can be tied to a team or cluster of teams working closely together for a common purpose. The performance, in this case, is the responsibility of one team. This helps in assigning ownership and accountability. Performance indicators are also called 'lead measures'.

In both of these measures, some are more important than others, so we add the extra word 'key' to show the relative importance of these measures. Thus, we have four types of measures:

- Key Result Indicators (KRIs) give the board and leadership team an overall summary of how the organization is performing. These are key results of actions taken by many teams, and leadership is ultimately responsible for these measures. Examples include, net profit, return on capital employed, net profit before tax, etc.
- Result Indicators (RIs) tell the management how the teams or departments are combining to produce results. These reflect the activities of more than one team and provide a good overview of how teams are working. The difference between a KRI and an RI is simply that the KRI is a more overall and important summary of activities that have taken place.
- Performance Indicators (PIs) show management what the teams are delivering. The difference between PIs and KPIs is that the latter are deemed fundamental to the organization's well-being. PIs help teams align themselves with the organization's strategy.
- Key Performance Indicators (KPIs) tell management how the organization is performing in its Critical Success Factors (CSFs), and by monitoring them, management can track and improve an organization's performance. KPIs are those indicators that focus on the aspects of organizational performance that are most critical for the current and future success of the organization.

It is important to understand the differences among the four types of measures and use appropriate measures as per the requirements. Also, please note that most of the financial indicators are RIs. In practice, we have seen people use PIs and RIs interchangeably without knowing the difference between the two.

Since KPI is the most commonly used term to denote performance measures, we will use this term unless the context calls for using a specific term (KRI, RI, PI, or KPI).

Why Do We Need Performance Measures?

Performance measures help us answer two of the most important questions (exhibit 9.1):

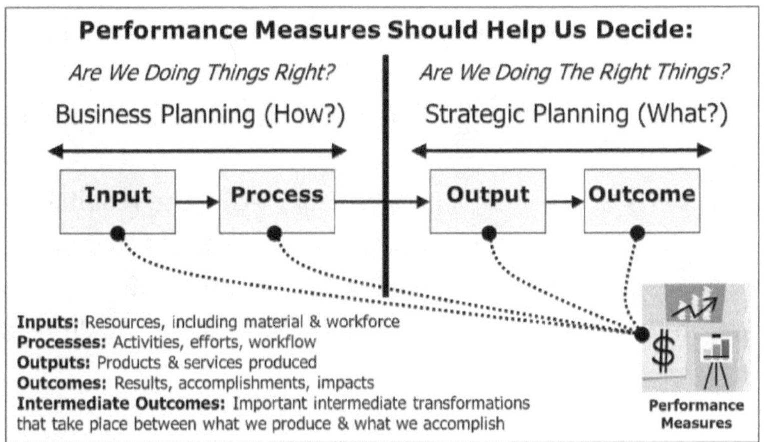

Exhibit-9.1

- Are we doing things right?
- Are we doing the right thing?
- Well-designed performance measures help the decision-makers in an organization to:
- Establish baseline information (current level of performance)
- Set performance standards and targets to motivate continual improvement
- Measure and report performance over time
- Determine if the basic business operations are functioning properly and are sustainable
- Compare performance across geographies, business units, departments, etc.

- Benchmark performance against regional and international norms/peers
- Evaluate if the underlying assumptions or hypotheses of the strategy are valid or need to change

Criteria for Selecting Measures:

The following criteria are generally used for selecting the right measures:

- *Validity* – Does the KPI measure what it is supposed to measure?
- *Reliability* – Does the KPI provide a consistent measure over a period?
- *Acceptability* – Are the measures acceptable to most of the people in the organization?
- *Feasibility* – Is it possible to collect the data, and is it worth the resources?
- *Sensitivity* – Are small changes reflected in the results?
- *Specificity* – Does the measure capture changes that occur in the performance for which the measure is intended?
- *Relevance* – What useful decisions can be made from the measure?

Characteristics of Great Measures

Great measures are:

- *Relevant* to and consistent with a specific organization's Vision, Strategy, and Objectives, and will impact one or more critical success factors/perspectives
- *Focused* on organization-wide strategic value rather than non-critical and/or local business outcomes
- *Appropriate* to the organization together with its operational performance
- *Realistic* – fits into the organization's constraints and overall strategy
- *Specific* – clear and focused to avoid any misinterpretation

- *Measurable* – can be measured and may be either quantitative or qualitative
- *Attainable* – achievable, reasonable, observable, and credible under expected conditions
- *Timely* – measured frequently and achievable within the given time frame
- *Limited Dark Side* – instigates appropriate actions and desired behaviour

Lead and Lag Measures

The Balanced Scorecard development process uses two main types of measures: lead measures and lag measures. Lead measures (drivers) are used for measuring immediate processes, activities, or behaviours. They are more predictive in nature and allow organizations to adjust (or drive) behaviours for performance. Whereas, lag measures assess or evaluate the performance results (outcome) at the end of a time period or activity. As an example, for a strategic objective 'Grow customer loyalty', the lead measure would be 'hours spent with customers', and the lag measure would be 'customer retention'. To summarize:

Lead Measures:

- Are also called in-process, efficiency, or performance measures
- Are predictive of lag measures, results, or outcomes
- Are influenceable, i.e., some actions may be taken to influence the final outcome
- Lead indicators are always more difficult to determine than lag indicators
- Often, they require some kind of investment to implement
- Provide an early warning for achieving a relevant lag indicator

Lag Measures:

- Are also known as effectiveness, outcome, or result measures
- Are the ultimate goals or objectives we are trying to accomplish
- Nothing more can be done once you accomplish a lag indicator

- Essential for charting progress but useless when attempting to influence the future
- Traditionally, we tend to settle for lag indicators as they are easier to track

Determining Meaningful Measures

Once the strategic objectives are finalized and the strategy map is developed by the core team, it is time to determine the measures that will help us track progress or improvement on those objectives. Prework includes revisiting the work done so far and refining the strategy map if required. Organizations may already be using some measures to track progress. It is a good practice to check the existing measures for their usability and assign them to appropriate objectives. Some financial measures may already exist and serve as a structure for the development of the remaining measures. When defining measures, it is not unusual to revisit objectives for clarity and precision. Draft measures for new objectives are developed in one-off meetings with the executives. Although the whole process appears to be linear, the actual process is iterative in nature.

By the end of this workshop, 90% of the linkages in the strategy map would be complete, with 80%–90% of the objectives having measures. The development of the measures is done in a separate workshop. At this point, the core team may engage several measurement team members to help define applicable measures for the objectives. Typically, measurement team members are functional or line experts. A good rule of thumb is to identify 50% of your Balanced Scorecard measures in existing management systems. This is particularly true for outcome or lag measures.

Three different models may be used to get to the measures that matter most:

- *The Logic Model:* Exploring the relationship among four types of performance measures: inputs, processes, outputs, and outcomes. The logic model reinforces the logic of the strategy map by showing activities that produce good results.

- *Process Flow:* Flowcharting a process helps identify the activities (and measures) that matter most to produce good outcomes. A process flow diagram also helps identify places where improvements in workflow are needed and possible. Applying this model also leads to new initiatives that can be used to validate the strategy.
- *Causal Analysis:* Causal analysis helps in identifying the causes and effects of good performance and identifying input and process measures that are leading indicators of future results. We typically start with the results (effect) and identify all the causes that contribute to good results.

Possible sources of measures include Strategic Objectives, Critical Success Factors, Customer Value Proposition, Customer Strategies/ Requirements, the Organization's Core Competencies, Strategic Advantages, the Organization's Value Chain, and Strategic Initiatives.

The following steps are involved in determining and finalizing measures and setting targets:

Developing a List of Potential Measures:

The following steps are involved in developing a list of potential measures:

- Step-1: Know what a KPI is and is not
- Step-2: Evaluate Existing KPIs and performance measures
- Step-3: Ensure that your goals are measurable (SMART Goals)
- Step-4: Use a deliberate technique to identify performance measures
- Step-5: Clearly define performance measures

Identifying and Finalizing Performance Measures:

This step involves reviewing all the potential measures and choosing the final measures:

- Sort all measures to remove duplicate and unnecessary measures
- Define measures to make them easy to understand, use the Measurement Detailing Matrix at this stage
- Assess the strengths and feasibility of the measures
- Sort measures to clearly identify KPIs, PIs, KRIs, and RIs
- Look for unintended consequences (the dark side) of all measures and refine them, if required
- Determine the measure's name and how it will be measured

By the end of this step, we should have a list of finalized and clearly defined performance measures. Next comes the target setting for each of the performance measures.

Setting Targets:

The next step is to set targets for each of the finalized performance measures.

- Targets serve as a link between the department/individual and the organizational strategy and goals. A Balanced Scorecard uses targets to motivate the organization, not to control or constrain it.
- Target-setting methods include deriving from overall business goals (e.g., revenue), benchmarking industry leaders, incremental improvement based on historical performance, establishing a baseline, and defining targets over time.
- The target-setting process involves reviewing the challenge or performance gap, setting targets for the financial performance first, and setting the remaining targets by theme against measures in the customer, internal, and learning & growth perspectives.
- Set only one target per measure and ensure that it clearly communicates expected performance.
- Show or illustrate the relationship between the target and corresponding measures, objectives, themes, and strategies.

Implementing, Interpreting, and Reporting

Implementing Measures:

Implementing the finalized measures involves:

- Defining the source of the data and the people responsible for the data
- Defining analysis, representation, and reporting requirements
- Establishing a current performance baseline
- Setting targets and thresholds (upper and lower limits of desired performance) for the measures, if not done already
- Designing, improving, and implementing a data collection system to optimize data availability and integrity
- Gathering and managing data so that it is easy and quick to access
- Launching a change management and communication process to reinforce a performance-driven culture

Interpreting Performance Measures:

Interpreting performance measures requires the following steps:

- Establish the current performance baseline (as-is performance level)
- Focus on the gaps between as-is and to-be performance
- Compare actual performance with that of other organizations or business units (if possible)
- Turn the data into information using appropriate analysis techniques
- Choose analysis techniques that produce performance information which answers driving business questions
- Translate the information into implications to decide if any action is needed (or not)

For Reporting Performance:

- Establish the reporting requirements for performance measures
- Present performance measures in ways that provide simple, relevant, trustworthy, and visual answers to their driving questions

- Design graphs and other visuals that facilitate interpretation and decision-making
- Design and develop performance reports for the owners and audiences of performance measures
- Report performance measures regularly, as per the agreed frequency, that support timely decision-making

The use of dashboards and other data visualization techniques is a common practice nowadays.

Chapter – 10

Strategic Initiatives

What are Strategic Initiatives?

Strategic Initiatives (or strategic projects) are collections of finite-duration discretionary projects and programs outside the organization's day-to-day operational activities, that are designed to help the organization achieve its targeted performance. Strategic initiatives enable the organization to align resources (people, time, money, equipment, etc.) to the strategic direction defined in the Balanced Scorecard development process. As measures and targets track our progress towards achieving and communicating the intent of the strategic objectives, initiatives help close the gap between our current and desired performance.

Strategic themes, objectives, measures, and targets represent WHAT the organization wants to accomplish. Strategic initiatives represent the HOW. Objectives, measures, targets, and initiatives all work together to achieve the strategic destination:

- The objectives articulate the components of the strategy.
- Measures and targets track progress towards achieving and communicating the intent of the objective against expected performance levels.
- Initiatives help close the gap between current and desired performance.

A 'Good' Strategic Initiative should have:

- Accountability at the leadership team level
- Clearly defined start and end dates and progress milestones

- Clearly defined deliverables
- A budget
- Committed resource allocation (e.g., real employee hours)

An organization can have many projects happening at the same time. Some of these projects are merely enhancements, business as usual, or tactical in scope. These are not strategic initiatives.

Managing Strategic Initiatives

The process of inventory and mapping initiatives is mainly driven by the core team. It is a consolidation and analysis task that considers the future vision. The core team gathers or collects the current initiatives within the organization and maps or links the initiatives to the objectives they support. One should avoid the tendency to map all initiatives to objectives. Only those initiatives with a business case that directly support objectives should be mapped. There needs to be a direct, logical relationship. Bear in mind that some initiatives are important even if they are not strategic. Compliance requirements are an example of such an initiative.

The management of Strategic Initiatives involves five steps:

Choosing Strategic Initiatives:

While selecting and finalizing the initiatives, the following points need to be kept in mind:

- Initiatives should not be selected in isolation from each other. Some initiatives may be complementary to each other.
- Initiatives should not be selected independently

Programs/Projects Strategic Themes/ Initiative Portfolio	Initiative 1	Initiative 2	Initiative 3	Initiative 4	Initiative 5
Theme 1 Objective 1 Objective 2	Yes				
Theme 2 Objective 1 Objective 2	Yes	No			
Theme 3 Objective 1 Objective 2					
Theme 4 Objective 1 Objective 2	Yes	Yes		Yes	

Exhibit-10.1

for each strategic objective. A single initiative may impact more than one objective.

- A portfolio of strategic initiatives should be developed for each strategic theme. This helps in creating synergies and optimizing resources at themes' levels.
- Each non-financial objective should have at least one initiative. If no initiative is assigned to an objective, it implies that no performance improvement is needed for that objective, which cannot be true.
- Strategic initiatives should be aligned with strategic themes and objectives through a formal rationalization process.
- Strategic initiatives should be reasonable in number. The more the numbers, the lesser the focus.

The Rationalization Matrix (exhibit 10.1) is used to ensure that all objectives have at least one initiative assigned to them and there are no initiatives without a corresponding objective.

Prioritizing the strategic initiatives

Once the initial list of initiatives is finalized, all initiatives need to be assessed and rated based on the selection criteria. The selection criteria will depend on the organization's requirements, constraints, and aspirations. Exhibit 10.2 shows the criteria used for prioritizing initiatives for a company.

Exhibit 10.3 shows the framework for evaluating and prioritizing strategic initiatives. Each criterion is assigned a relative weightage based on its criticality and importance. Each

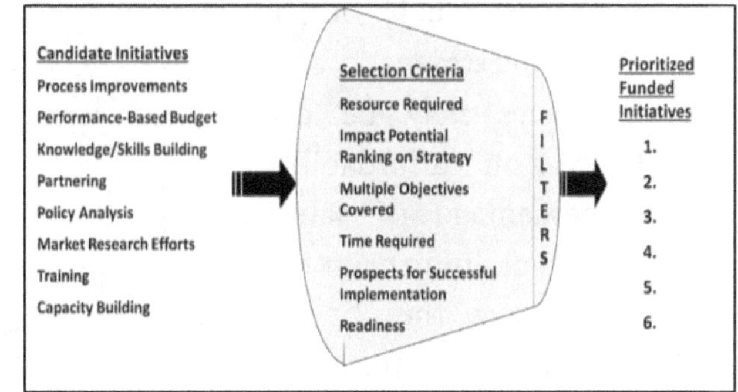

Exhibit-10.2

initiative is given a score out of ten for each of the selection criteria.

The score is then multiplied by the respective criterion weight. The weighted scores for all the criteria are added together to arrive at the total score for a particular initiative.

Funding the Strategic Initiatives

Strategic initiatives need to be both funded and linked to the budget. It is sometimes called Strategic Expenditure or StratEx, a budgeted item that specifically resources strategically important initiatives. StratEx can be maintained at multiple organizational levels (e.g., enterprise, functional, and departmental levels).

Strategic Initiatives	Initiative Selection Criteria							Total Score
	Strategic fit & benefit	Resource Demand	Time Required	Risks	Project Team/Skills	Depth & breadth of change		
Relative weightage	30	15	15	10	10	20		100
Initiative 1	8	5	5	5	6	8		660
Initiative 2								
Initiative 3								
Initiative 4								

Exhibit-10.3

- Exhibit 10.4 shows the process for finalizing the funding for the strategic initiatives. Both top-down and bottom-up approaches are used for estimating the total requirements and budget for individual initiatives. Total investment in strategic initiatives may be decided based on affordability as a percentage of sales and historical information. The budget may then be divided for each of the strategic themes and strategic initiatives under each theme.

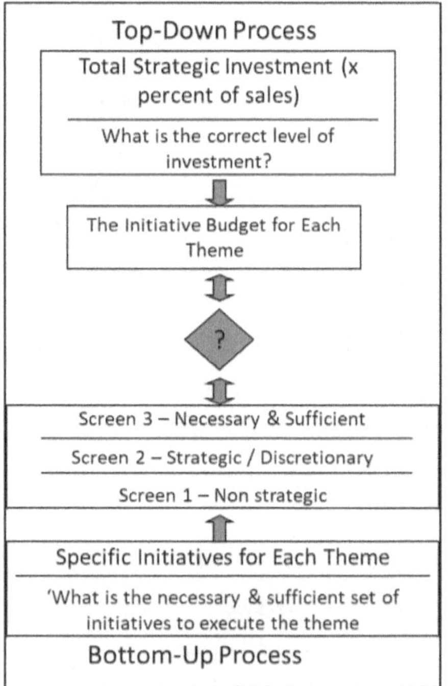

Exhibit-10.4

Screening all strategic initiatives helps us eliminate non-strategic and discretionary initiatives.

Performance Budgeting

After rationalization and prioritization, many organizations use performance budgeting techniques to allocate budgets to initiatives. Performance budgeting is based on the results that are expected to be realized from each initiative. Performance budgeting can:

- change the entire focus of the budgeting process from activities to results.
- be used to develop a rational and supportable case for new resources and to defend against budget cuts.
- help in identifying issues during budget analysis and review.
- assist improvement programs in coping with declining resources.
- be useful for incentive funding.
- it can be instrumental in achieving program results without additional resources.

Establishing Accountability

Each of the strategic initiatives needs to be owned and driven by a senior executive from the department that will benefit the most from the outcomes of the specific initiative. Depending on the nature of the initiative, a team of people (on a full-time or part-time basis) is assigned for each initiative. The progress of all initiatives is reviewed periodically, and progress and results are reported to the core team.

Chapter – 11

Implementing Balanced Scorecard

By now, you must have realized that implementing a Balanced Scorecard requires sustained effort and the involvement of the whole organization. Moreover, it is not a project with a finish line and requires a long-term commitment. Additionally, the leadership team's visibility and involvement are critically important for successful implementation and realizing the benefits. *'Build it and they will come'* works for products, brands, and many other new things, but it does not work so well with a Balanced Scorecard. *'Let them build it and they will use it'* works much better. This means involving and getting buy-in from as many employees as possible. And 'implementing' involves turning the strategy and Balanced Scorecard into a true management system and deploying, managing, and sustaining the newly created system.

The complete process and activities involved in implementing a strategy using a Balanced Scorecard are shown in exhibit 11.1.

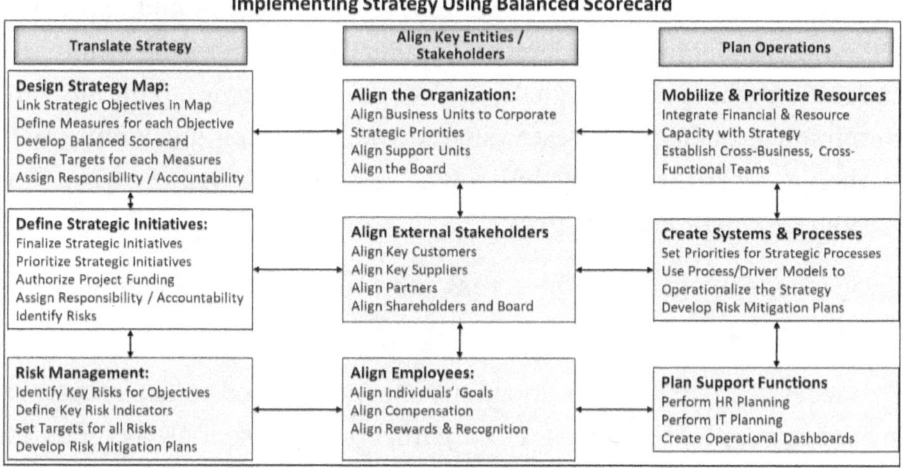

Exhibit-11.1

Implementing a Balanced Scorecard involves:

- Cascading the Balanced Scorecard to lower-level hierarchies
- Aligning key stakeholders and support functions
- Evaluating the relevance and efficiency of the Balanced Scorecard regularly
- Conducting regular strategic reviews using a Balanced Scorecard

These topics will be covered in the next section of the book.

Managing Change

Moving from traditional business planning and performance management to using a Balanced Scorecard requires a change in the mindset of the leadership team and employees. To support the shift in the mindset and instigate performance-driven culture leadership, the management needs to have regular communication with all employees, supported by relevant training and feedback. The following practices are useful in managing the shift to the new system.

Continued communication of the vision and rationale behind the scorecard

Continued communication of the vision and rationale behind the scorecard is crucial for maintaining organizational alignment and understanding. By regularly communicating the vision and explaining the rationale behind the scorecard, leaders can ensure that employees understand the purpose, goals, and desired outcomes. This ongoing communication helps to create a shared understanding and commitment to the scorecard, enabling individuals to connect their work to the broader organizational strategy.

Involvement of people from across the organization in planning and implementing the changes:

To successfully plan and implement changes related to the scorecard, involving people from across the organization is essential. By including diverse perspectives and expertise, organizations can tap into a broader pool of knowledge and generate innovative solutions. Involvement also fosters a sense of ownership and engagement among employees, as they have a voice in shaping the changes. This collaborative approach enhances the likelihood of successful implementation and minimizes resistance to change.

Communication of results to all employees and drawing comparisons to expected results

Regular communication of results to everyone in the organization is vital for transparency and accountability. By sharing scorecard results, organizations create a culture of openness and enable individuals to see the impact of their contributions. Drawing comparisons to expected results allows employees to evaluate their performance and identify areas for improvement. This information can also stimulate discussions and encourage collective learning, enabling the organization to make data-driven decisions and continuously enhance performance.

Ongoing scorecard training, especially for new people

Continuous scorecard training, especially for new employees, ensures that everyone understands the purpose, mechanics, and significance of the scorecard system. By providing comprehensive training, organizations can equip individuals with the knowledge and skills necessary to contribute effectively to the scorecard's objectives. Ongoing training also facilitates a consistent understanding of performance metrics and encourages alignment with organizational goals, fostering a culture of continuous improvement.

Employing process teams to improve throughput

Employing process teams is a powerful strategy for improving throughput and efficiency within an organization. By assembling cross-functional teams focused on specific processes, organizations can identify bottlenecks, streamline workflows, and implement process improvements. Process teams enable employees to collaborate, share best practices, and collectively solve problems. This approach promotes a culture of continuous improvement and empowers employees to take ownership of optimizing their work processes.

Use of reward and recognition to emphasize and reinforce desired behaviours

The use of reward and recognition programs is an effective way to emphasize and reinforce desired behaviours aligned with the scorecard objectives. By acknowledging and rewarding individuals or teams that demonstrate exemplary performance, organizations reinforce a culture that values and encourages the behaviours needed to achieve strategic goals. These programs not only motivate employees to excel but also foster a sense of appreciation and engagement, driving sustained performance improvement. Both monetary and non-monetary incentives may also be used to achieve long-term positive impacts on the behaviours of employees. While monetary rewards, such as bonuses or profit-sharing, provide tangible recognition, non-monetary incentives, such as flexible work arrangements, professional development opportunities, or public recognition, cater to different employee motivations. By offering a combination of incentives, organizations can appeal to diverse preferences, promote holistic employee well-being, and encourage sustained behavioural change aligned with the scorecard goals.

Performance Management System Challenges

Since implementing a Balanced Scorecard involves a new way of thinking and working, certain challenges and roadblocks are bound to occur.

Some of the challenges in implementing the performance management system include:

Fear of measurement and new systems

One common challenge in implementing a performance management system is the fear of measurement and new systems. Employees may be apprehensive about being evaluated and measured, especially if they perceive it as a threat to their job security or personal reputation. This fear can hinder the adoption and acceptance of the system, making it essential for organizations to address concerns, provide clear communication about the purpose and its benefits, and create a supportive environment that encourages learning and growth.

Lack of common definitions and terms

Effective performance management relies on a shared understanding of key definitions and terms. When there is a lack of common definitions, confusion and misinterpretation can arise, leading to inconsistent assessments and misaligned expectations. Organizations should establish clear and well-communicated definitions and provide training to ensure everyone understands the terminology and concepts associated with the performance management system.

Inconsistent or weak buy-in, and lack of understanding

Without consistent buy-in and understanding across the organization, the implementation of a performance management system may face resistance or limited engagement. When employees do not fully grasp the purpose, benefits, and mechanics of the system, they may perceive it as an administrative burden rather than a tool for improvement. Leaders should invest in comprehensive communication, education, and engagement initiatives to foster a shared understanding and generate strong buy-in throughout the organization.

Visions and strategies that are poorly defined and understood, and are not linked to individual actions

A significant challenge in performance management is when visions and strategies are poorly defined and not effectively cascaded to individual actions. If organizational goals are vague, disconnected, or lack clarity, it becomes challenging for employees to align their efforts with strategic objectives. Organizations should ensure that visions and strategies are well-defined, actionable, and communicated effectively at all levels. Connecting individual actions to larger organizational goals helps employees see the relevance of their contributions and promotes alignment.

Treating budgeting as a separate activity from strategy development

When budgeting is treated as a separate process from strategy development, it can lead to a misalignment between financial targets and strategic objectives. Organizations should integrate budgeting and strategy development to ensure that financial goals and resource allocation align with strategic objectives. This integration enables a holistic approach to performance management, where financial considerations are linked to the achievement of strategic outcomes.

Measures that are set independently of the performance framework or measures with no ownership

Another challenge is setting independent measures of the performance framework or lacking ownership over the measures. This can result in misaligned or ineffective PIs that do not reflect the strategic priorities. It is crucial to establish a robust performance framework that aligns measures with strategic objectives and ensures clear ownership and accountability for each measure. This approach enhances the relevance and reliability of performance data for decision-making and improvement efforts.

No performance targets, or targets that are set too high or too low

Setting appropriate performance targets is critical for driving motivation, improvement, and accountability. The absence of performance targets or setting targets that are either too high or too low can undermine the effectiveness of a performance management system. Organizations should establish realistic and challenging targets that inspire employees to stretch their capabilities while remaining attainable. Regular review and adjustment of targets based on feedback and organizational context are also essential for maintaining relevance and promoting continuous improvement.

Little or no strategic feedback

A lack of strategic feedback can impede the effectiveness of a performance management system. Employees need feedback on their performance relative to strategic objectives to understand their strengths, areas for improvement, and contribution to the overall organizational goals. Regular and timely strategic feedback helps employees make informed decisions, adjust their actions, and enhance their performance. Organizations should prioritize the provision of meaningful feedback to facilitate growth and development.

Lack of meaningful involvement

A performance management system's success relies on meaningful involvement from all stakeholders, including employees, managers, and leaders. When individuals feel excluded or have limited involvement in the system's design and implementation, they may perceive it as imposed or irrelevant to their work. Organizations should promote meaningful involvement by seeking input, encouraging collaboration, and creating opportunities for dialogue and participation. This inclusive approach fosters ownership, engagement, and a sense of shared responsibility for performance improvement.

PART – 3

Balanced Scorecards for Corporate and Support Functions

Chapter – 12

Evolution of Corporates

The industrial revolution started somewhere in the 17th century in the United Kingdom with the advent of small factories that focused on a narrow range of products. The second industrial revolution, which started in the 19th century, saw much more complex, capital-intensive industries, such as metals, chemicals, petroleum, machinery, and transportation. They needed more elaborate and centralized functions to coordinate and gain scale of economies, from procurement, manufacturing, and marketing to distribution functions. In these large, centralized organizations, production and sales were the primary value-adding activities. The finance department provided financial information to managers for monitoring, decision-making, and coordinating the flow of funds within the organization.

By the early 20th century, these large manufacturing companies had become multiproduct, multifunctional, and multiregional corporations. With an increase in size, it became more difficult and cumbersome to coordinate and collaborate between departments and multiple locations.

In the 1920s and 1930s, large companies such as General Motors and General Electric introduced a new form of organization called a multidivisional company, which was organized around specific product lines and geographic locations. And each product or geographic division became a replica of the original division. All these divisions were managed by senior executives at the corporate headquarters. Operations at the individual divisions were managed by divisional heads, and executives at the headquarters reviewed the performance of the individual divisions along with strategic planning and resource (funds, facilities, personnel, etc.) allocation.

The 1950s and 1960s saw a new form of organization called a Conglomerate. A conglomerate is a group of autonomous operating companies with no apparent commonalities or synergies. The apparent purpose was to reduce the risk of business cycles by investing in a diversified portfolio of businesses. This led to the development of a matrix organization, where a manager reports to both a senior corporate functional executive (at the corporate office) and a line or business unit manager. In practice, matrix organizations have proven difficult to manage because of the inherent tension or conflict between the interests of the corporate executive and the business unit manager.

Cascading Corporate Scorecards to Business Units

Cascading the corporate Balanced Scorecard to business units is a strategic approach that ensures alignment and consistency in organizational performance management. By extending the Balanced Scorecard framework to individual business units, companies can effectively translate high-level corporate objectives into actionable goals and measures at the operational level. This process involves breaking down the corporate's overall strategy and objectives into specific targets and KPIs that are relevant to each business unit. By cascading the scorecard, organizations can foster a sense of ownership and accountability among business-unit leaders, who can then develop tailored strategies and initiatives to drive performance and contribute to the overall success of the organization. This alignment of objectives across different levels of the organization enables a cohesive and integrated approach to performance management, ensuring that all business units are working towards common goals and driving progress in a coordinated manner.

Aligning Support Functions

Aligning support units with the business strategy is crucial for organizations to optimize their operational efficiency and effectively support the achievement of strategic objectives. Support units, such as HR, finance, IT, and procurement, play a vital role in enabling business functions to operate smoothly and contribute to overall organizational success. By aligning these support units with the business strategy, organizations ensure that their resources and capabilities are focused on activities that directly support the strategic goals. This alignment involves understanding the specific needs and requirements of each business unit and tailoring support services accordingly. For example, HRs may align their talent acquisition, development, and retention efforts with the skills and competencies required by the business units. Similarly, finance can align its budgeting and financial management processes to ensure the optimal allocation of resources to support strategic initiatives. By aligning support units with the business strategy, organizations can enhance collaboration, streamline processes, and maximize the value and impact of these units in driving overall organizational performance.

Aligning support units' strategies to business strategies is a critical element of overall strategy management for the following reasons:

- The resources provided by support units such as HR, IT, and procurement are fundamental to strategic success
- Support units develop a clear understanding of business-unit strategies
- Efficient, well-qualified support units do not necessarily contribute to the organization's strategy (unless they are fully aligned with the business strategy)
- Historically, support units have not been focused on strategy
- Proper cascading and alignment help in showing the contributions made by the support functions to the business strategy

Chapter 22 provides a case study based on one of our clients' assignments. It describes the whole process of developing key elements of the strategy, developing a Corporate Scorecard, cascading the same to the business units, and aligning scorecards for the support functions with the business units' scorecards.

Chapter – 13

Alignment and Cascading of Strategy

Why are Alignment and Cascading of Strategy Important?

Developing a robust business strategy is essential for organizations to achieve their long-term goals and stay competitive in today's dynamic market. However, formulating a strategy is just the first step. To turn strategy into action and achieve tangible results, organizations must effectively implement their business strategy throughout the organization.

Cascading and alignment are two key concepts in the implementation of a Balanced Scorecard framework. They are both important for ensuring that organizational strategies are effectively translated into actionable objectives and initiatives and implemented throughout the organization. However, they differ in terms of their focus and scope.

Alignment

Alignment in the context of the Balanced Scorecard refers to ensuring that the objectives and measures across different levels of the organization are consistent and mutually supportive. It involves aligning the goals and metrics of individual business units, departments, and teams with the overall strategic objectives of the organization. Alignment helps create a coherent and integrated approach to performance management. For example, a retail company has multiple departments, such as sales, marketing, and operations. Alignment would involve ensuring that the objectives and measures of each department are aligned with the overall strategic objective of improving customer satisfaction. For instance, the marketing department might have the objective of enhancing brand perception, while the operations department may have the objective of improving product quality. Both of these objectives contribute to the overall goal of customer satisfaction and are aligned with the strategic direction of the organization.

Cascading

Cascading business strategy involves translating the overarching strategic vision into actionable objectives and initiatives at various levels within the organization. It involves aligning the strategic objectives of top-level management with the operational goals of various departments, teams, and individuals. By cascading the strategy, organizations align all levels of the workforce towards common goals, ensuring that each employee understands his or her role and contribution in achieving the strategic objectives. The aim is to create a clear line of sight between the overall strategy and the day-to-day activities of employees. This alignment fosters a sense of purpose, improves collaboration, and enhances overall organizational performance. Let us consider the same retail company with a strategic objective of improving customer satisfaction. To cascade this objective, the company may set specific targets for its sales team, such as increasing the number of positive customer reviews, improving customer service response time, or achieving a certain level of customer retention. These targets directly support the higher-level strategic objective and provide a clear direction for the sales team's efforts.

In summary, cascading focuses on the vertical translation of strategic objectives from the top to the bottom levels of the organization, while alignment emphasizes the horizontal integration of objectives and measures across different units. Both cascading and alignment are crucial in ensuring a cohesive and effective implementation of the Balanced Scorecard framework.

Cascading Corporate Strategy to Business Units

A customized cascaded system of linked strategy maps and Balanced Scorecards align organization structure with corporate-level strategy.

Since strategy precedes structure and systems (Michael Porter), we need to first decide on the strategy and its usefulness. Similarly, when articulating a value proposition for a business, we need to have clarity on how a corporate will create more value from its business units if the same businesses operate completely independently. The four Balanced Scorecard perspectives provide a natural way to categorize the various enterprise value propositions that will support the business units' strategies.

Organization Change Agenda

Apart from the support services, 'organization capital' also plays a critical role in successful strategy execution. Organizational capital includes intangible factors such as culture, leadership style, systems, people's behaviour, alignment, teamwork, etc.

Organizational Change Agenda		
From...	**Element**	**....to**
Top-down	Leadership	Identify, develop, empower
Focus on tasks	People	Connected to the strategy
Operational silos	People	Integrated team approach
Budget drives strategy	Budget	Strategy drives budget
Practice Driven	Systems	Procedure Driven
Effort Driven	Culture	Performance Driven
Relationship Driven	Customer	Relationship & Credibility
Contributor	Partner / Supplier	Full Partner
Presence in Qatar	Geography	GCC & MENA
Satisfied Employee	People	Engaged Employee

Exhibit-13.1

Depending on the strategy, changes may be required in these attributes. The organizational change agenda is derived from the strategy and shapes the new desired culture in the organization (exhibit 13.1).

Aligning Support Units

Support units, like business units, have missions, customers, services, and employees. When developing a strategy map and Balanced Scorecard for the support unit, it is useful to think of the support unit as a 'business within a business'.

The financial perspective of a support unit will have two components: efficiency (cost of service) and effectiveness (impact on enterprise strategy). The customer perspective will have two classes of customers: business-unit managers to whom they provide services directly, and employees, who are the recipients and beneficiaries of the services. The internal process perspective of a support unit scorecard has three themes: operational excellence, business-unit partnership (efficiency), and providing strategic support (effectiveness). The learning & growth perspective of a support unit will have its own specific needs in terms of staff, technology, and work climate.

Support units' strategies will depend on whether they are considered a 'Cost Centre' or a 'Profit Centre.' Support Units can create a competitive advantage by excelling in any of the strategy archetypes: Operational Efficiency, Product Leadership, or Customer Intimacy. Exhibit 13.2 shows a typical portfolio of strategic services.

Strategic HR Service Portfolio	Strategic Information Capital Portfolio	Strategic Financial Service Portfolio
• Strategic Competency Development • Organization & Leadership Development • Performance Management Process	• Analytic & Decision Support Applications • Transaction-Processing Applications • Technology Infrastructure	• Transactions, Controls, and Processing • External Compliance & Communication • Planning & Decision Support Services

Exhibit-13.2

The objectives in these three portfolios must be aligned with the objectives of the 'internal process' perspective and integrated. Alignment and integration provide the opportunity for developing strategic objectives for human capital, information capital, financial portfolios, and organizational capital. The following techniques are used to establish a relationship between the strategy map and intangible assets:

Strategic Job Families: Strategic jobs will have the greatest impact on strategic outcomes. Organizations need to identify these job families, define the required competencies, and ensure their development to accelerate strategic outcomes.

Strategic IT Portfolio: The Strategic IT portfolio should receive priority in funding and other resources, as this will support and expedite strategy implementation.

Strategic Financial Portfolio: A Strategic financial portfolio helps in planning and decision support, external compliance, communication, and other transactional-level processes.

Key steps involved in aligning and cascading the Corporate/Enterprise strategy are:

- ***Clarifying Strategy Through Corporate Strategy Map:*** Getting consensus on the strategic priorities.
- ***Adopting Common Strategic Themes:*** Focusing on the critical outcomes needed to achieve the Vision.
- ***Developing Scorecards Across the Business Units/Functions:*** Cascaded from and aligned with Corporate Balanced Scorecard, ensuring understanding of the actions and resources needed.
- ***Developing Virtual Balanced Scorecards for the three Sectors:*** Promoting horizontal responsibility and shared management.
- ***Refining the Cascading of Objectives:*** Through exact, derived, and/or new objectives reflecting corporate objectives.
- ***Leveraging the Balanced Scorecard to Improve Business Planning:*** Through Performance-based Budgeting and Stratex (Strategy Expenditure).
- ***Forming Working Groups to Manage Strategic Priorities (Themes):*** Transitioning from 'Management by Business Lines' to 'Management by Mandate'.

Creating a Linkage Scorecard (exhibit 13.3) between the strategic business unit and shared service unit helps in identifying and defining the support unit's contribution to the business unit.

Service Level Agreement (SLA) defines the level of service that will be provided by the support unit and is reviewed every month. Support units also seek feedback from the business unit regarding the quality of service provided by the support unit and take appropriate actions if required.

Creating Support Unit Linkage

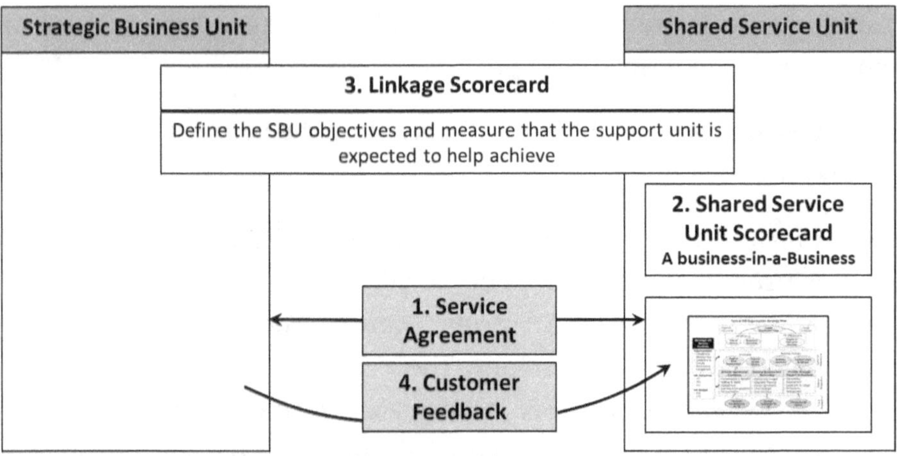

Source: The Strategy Focused Organization by Robert Kaplan & David Norton. Pp 193

Exhibit-13.3

Cascading business strategy is a vital process for organizations to effectively translate their strategic vision into actionable outcomes. By aligning objectives, initiatives, and activities at different levels, organizations can drive collaboration, enhance performance, and achieve their long-term goals. Organizations that master the art of cascading strategy can gain a competitive edge and navigate the ever-evolving business landscape with confidence.

Chapter – 14

Corporate Scorecard

Since the purpose of a corporate or enterprise is to create synergies among the entities it operates under its umbrella, this should lead to financial and non-financial benefits for the individual business units. The corporate needs to have an enterprise value proposition and should be able to figure out how it will create more value from the businesses it owns and operates in comparison to the stand-alone outcomes of individual businesses. Depending on the scope, a corporation can play multiple roles, such as allocating economic resources, sharing customers across businesses, having common branding, creating a common value proposition, integrating a value chain, etc.

Exhibit 14.1 shows various opportunities for and sources of corporate or enterprise-derived synergies and values. For example, a shared customer interface can be optimized for increasing total customer value through cross-selling and common customer value propositions.

Developing Synergies Through Corporate Scorecard

The four perspectives of the Balanced Scorecard provide us with various types of enterprise value propositions that would contribute to corporate synergies:

Financial Synergies:

- Effective acquisition and integration of business units.
- Excellent monitoring and governance across diverse business units.
- Leveraging a strong common brand across business units.
- Economising on the overall cost of production and delivery of products or services.

- Acquiring expertise in specialized skills to manage and synergize with external entities.

Customer Synergies:

- Consistent delivery of a strong and common value proposition to customers.
- Combining multiple products and services and delivering them to common customers.
- Using common channels for customer communication and delivery of products or services to reduce overall costs for acquiring and serving customers.

Internal Processes Synergies:

- Developing common core competencies in product and process technologies across business units.
- Achieving economy of scale through centralized sourcing and merchandising.

The Enterprise Scorecard	The Source of Enterprise-Derived Value
Financial Synergies 'How can we increase the shareholder value of our SBU portfolio?'	• **Internal Capital Management:** Create synergy through effective management of internal capital & labour markets. • **Corporate Brand:** Integrate a diverse set of businesses around a single brand, promoting common values or themes.
Customer Synergies 'How can we share the customer interface to increase total customer value?'	• **Cross Selling:** Create value by cross selling a broad range of products & services from several business units. • **Common Value Proposition:** Create a consistent buying experience, conforming to corporate standards at multiple outlets.
Internal Process Synergies 'How can we SBU processes to achieve economies of scale or value chain integration?'	• **Shared Services:** Create economies of scale by sharing the systems, facilities, & personnel in critical support processes. • **Value-Chain Integration:** Create value by integrating continuous processes in the industry value chain.
Learning & Growth Synergies 'How can we develop & share our intangible assets?'	• **Intangible Assets:** Share competency in the development of human, information, and organizational capital.

Exhibit-14.1

Learning and Growth Synergies:

- Leveraging common technologies for support functions and for providing a common platform to customers for accessing a wide variety of products or services.

- Sharing best practices through knowledge management, business excellence, and other mechanisms across business units.
- Enhancing human capital through excellence in HR recruiting, training, and leadership development practices across business units.

A good corporate strategy aligns and integrates all the elements (resources, processes, businesses, and organizations) into one system of interdependent parts. Exhibit 14.2 shows a typical Corporate Strategy Map.

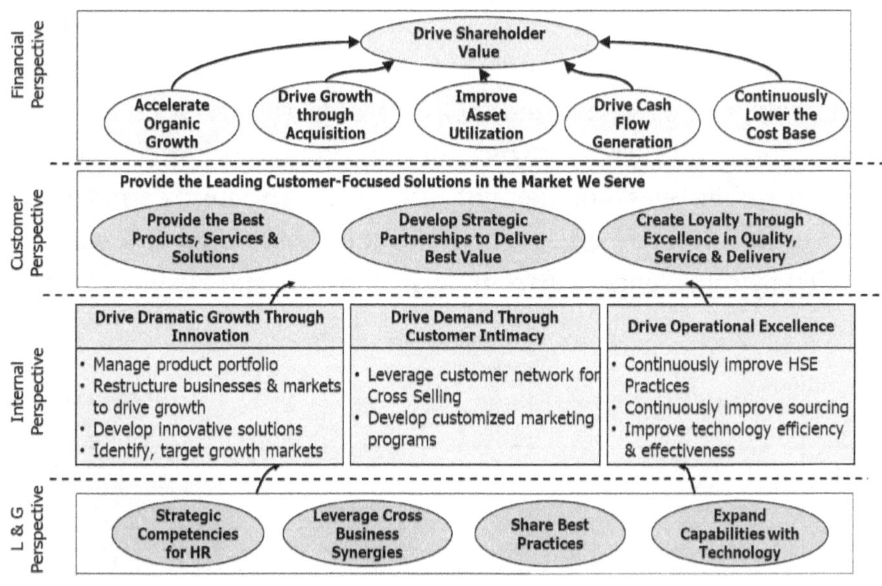

Exhibit-14.2

Aligning Business Units to Corporate –Vertical Alignment

Aligning the business units' strategy and Balanced Scorecard to the Corporate Strategy is a three-step process:

Step 1: After the development of the Corporate (parent) Balanced Scorecard, the organization communicates the function, structure, and content of the strategy throughout the organization. This ensures that all business units understand the overarching strategy of the corporate and what the corporate is trying to achieve as a parent organization.

Step 2: With an understanding of the parent scorecard function, structure, and content, the child organization builds a strategy map to align with and support the parent. The child's scorecard will consist of strategic themes and linked objectives.

Step 3: In step 3, both the child and parent organization use the Objective Matrix Template, as shown in exhibit 14.3, to visually clarify the relationship between the objectives of the parent and child.

It is important that the business unit gains approval to proceed to the next step in the cascading and alignment process.

The business unit has the responsibility to describe its contribution to corporate objectives, identify objectives that are not relevant to the unit's strategy, and recommend additional objectives relevant to the unit. The corporate, in turn, confirms contribution to corporate objectives, reconciles objectives not thought relevant to the unit's strategy, and approves new objectives relevant to the unit. This is done in a workshop attended by representatives from both corporate and business units.

Objective Matrix (Corporate-Business Unit Alignment)

	Corporate BSC Objectives	Identical	Contributory	New	N/A	Unit BSC Objectives
Financial						
Customer						
Internal						
Learning & Growth						

Exhibit-14.3

In the second workshop, alignment on measures, targets, and strategic initiatives is achieved. In this workshop, the business unit confirms its contribution to corporate Balanced Scorecard, develops a strategic business plan, and proposes cross-unit coordination where applicable (shared objectives). The corporate board approves the unit Balanced Scorecard and strategic plan and assists in cross-unit coordination for shared objectives. The meeting is often informal. The Cascading Unit Coordinator and the leader of the unit meet with the Balanced Scorecard Corporate Cascading Facilitator and/or the Balanced Scorecard Cascading Steering Team to review progress and gain agreement to proceed. Deliverables of this meeting include agreement on measures and targets and approval of the next steps. The sequential steps are given in exhibit 14.4.

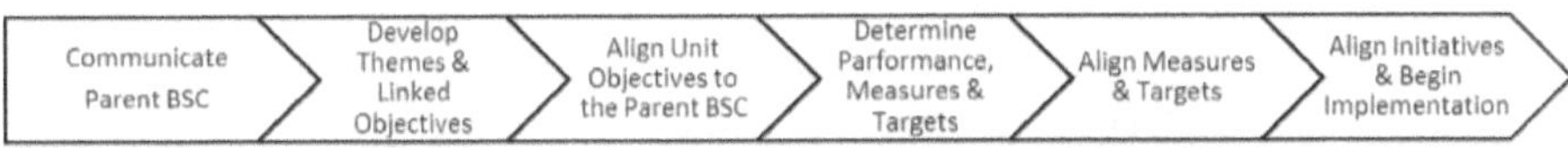

Exhibit-14.4

Aligning Support Units to Corporate – Horizontal Alignment

As we saw above, vertical alignment results from cascading the Balanced Scorecard from the enterprise level to business unit levels, while horizontal alignment results from cascading the Balanced Scorecard from enterprise/SBU levels to support units and external partners (exhibit 14.5). A cascaded Balanced Scorecard ensures that support units and external partners actively support the strategy of the SBUs and the enterprise. This is especially important if your organization works closely with external partners such as suppliers, distributors, or long-term customers, whose support is critical for your organization's success.

The resources and/or services provided by the support units, such as HR, IT, and purchasing and distribution, are fundamental to strategic success. However, alarmingly, studies show that support organizations are aligned with the organization's strategy less than 40% of the time. Though the support units may have efficient internal systems and

		SBU	Support Unit
"External" Constituencies	**Financial Perspective** XXX XXX XXX	Public Shareholders	Corporate & Business Units
	Customer Perspective XXX XXX XXX	External Customers	Internal Customers
"Internal" Constituencies	**Internal Perspective** XXX XXX XXX	SBU Work Process	Support Unit Work Processes
	Learning Perspective XXX XXX XXX	Work Enablers	Work Enablers

Exhibit-14.5

processes, they do not necessarily contribute to the organization's strategy. Strategy alignment helps create synergies between support units and organizations. Moreover, support units need to align themselves with the strategic conditions of the organization and the industry it operates in to plan their functions properly.

Before cascading the corporate/SBU scorecard to support functions, it is important to develop strategic themes for the support functions based on corporate/SBU themes. If the themes are directly applicable, transfer them directly. If they are not directly applicable, transfer them so they make sense for the business. Finally, develop themes that make sense for your business. Sharing themes among SBU and support units helps in having the same language/terminology and understanding of strategic directions and affords a clear 'line of sight'.

Bear in mind that support units' horizontal alignment differs significantly from SBU's vertical alignment in how they view internal and external stakeholders. From a financial perspective, public shareholders are the customers of the SBU, and SBUs are the customers of the support units. The support unit must shift its thinking towards internal constituents and how best it can support/enable strategy from an internal perspective. The SBU has external customers, and the support unit has internal customers (the SBU). The cascading question for the support unit from a financial perspective will be, '*How does our support unit contribute to the cost, revenue, or asset utilization?*' And the question from the customer perspective will be, '*Who are our customers, and what are their needs and expectations?*' The internal perspective of the support unit will have objectives that support the SBU, and the learning perspective will include the support unit's own need for skills, technologies, and means to contribute to corporate objectives for culture and climate. The scorecard of the support unit must strike a balance between reflecting the organization's overall strategy and capturing the unit's own operation and success metrics.

Chapter – 15

HR Function Scorecard

In today's knowledge economy, intangible assets have become decisive factors for sustainable value creation. As we covered in the earlier chapter, the difference between the market value and book value of a firm is due to intangibles. In recent times, many financial analysts have started including intangibles in their valuation models. The dictionary defines 'intangible' as 'incapable of being realized or defined', and something that cannot be defined or realized cannot be managed. How can you manage something that cannot be defined? This is the challenge that is faced by all strategists. And human capital is the most important intangible asset, as the other two intangible assets (information capital and organization capital) are also created by human capital. The learning & growth perspective of the Balanced Scorecard highlights the role of aligning these intangible assets with its strategy.

Strategic HR deliverables include those outcomes of the HR architecture that serve to execute the firm's strategy. These deliverables come in two categories: performance drivers and enablers. HR performance drivers are the core people-related capabilities or assets, such as employee productivity or employee satisfaction. Enablers reinforce performance drivers. For example, a change in the company's reward structure might encourage employees to produce more. Producing more might, in turn, 'enable' more deliveries to the customer. Any performance driver may have several enablers. The enablers themselves, in isolation, may seem mundane, but their cumulative effect can have strategic importance.

Similarly, if employee productivity is a core performance driver, then 're-skilling' might be an enabler.

Strategic Role of the Human Resource Function

HR is often perceived as a function that consumes resources without adding much value to the organization. However, this perception is outdated and inaccurate. In today's competitive and dynamic environment, HR can be a source of competitive advantage that contributes to the organization's strategy and performance. To do so, HR needs to align its activities with the business outcomes that matter most to the organization.

The HR portfolio of strategic activities includes:

1. Strategic Competency Development Programme
   - Identifying strategic job families and their competencies
   - Analysing gaps between job requirements and existing competencies
   - Developing training programs for employees to close the gap

2. Organization and Leadership Development:
   - Developing Leaders, promoting teamwork, fostering organizational synergy, and enhancing the climate and values of the organization
   - Developing Leadership Competency Model and leadership training
   - Succession Planning
   - Job rotation and development of the key employees

3. Performance Management Process:
   - Defining, motivating, appraising, and rewarding the performance of individuals and teams
   - Aligning employees' incentive and reward systems with strategic objectives
   - Facilitating change management

Implementing HR's Strategic Role

The HR scorecard is a tool that helps to measure, manage, and improve the strategic role of the HR department. How can HR formalize this kind of strategic role? Dave Ulrich et al., in their book, The HR Scorecard[6], suggested a 7-step model for implementing HR's strategic role as summarized below:

Step 1: Clearly define business strategy: While developing the business strategy, HR leaders provide an essential perspective. By focusing on how to implement the strategy rather than solely on what the strategy consists of, they can facilitate a discussion about how to communicate the organization's goal throughout the organization. When strategic goals are not developed with an eye towards how they will be implemented and communicated throughout the organization, they tend to become very generic; for example, maximizing operational efficiency, improving productivity, or increasing presence in international markets. An organization's goals should be stated in such a way that employees understand their role and the organization knows how to measure its success in achieving them.

Step 2: Build a business case for HR as a strategic asset: Once the organization's strategy is clearly defined, HR needs to build a case for 'why' and 'how' HR can support that strategy. Various studies in the last three decades indicate that a high-performance work system has a distinct positive influence on an organization's financial performance. The business case must also incorporate HR's key influence on strategy implementation and the role of a strategically focused measurement system. The ultimate HR performance driver and the cornerstone of successful strategy implementation is a *strategically focused workforce.*

---

6   The HR Scorecard: Linking People, strategy, and, Performance by Becker, Brian E., Huselid, Mark A, and Ulrich, Dave Harvard Business School Press, 2001

Step 3: Create a strategy map: Once the business strategy is clearly articulated and a business case is built for HR, the next step is to create the business strategy map and Balanced Scorecard for the organization. While developing the business case for the HR function, one should seek answers to the following questions:

- Which strategic goals or objectives are critical for the organization rather than nice to have?
- What are the performance drivers for each of those goals?
- How would we measure progress towards these goals?
- What are the barriers and enablers to the achievement of each goal?
- What should be the employees' behaviour to achieve these company's goals?
- Do employees have the required competencies and behaviours to achieve these goals?
- If not, what needs to change?

Answering the above-mentioned critical questions while developing the business strategy helps organizations articulate the HR value proposition, how HR functions have contributed in the past, and how they will improve in the future.

Exhibit 15.1 shows a typical strategy map for the HR department with generic strategic themes.

Step 4: Identify HR deliverables within the strategy map: Based on the organization's strategy, HR managers need to identify both HR performance drivers and HR enablers that would help in achieving the strategic outcomes and subsequently articulate HR deliverables that support company-level performance drivers in the strategy map. For example, if the employees' low turnover positively impacts customer satisfaction, employee stability is a key HR enabler. Based on this insight, a company can design policies that would encourage employees to have lengthy tenure.

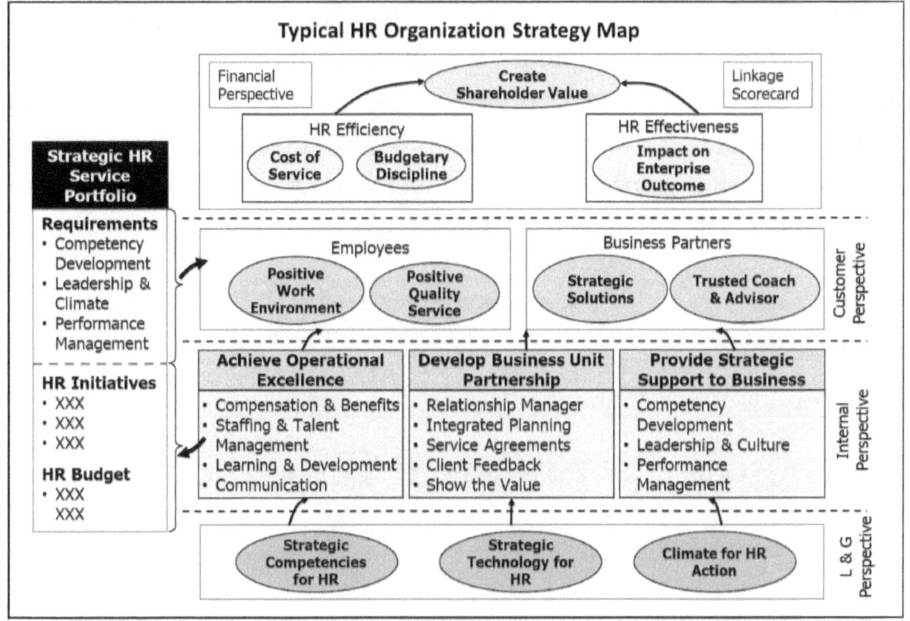

Exhibit-15.1

Step 5: Align the HR architecture with HR deliverables: The next step is to align the HR architecture or systems (rewards, competencies, work environment, etc.) to provide those deliverables that impact the corresponding performance driver. This step helps in bringing the organization's value-creation story to life by aligning the HR system with the company's larger strategy-implementation system. However, the HR systems must be aligned internally (fit together) and externally with the other elements of the value chain of the organization. Misalignment between the HR system and the strategy implementation system can actually destroy value.

Step 6: Design the strategic HR measurement System: Once the architecture and layout of the HR system are developed (Steps 1 through 5), in Step 6, we design the HR measurement system. This includes developing the Balanced Scorecard and Strategy Map for the HR function or department. If we have chosen the correct performance drivers and enablers in the previous steps, we will arrive at the correct deliverables. Most HR systems fail as the focus is on operational metrics, such as cost per hire, average tenure, etc. Just because you are not able to capture the full impact of HR on organizational performance, that does not mean that you should not measure part of the impact. The more sophisticated the measurement system, the greater the eventual benefit. Exhibit 15.2 shows a sample of one of the matrices that we used for showing an organization's 'overall strategic HR readiness' for critical resources for a construction company.

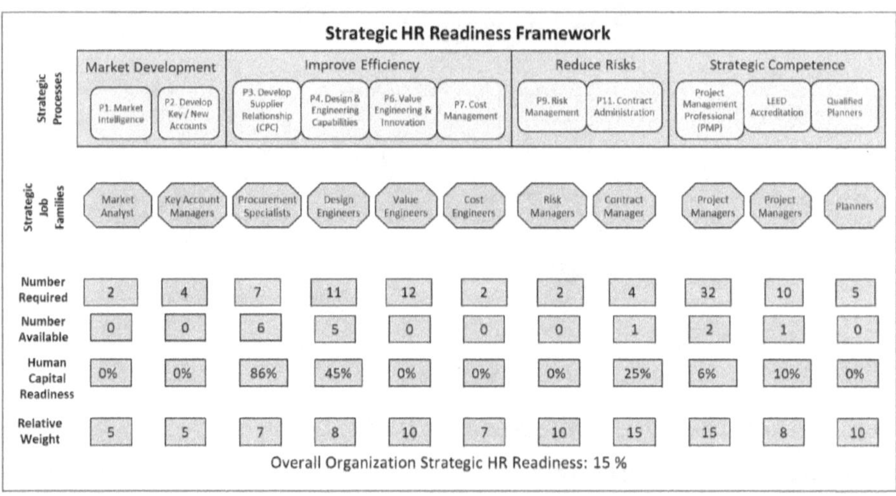

Strategic Job Families	Market Analyst	Key Account Managers	Procurement Specialists	Design Engineers	Value Engineers	Cost Engineers	Risk Managers	Contract Manager	Project Managers	Project Managers	Planners
Number Required	2	4	7	11	12	2	2	4	32	10	5
Number Available	0	0	6	5	0	0	0	1	2	1	0
Human Capital Readiness	0%	0%	86%	45%	0%	0%	0%	25%	6%	10%	0%
Relative Weight	5	5	7	8	10	7	10	15	15	8	10

Exhibit-15.2

Step 7: Implement management by measurement: If the above steps are followed stringently, the outcome will be a powerful new management tool. And if the HR scorecard is aligned with the organization's strategy, the HR function will be able to afford new insights into what it takes to manage HR as a strategic asset.

Chapter – 16

IT Function Scorecard

Over the past decade, many CIOs have realized that it is not sufficient to manage merely the IT end of the business. The continued evolution and advancement of IT offer every organization the opportunity to achieve performance breakthroughs and competitive advantage through the effective alignment of this resource with corporate and business-unit strategies. In recent times, IT has become one of the most critical functions for running an organization smoothly. For this reason, the integration of IT strategy into business strategy must be managed as well. Implementation of a Balanced Scorecard for the IT function that is aligned with the business strategy helps us achieve this objective.

IT as a Strategic Partner

Before IT dives into planning the function, everyone must have the same assessment of current IT output. This is important, especially if the IT strategy or annual plan calls for dramatic change. It is possible that either the IT function or the business, or both, may not be ready for dramatic change. Moreover, IT needs to understand the organization's strategy and business priorities prior to beginning the planning process. Setting appropriate expectations is critical in IT planning. And this requires stepping out of the function and diving into the business strategy.

There is a huge difference between IT being a Service Provider and IT becoming a Strategic Partner Service Provider:

IT as a Service Provider	IT as a Strategic Partner Service Provider
Strategic Partner IT is for efficiency	IT is for business growth
Budgets are driven by external benchmarks	Budgets are driven by business strategy
IT is separable from the business	IT is inseparable from the business
IT is seen as an expense to control	IT is seen as an investment to manage
IT managers are technical experts	IT managers are business problem solvers

Jessica Keyes, in her book entitled 'Implementing the IT Balanced Scorecard', lists following goals of the IT Balanced Scorecard:

- Align IT plans with business goals and needs.
- Establish appropriate measures for evaluating the effectiveness of IT.
- Align employees' efforts towards achieving IT objectives.
- Stimulate and improve IT performance.
- Achieve balanced results across stakeholder groups.

Every organization must identify and deliver a portfolio of IT services to execute its strategy that has four components: business analytics and decision support, transaction processing, infrastructure for delivery, and the use of information capital to provide strategic support. In developing a Balanced Scorecard, it is not enough to use the usual IT metrics. To be effective, the IT scorecard must incorporate measures that demonstrate the value IT provides to the business and that directly support the organization's strategies and goals. The key to achieving this is to view IT as a strategic partner of the business rather than simply a cost centre or utility. Moreover, IT investments should be evaluated beyond cost, based on the expected benefits they bring to the organization.

IT Strategy Map

From a planning perspective, creating an IT strategy map can be of great help. It helps to:

- Understand and articulate your value proposition to the organization

- Prioritize the objectives (between the basic and advanced)
- Prioritize funding and resource allocation
- Communicate the IT strategy to internal stakeholders
- Provide a tool for measurement

Exhibit 16.1 shows an organization's typical IT strategy map.

As one can see, the organizational structure of the IT department roughly parallels that of the four perspectives of the Balanced Scorecard:

- Financial perspective – management services
- Customer perspective – account management
- Internal perspective – application delivery, technology services, corporate technology, and e-business solutions
- Learning & growth perspective – career centres

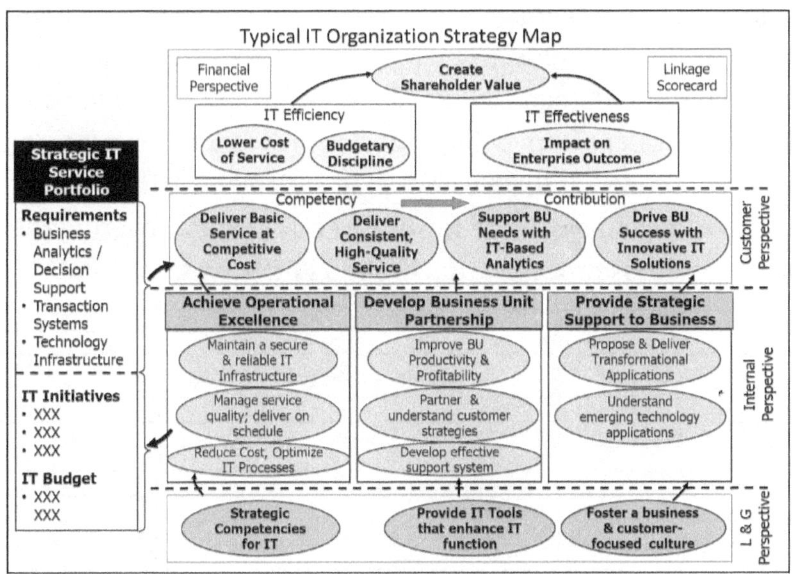

Exhibit-16.1

Great-West Life's IT scorecard, as described by Van Grembergen, Saull, and De Haes (2003), encompasses the following four orientations:

- ***Customer orientation:*** to be the supplier of choice for all information services, either directly or indirectly through supplier relationships.

- ***Corporate contribution:*** to enable and contribute to the achievement of business objectives through the effective delivery of value-added information services.
- ***Operational excellence:*** to deliver timely and effective services at targeted service levels and costs.
- ***Future orientation:*** to develop the internal capabilities to continuously improve performance through innovation, learning, and personal organization growth.

The above can be used to make sure that the IT function delivers IT services in line with the business requirements and recipients of its services.

Measuring Progress

Replacing existing systems and/or implementing new IT systems may take a lot of time. Moreover, most of these tasks are outsourced to IT vendors as projects. Organizations can track the progress of the transition of the IT department from being a service provider to a strategic partner and progress on new initiatives by using suitable matrices. Exhibit 16.2 shows the IT Readiness Score for one of our clients, covering the most important business processes and desired IT systems.

	Business Process	Desired System	Score	FY 18 - 19 Target	
				Weightage	Weighted Score
1	Txn Processing	SAP ERP	87	15%	13
2	Project Monitoring	Primavera 6 Online & Contract Manager	83	15%	12
3	Communication	Lotus / Open / Cloud Computing Mail	65	12%	8
4	Design & Drawing	AutoCAD & 3D Tools	85	10%	9
5	HCM & Payroll	SAP HCM	85	10%	9
6	Documentation	DMS / ACONEX / P6 CM / Email	61	8%	5
7	Tendering & Estimation	CANDY / Online System	50	7%	4
8	Contract Management	P6 Contract Manager	75	7%	5
9	Employee Engagement	SAP ESS / MSS / Intranet Portal	90	7%	6
10	Sourcing	MS Office / Mail / E-Sourcing	75	4%	3
11	Asset / Inventory Management	Barcode / RF ID	40	1%	0
12	Cycle Time Reduction	Mobility Solution	40	1%	0
13	Compliance Management	Active Directory / Software License Mgt	40	1%	0
14	KPI Monitoring	Dashboards / System Reports	30	2%	1
	Total			100%	75

IT Readiness -Actual Q1 FY 18-19

Exhibit-16.2

Chapter – 17

Finance Function Scorecard

Finance is probably the most powerful of all support units. Finance is responsible for measuring and controlling the organization's financial resources. It is also responsible and accountable for interpreting and enforcing all the accounting standards and compliance requirements imposed by the external regulatory authorities. It also communicates with the organization's diverse stakeholders including, shareholders, analysts, the board of directors, the company secretary, tax authorities, regulators, creditors, etc.

On the other hand, the financial function has also undergone dramatic change due to corporate reporting scandals in the past, changes in electronic technologies, the increasing value of intangible assets, new measurement approaches, etc. All these changes call for departing from the finance department's traditional scorekeeping function and forging new partnerships with the business units and corporate executives. According to various surveys, Chief Financial Officers are viewed by their CEOs as their primary aides in driving company-wide transformation efforts. Moreover, a CEO's role is increasingly linked to operations.

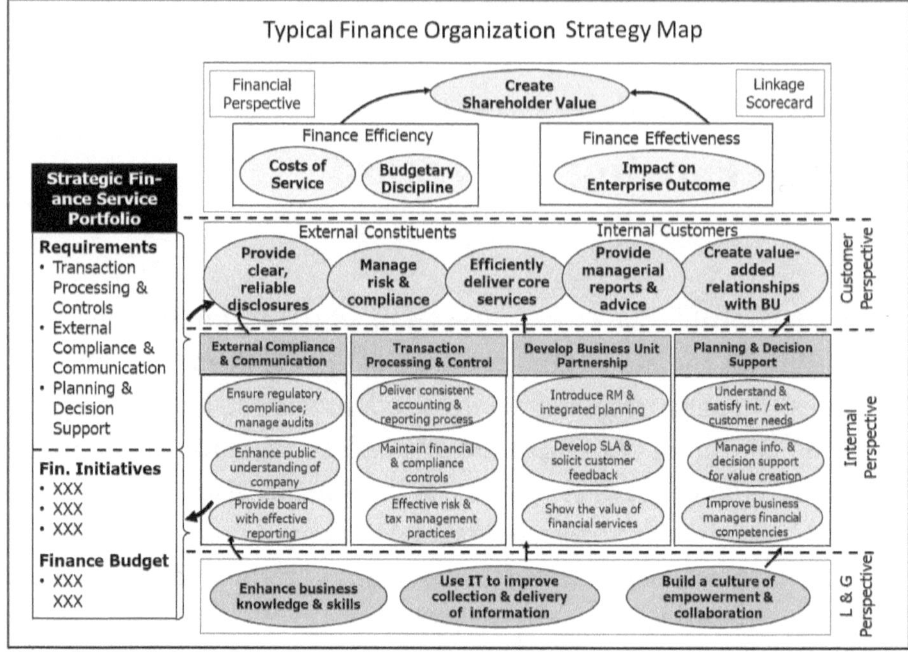

Exhibit-17.1

These multiple responsibilities are captured in the generic finance organization scorecard in exhibit 17.1.

The financial perspective includes objectives related to efficiency and effectiveness. The efficiency objective calls for providing services to the business unit at a minimum cost and keeping the department's overall spending within the allocated budget. It also includes assisting the business unit in achieving its cost reduction and productivity objectives through effective budgeting, resource allocation, reporting, and feedback. Effectiveness objectives have an impact on enterprise outcomes by optimizing the cost of financing and maximizing returns on surplus funds.

The customer perspective includes two types of customers: external constituents and internal business partners. External constituents (shareholders, analysts, the board of directors, company secretary, tax authorities, regulators, creditors, etc.) look at the finance function for high-quality periodic financial reports, corporate risk management, controls, and compliance ensuring that the organization is complying with all the legal and ethical requirements. The internal customers want low-cost execution of required finance functions and reporting of consistent quality.

The internal perspective includes processes that deliver these services and benefits to internal and external customers. Broadly speaking, these responsibilities and processes are built around four themes:

- *Transaction Processing and Control:* includes financial transaction management, such as accounts receivable, accounts payable, payroll management, regulatory reporting, etc. Responsibilities also include improvements in the structure and effectiveness of the transaction system, working capital management, and risk analytics that facilitate the effective use of financial assets, and minimize the risks through appropriate risk mitigation strategies.
- *External Compliance and Reporting:* ensures compliance with statutory and regulatory requirements and external communication, and makes sure that external reports and disclosures adequately reflect the company's strategy and financial standing.
- *Planning and Decision Support:* includes consulting, analytics, and systems that improve the management of strategy and financial functions across the organization.
- *Develop Business-Unit Partnership:* Understand the business-unit requirements for financial management support, and build and implement systems/processes to meet those requirements.

The learning & growth objectives of the finance function describe the transformation requirements of its new role. These include traditional competencies, knowledge of new reporting and disclosure requirements, strong IT capabilities to meet business objectives, and a culture conducive to empowerment, collaboration, and cooperation.

We have discussed here a generic scorecard for finance as a support function for a business unit. The finance function of a corporate or enterprise will play a more strategic role. Such a role will be more concerned with increasing the shareholder value of the business units in their SBU portfolio. Corporate finance strategy revolves around issues such as where to invest, where to harvest, how to balance risk and reward, and how to create a compelling brand for investors.

Chapter – 18

Procurement Function Scorecard

Procurement has become an important part of any organization. Depending on the industry, the cost of procured material may be more than 50% of the total cost of the final product. Procurement not only helps in the acquisition of goods and services at a reasonable price and quality, but it also supports risk management and compliance.

The procurement function is both inter-functional and inter-organizational. It is inter-functional because the effective production and supply of goods require close coordination with other functions, such as marketing, operations, sales, logistics, etc. It is inter-organizational because systems and processes among all participants (raw material provider, manufacturer, distributor, and retailer) must be integrated and coordinated for efficient performance. If used properly, the Balanced Scorecard as an alignment tool may be able to positively impact the performance of the entire supply chain.

The Chartered Institute of Procurement and Supply (CIPS) suggests five attributes that are important in procurement. These are Quality, Quantity, Price, Place, and Time. These five attributes can be used (along with others) as PIs for measuring the performance of the procurement function.

According to the surveys done by Deloitte in 2018 and 2021, the top two priorities of the Chief Procurement Officers are: driving operational efficiency and reducing costs. The same survey concluded that procurement has continued to successfully deliver short-term savings and manage risk to support growth during a period of uncertainty. As national and global economies improve, procurement has a pivotal role to play in increasing supply chain transparency, accessing supplier innovation, and delivering enterprise-wide cost reduction. Cost reduction continues to be the number one priority for procurement leaders, with 78 per cent of respondents in the survey identifying reducing costs as their top priority. Exceptional procurement suppliers, businesses, and digital leadership will differentiate those organizations that deliver an impact that matters. The research on high-performing procurement leaders shows that there are seven key capabilities where high performers outperform other procurement leaders. These include:

- Executive advocacy
- Leadership – supplier and procurement
- Strategic decision-making
- Talent capability
- Digital procurement
- Supply chain transparency
- Balanced Scorecard

The same survey concludes:

Improved transparency of pricing, supplier locations, and critical dependencies can help procurement functions deliver greater value.

There is a direct correlation between stronger leadership capabilities, higher spending on training, and enhanced performance of procurement functions.

Digital transformation is inevitable, and high-performing organizations are leading the way in adoption.

The key stakeholders (on the organization side) include:

- ***Procurement team led by the chief procurement officer or manager:*** They are the process owners. They are interested in maintaining an effective procurement process and are expected to achieve the performance targets they own. They are also interested in getting regular training appropriate for their respective functions (technical, management, or commercial).

- ***Internal Customers:*** Internal customers of procurement are the people who will actually use the procured material for further processing to manufacture finished goods or supply them to the organization's customers directly (e.g., to a trading company). They are interested in the timely availability of materials that comply with the quality requirements.
- ***Management or Board of Directors:*** Management is interested in improving the performance of the procurement department and increasing the organization's profit. Depending on the material being procured, the procurement team also needs to comply with the legal and statutory requirements.

Procurement Process

We generally look at procurement from the viewpoint of the procurement team, although the process depends on the type of organization and the industry. A typical procurement process involves these steps:

- Requirement analysis
- Market analysis
- Supplier identification and communication of the requirements
- Negotiation and finalization of the order
- Performance management (logistics and quality management)

Procurement Scorecard

The procurement department may have its own mission statement and will generally include effective procurement and cost-saving as key objectives. A typical strategy map for the procurement function is given in exhibit 18.1.

Similar to the strategy maps for other support functions, the financial perspective of a procurement function will have performance objectives related to the efficiency and effectiveness of the procurement department. The efficiency measures will include the overall departmental costs of the procurement function and whether they can provide services within the budget (since procurement is a support function, it will have an allocated budget). The effectiveness measures from the financial perspective of the Balanced Scorecard will have measures related to the impact the procurement department has on enterprise outcomes (typically gross profits).

The customer perspective will include objectives for service attributes of the procurement function and its contribution to the business's success. Measures will include cost savings due to procurement at lower material costs against budgeted costs, reduced procurement cycle time, quality of procured materials, minimum reorder quantity, etc.

The internal perspective will have objectives and measures related to the procurement department's own processes that provide operational and strategic support to the business unit. These can be grouped into three strategic themes:

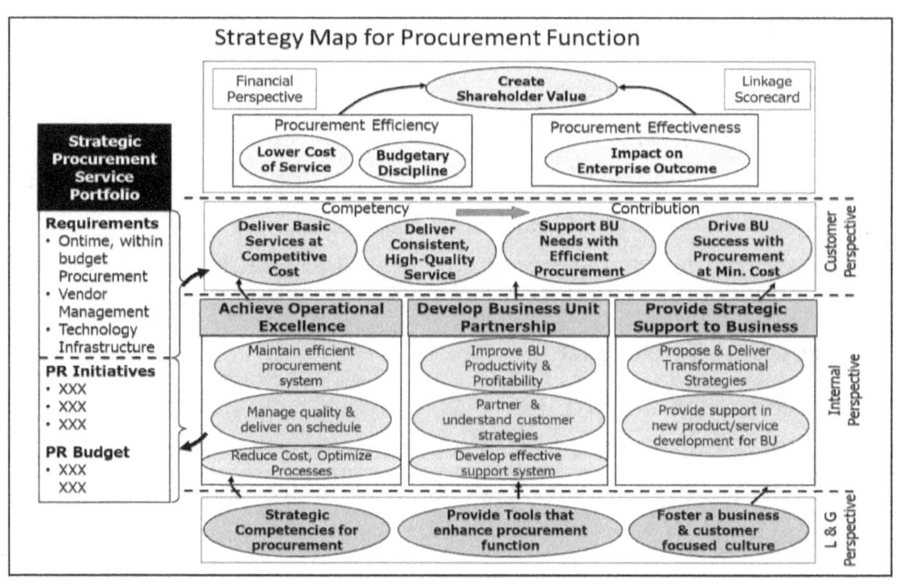

Exhibit-18.1

- ***Achieving operational excellence:*** Operational excellence includes objectives related to an efficient procurement system, quality, and on-time delivery of procured material, and buying at minimum costs.

- **Developing business unit partnership:** Building a partnership entails helping the business unit perform better, understanding the business unit's strategies, and developing an effective support system.
- **Providing strategic support to business:** Strategic support includes suggesting and implementing transformational strategies to make the internal value chain more efficient and providing support for new products and service development.

The learning & growth perspective will include the department's own developmental needs. Objectives and measures in this perspective include developing strategic competencies, having relevant tools and technologies, and fostering the right culture.

In summary, developing a Balanced Scorecard for the procurement function ensures alignment with business objectives, provides comprehensive performance measurement, focuses on value creation, promotes continuous improvement, and enhances decision-making capabilities. It enables the identification and measurement of key value drivers, such as cost savings, supplier performance, and process improvements. By tracking these metrics, organizations can ensure that procurement activities contribute directly to the bottom line and generate tangible benefits for the business.

Chapter – 19

Implementing and Evaluating the Balanced Scorecard

The Balanced Scorecard is a strategic management framework that helps organizations align their activities with their vision and strategy. It provides a holistic view of organizational performance by measuring key indicators across four perspectives: financial, customer, internal processes, and learning & growth. In this chapter, we will explore the implementation process of the Balanced Scorecard and discuss the methods for evaluating its effectiveness in organizations.

Prerequisites for Implementation of the Balanced Scorecard

Clearly Articulate the Strategy:

Before implementing the Balanced Scorecard, it is important to ensure that the organization's strategy is clearly articulated and well-understood by all stakeholders. This includes communicating the vision, mission, and strategic objectives of the organization. When employees have a clear understanding of the strategy, it becomes easier to align their objectives and KPIs with the broader goals of the organization.

Engage Leadership and Stakeholders:

Successful implementation of the Balanced Scorecard requires strong leadership commitment and active engagement from key stakeholders. Top management should champion the initiative and demonstrate their support through their actions and decisions. Involving stakeholders from different levels and departments in the development and implementation process helps to build ownership and ensure that diverse perspectives are considered. Inputs should also be sought from external stakeholders (customers, suppliers, channel partners, and other service providers).

Develop a Balanced Scorecard Team:

Forming a dedicated Balanced Scorecard team can greatly facilitate the implementation process. This team should consist of individuals with knowledge and expertise in strategy, performance management, and data analysis. The team will be responsible for driving the implementation, coordinating efforts, and providing guidance and support to departments and individuals throughout the organization.

Conduct a Strategy Review:

Before developing the Balanced Scorecard, conduct a comprehensive review of the organization's strategy. This review should involve assessing the external environment, analyzing the internal strengths and weaknesses, and identifying CSFs. By understanding the strategic landscape, organizations can ensure that the Balanced Scorecard focuses on the most relevant and impactful objectives and measures.

Tailor the Balanced Scorecard to the Organization:

The Balanced Scorecard should be customized to fit the unique needs and characteristics of the organization. Avoid using generic templates or adopting a one-size-fits-all approach. Instead, tailor the Balanced Scorecard framework to align with the industry, organizational culture, and strategic priorities. This customization ensures that the Balanced Scorecard becomes a meaningful and relevant tool for performance management.

Prioritize Key Objectives and KPIs:

Not all objectives and KPIs are equally important or feasible to measure. Prioritize the key objectives and focus on a limited number of high-impact KPIs from each perspective. This helps to avoid information overload and ensure that resources are allocated effectively. The prioritization should be based on strategic significance, alignment with the organization's goals, and the availability of reliable data for measurement.

Methodology for Implementing the Balanced Scorecard

Phased Implementation:

Implementing the Balanced Scorecard is a complex and time-consuming process. To manage the implementation effectively, consider adopting a phased approach. Break down the implementation into manageable stages and set clear milestones and timelines. This allows focused efforts, learning from each phase, and making necessary adjustments before progressing to the next stage. More details are provided in the respective chapters.

Pilot Testing:

Before rolling out the Balanced Scorecard organization-wide, conduct a pilot test in a specific department or business unit. This provides an opportunity to test the effectiveness of the Balanced Scorecard framework, identify any challenges or gaps, and refine the implementation approach. The pilot phase also allows for valuable feedback from participants, which can be used to improve the Balanced Scorecard design and implementation strategy.

Establish Performance Review Processes:

To ensure ongoing monitoring and review of performance, establish robust performance review processes. This includes regular meetings, such as monthly or quarterly, where departments and individuals discuss their progress, challenges, and initiatives related to the Balanced Scorecard. These performance review sessions provide a platform for accountability, learning, and problem-solving.

Provide Training and Support:

Effective implementation of the Balanced Scorecard requires that employees have a clear understanding of its purpose, methodology, and role in the process. Provide training and support to employees at all levels to ensure they are equipped with the necessary knowledge and skills. This may include training sessions, workshops, and access to resources and tools for measurement and analysis.

Aligning Incentives and Recognition:

To reinforce the importance of the Balanced Scorecard and motivate employees to actively participate, align incentives and recognition programs with the achievement of Balanced Scorecard objectives. This could involve tying performance bonuses or rewards to the attainment of specific KPI targets or recognizing teams and individuals who consistently demonstrate exceptional performance aligned with the Balanced Scorecard.

Continuous Communication and Improvement:

Throughout the implementation process, maintain open and transparent communication with all stakeholders. Regularly communicate the progress, results, and benefits of the Balanced Scorecard implementation. Actively seek feedback from employees and make necessary improvements based on their input. Continuous communication and improvement foster engagement, collaboration, and a culture of continuous learning and growth.

In summary, Implementing the Balanced Scorecard requires a combination of tactical approaches and a well-defined methodology. By following these tactics and methodologies, organizations can effectively implement the Balanced Scorecard and drive performance improvement aligned with their strategic objectives. Remember that successful implementation is an iterative process that requires ongoing monitoring, evaluation, and adaptation to ensure its long-term effectiveness.

Evaluating the Balanced Scorecard

Although performance measures or indicators need to be evaluated regularly as per agreed frequencies, the Balanced Scorecards should be evaluated at least quarterly (if not monthly).

Data Collection:

To evaluate the effectiveness of the Balanced Scorecard, organizations need to collect relevant data for each perspective and KPI. This data can be collected through various sources, such as financial reports, customer surveys, internal process measurements, and employee feedback. It is essential to establish a systematic and reliable data collection process to ensure the accuracy and consistency of the information.

Analysis and Interpretation:

Once the data is collected, it needs to be analyzed and interpreted to assess the performance from each perspective. This involves comparing the actual performance against the targets set for each KPI. Deviations from the targets can highlight areas for improvement or potential issues that need to be addressed. The analysis should also consider trends over time to identify patterns and evaluate the effectiveness of the initiatives implemented.

Feedback and Communication:

The evaluation process should not be confined to the top management; it should involve all levels of the organization. Regular feedback and communication are crucial for engaging employees and fostering a culture of continuous improvement. The Balanced Scorecard results should be shared with employees, and discussions should take place to identify potential solutions, celebrate successes, and address any challenges.

Adaptation and Continuous Improvement:

The evaluation process should lead to adaptation and continuous improvement of the Balanced Scorecard. If certain objectives or initiatives are not delivering the expected results, they may need to be revised or replaced. The evaluation results can also guide the allocation of resources and inform strategic decisions. Organizations should be open to feedback and make necessary adjustments to ensure the effectiveness of the Balanced Scorecard.

Avoid Making These Mistakes

The whole process of developing and implementing the Balanced Scorecard is intuitive, with logical steps, and involves the whole organization. While implementing the 'new way of working', making mistakes should be avoided at all costs.

Overcomplicating the Process

One common mistake in implementing performance management initiatives is overcomplicating the process. This can happen when organizations create complex and convoluted performance measurement systems that are difficult for employees to understand and navigate. When the process becomes overly complicated, it can lead to confusion, frustration, and resistance among employees. It may also result in a lack of clarity regarding performance expectations and objectives, making it harder for employees to align their efforts with organizational goals.

Measuring the Wrong Things

Another fatal mistake is measuring the wrong things. Performance management initiatives should focus on measuring and evaluating the key drivers of success and the outcomes that truly matter to the organization. However, organizations sometimes make the error of emphasizing metrics and indicators that do not align with strategic objectives or fail to capture the full picture of employee contributions. This can lead to a distorted understanding of performance and may incentivize behaviours that are not in line with the organization's long-term goals.

Failing to Engage the Workforce

Effective performance management requires active engagement and participation from the entire workforce. However, organizations often make the mistake of not involving employees in the design and implementation of performance management initiatives. When employees are not engaged in the process, they may perceive it as a top-down imposition and resist its implementation. Additionally, without employee input, organizations may overlook valuable insights and suggestions that could improve the effectiveness and fairness of the performance management system.

Perpetuating 'Siloed Thinking'

A significant challenge in performance management is overcoming 'siloed thinking' or the tendency for departments or teams to operate in isolation, focusing solely on their own objectives without considering the broader organizational goals. When performance management initiatives reinforce this siloed mindset, it can lead to conflicting priorities, a lack of collaboration, and suboptimal performance. Organizations need to ensure that performance management processes encourage cross-functional cooperation and align individual and team goals with the overall organizational strategy.

Declaring Victory at the Wrong Time

It is crucial to accurately assess and evaluate performance in a timely manner. However, organizations may make the mistake of prematurely declaring victory or drawing conclusions based on incomplete or insufficient data. This can lead to complacency and a false sense of achievement. Performance management initiatives should include regular and ongoing assessments, allowing for adjustments and improvements based on reliable and comprehensive information. Declaring victory too soon may hinder continuous improvement efforts and limit the potential for organizational growth.

Failing to Institutionalize the Performance Initiative Throughout the Enterprise

One of the most fatal mistakes in implementing performance management initiatives is failing to institutionalize them throughout the organization. Often, performance management systems are treated as short-term projects or initiatives without a long-term perspective. Organizations must integrate performance management into the fabric of their culture, ensuring that it becomes an ongoing process embedded in daily operations. This involves providing regular feedback, training managers and employees on performance management best practices, aligning performance goals with rewards and recognition, and continuously monitoring and refining the system to adapt to changing business needs.

Overall, avoiding these six fatal mistakes requires organizations to prioritize simplicity, alignment, engagement, collaboration, accurate assessment, and long-term integration when implementing performance management initiatives.

Best Practices in Performance Management

Based on our experience, listed below are the best practices for developing and implementing Balanced Scorecards.

Limit the Number of Measures

To ensure clarity and focus, it is advisable to limit the number of measures used in performance management initiatives. Too many measures can lead to confusion and dilute the importance of key indicators. By selecting a few critical measures that directly align with strategic objectives, organizations can streamline the process and enhance understanding and accountability.

Include Measures for All Perspectives and All Strategies

Performance management should consider all relevant perspectives and strategies within the organization. This means incorporating measures that reflect not only financial outcomes but also other aspects such as customer satisfaction, employee engagement, process efficiency, and innovation. By including a balanced set of measures, organizations gain a comprehensive view of performance and can make informed decisions across various areas.

Seek Balance Among Measures

A well-designed performance management system seeks balance among measures. This balance ensures that organizations do not focus excessively on one area at the expense of others. For example, solely emphasizing financial metrics may neglect important aspects like customer service or employee development. Balancing measures provides a more holistic and integrated view of performance, promoting overall organizational success.

Develop Solid Baseline Data

To effectively measure performance over time, it is crucial to establish solid baseline data. Baseline data serves as a reference point against which future performance can be evaluated. It provides a benchmark to assess progress and identify areas for improvement. By collecting accurate and reliable baseline data, organizations can track trends, set realistic targets, and measure the impact of performance management initiatives.

Develop Measures for the Past, Present, or Future

Performance management initiatives should include measures that cover different time perspectives—past, present, and future. Past measures help evaluate historical performance and identify patterns and trends. The present measures enable real-time monitoring and provide immediate feedback to support decision-making. Future measures will allow organizations to set goals and track progress towards desired outcomes. A balanced approach to time perspectives ensures a comprehensive understanding of performance.

Do not over-rely on output; include process and input measures

While output measures, such as sales revenue or production output, are essential indicators of performance, organizations should not solely rely on them. It is important to include process and input measures as well. Process measures assess the efficiency and effectiveness of internal operations, while input measures track the resources and capabilities invested in achieving desired outcomes. A well-rounded approach considers the entire performance ecosystem, from inputs to processes to outputs.

Set Stretched Targets

Setting stretched targets is a best practice that encourages continuous improvement and pushes employees to reach beyond their comfort zones. Stretch targets challenge individuals and teams to aim for ambitious goals that require innovation and creativity. While stretch targets should be realistic, they should also be challenging enough to motivate and inspire high performance. By setting stretch targets, organizations can unlock the full potential of their workforce.

Watch for Unintended Incentives

When designing performance measures, it is essential to be mindful of any unintended incentives that may arise. Sometimes, certain measures or targets can inadvertently drive undesirable behaviours or create perverse incentives. For example, if a sales team is solely rewarded based on revenue without considering customer satisfaction, they may prioritize short-term sales volume over long-term customer relationships. Organizations should carefully consider the potential unintended consequences of their performance measures and adjust as necessary.

Hold People Accountable for Results

Accountability is a crucial aspect of performance management. Organizations should establish clear lines of responsibility and hold individuals and teams accountable for achieving results. This includes setting performance expectations, providing regular feedback, and linking rewards and consequences to performance outcomes. Holding people accountable ensures that performance management initiatives have a meaningful impact on driving improvement and achieving organizational objectives.

By following these best practices, organizations can establish effective performance management initiatives that align with their strategic goals, provide a balanced view of performance, motivate employees, and drive continuous improvement.

PART – 4

Balanced Scorecard for Nonprofit Organizations and the Triple Bottom Line

Chapter – 20

Balanced Scorecard for Nonprofit Organizations

While the Balanced Scorecard framework can be applied to both for-profit and nonprofit organizations, there are some key differences in how it is implemented and the metrics used. These differences arise due to the distinct goals and nature of these two types of organizations.

In the realm of nonprofit organizations, success is not merely defined by financial performance but also by the achievement of their social missions. While financial sustainability remains crucial, these organizations must also focus on delivering value to their stakeholders, including beneficiaries, donors, volunteers, and the community at large. To effectively measure and manage their performance, nonprofit organizations can also adopt the Balanced Scorecard framework. This chapter explores how the Balanced Scorecard can be applied to enhance performance management in the nonprofit sector.

Nonprofit Organizations' Scorecard

As you know by now, a Balanced Scorecard is a strategic management tool that goes beyond financial measures by incorporating a broader set of PIs. It provides a comprehensive view of organizational performance considering multiple dimensions, including financial, customer, internal processes, and learning & growth perspectives. By examining these interconnected areas, nonprofit organizations can better align their activities with their mission and strategic objectives. As the name suggests, the focus of nonprofit and government organizations is not profit. Moreover, generally, they have a mission. For this reason, initially, the focus of such institutions is on operational excellence. Hence, the scorecards of such organizations resemble a set of operational KPIs.

Since achieving financial success is not the primary objective for such organizations, the architecture can be rearranged to place customers or communities at the top of the hierarchy. In a private sector transaction, the customer pays for the product or service and also receives

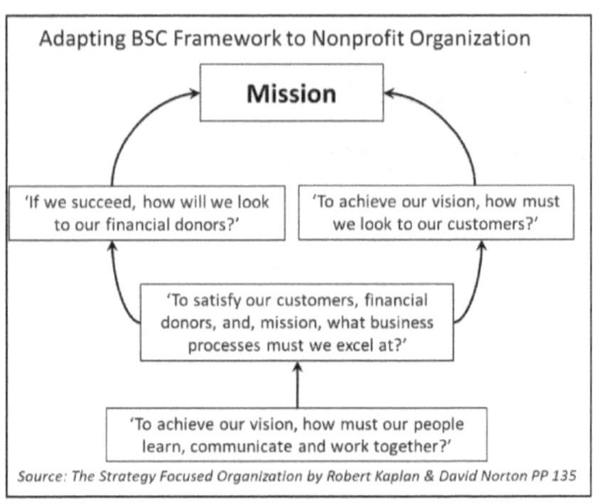

Source: The Strategy Focused Organization by Robert Kaplan & David Norton PP 135

Exhibit-20.1

the service. In a nonprofit organization, donors provide the financial resources, and constituents receive the services. Hence, both the recipient perspective and the donor perspective are placed on the top of the Balanced Scorecard, where objectives are developed for donors and recipients, and then internal processes are identified that will deliver desired value propositions for both groups of 'customers'. Nonprofit and government organizations may also put overarching objectives at the top, for instance, imparting quality education to the most disadvantaged, victimized, and marginalized children. Then the objectives within the scorecard can be oriented towards improving such a high-level objective. Such a mission is placed and measured at the highest level of the scorecard, resulting in the Balanced Scorecard structure shown in exhibit 20.1.

The Balanced Scorecard of a nonprofit organization also has four perspectives with an overarching mission. For the reasons explained above, the customer perspective is at the top, followed by the financial perspective, the internal perspective, and the learning & growth perspective. Exhibit 20.2 shows a standard Balanced Scorecard template for a nonprofit organization.

Strategy Map of a Nonprofit Organization

Value to Taxpayer

Customer

Safe and Convenient Services | Improve Service Quality | Increase outreach and scope | Improve Service Quality

Financial

Expand Funding | Maximize Benefit to Cost Ratio | Grow Tax Base | Maintain AAA Rating

Internal

Increase Positive Contacts | Promote Community Based Problem Solving | Secure Funding / Service Partners | Streamline Customer Interaction | Increase Infrastructure Capacity

Learning & Growth

Enhance Knowledge Management Capabilities | Achieve Positive Employee Climate | Close Skill Gap

Exhibit 20.2

Financial Perspective

Although nonprofit organizations may not aim for profit maximization, financial sustainability is essential for their long-term survival. The financial perspective of the Balanced Scorecard for nonprofit organizations includes key indicators such as revenue diversification, fundraising effectiveness, cost management, and resource allocation. The goal is to ensure that the organization has the necessary financial resources to fulfil its social mission effectively. Tracking these metrics enables organizations to ensure that they are efficiently utilizing their resources to support their mission.

Customer Perspective

The customer perspective of the Balanced Scorecard focuses on measuring the organization's impact and effectiveness in delivering services. In a nonprofit organization, the customer perspective is broader and encompasses the organization's impact on beneficiaries and the community. Key indicators may include satisfaction survey outcomes, client retention rates, the number of beneficiaries reached, and the extent of social impact. The emphasis is on delivering value to the target population and fulfilling the organization's social mission. By continuously monitoring these metrics, organizations can assess their performance in meeting the expectations and needs of their beneficiaries.

Internal Processes Perspective

The internal processes perspective examines the efficiency and effectiveness of an organization's internal operations. In a nonprofit organization, the process of internal perspective extends beyond operational efficiency to encompass activities such as programme delivery, volunteer management, and partnerships. By identifying critical internal processes and measuring their performance, nonprofit organizations can identify areas for improvement and optimize their operations to maximize their social impact and effectiveness. Key metrics may include programme effectiveness, volunteer satisfaction, collaboration with stakeholders, and the efficiency of resource utilization.

Learning & Growth Perspective

The learning & growth perspective recognizes that the success of nonprofit organizations relies on the knowledge, skills, and capabilities of their staff and volunteers. By fostering a supportive learning environment and investing in the growth of their people, organizations can enhance their ability to achieve their mission. In a nonprofit organization, the learning & growth perspective also emphasizes on employee development and organizational culture, but with a focus on fulfilling the social mission. Key metrics may include staff satisfaction, training and development, volunteer engagement, capacity-building initiatives, and cultural alignment with the organization's values.

The objective is to cultivate a supportive learning environment that empowers staff and volunteers to drive social change.

Developing a Balanced Scorecard for Nonprofit Organizations

The process for developing a Balanced Scorecard for a nonprofit organization is very similar to that for a for-profit organization. The process includes defining the mission, vision, and values of a nonprofit organization; developing strategy based on vision and mission; defining strategy objectives; selecting PIs for the objectives; setting targets and benchmarks; implementing measurement and data collection systems; monitoring and analyzing performance; and using performance data for decision-making and improvements.

The financial perspective of the Balanced Scorecard for nonprofit organizations will have key indicators such as revenue diversification, fundraising, budget, and resource allocation. The customer perspective will measure the impact on beneficiaries to whom the services are delivered. The internal process perspective will have efficiency and effectiveness measures for the processes of programme delivery, volunteer management, and other internal processes. The learning & growth perspective will include measures related to building capabilities, work culture, environment, etc.

The Balanced Scorecard provides a comprehensive framework for nonprofit organizations to measure and manage their performance effectively. By considering financial, customer, internal processes, and learning & growth perspectives, organizations can holistically evaluate their impact and ensure alignment with their mission and strategic objectives. By adopting the Balanced Scorecard, nonprofit organizations can enhance their ability to fulfil their social mission, improve stakeholder engagement, and sustain long-term success.

Chapter – 21

Incorporating the Triple Bottomline and CSR in the Balanced Scorecard

All business entities are required to develop a strategy and execute that strategy. An effective business strategy needs to clearly identify where the business is headed and create cohesion within an organization to achieve the targeted goals. It should not only define the destination but also set out the best route and provide the tools with which progress can be measured along the way. It is critical to continually assess progress and, if warranted, realign the strategy and business. In this context, organizations need to have the tools and means to develop a robust strategy and translate, communicate, and execute the chosen strategy, and track its performance against the strategic goals or objectives. As we have seen, the Balanced Scorecard emerges as the most appropriate framework for executing and monitoring business strategy.

On the other hand, the business entity is required to comply with local rules and regulations pertaining to doing business in a specific country and meet the requirements set by respective countries, regulators, and other international bodies. In India, numerous frameworks and laws exist to address governance and CSR in the Company's Laws and Securities and Exchange Board of India's (SEBI) listing guidelines. Almost all organizations deal with these statutory requirements as individual elements of obligations that need to be dealt with for continued business, not as part of their strategy.

Mandatory Listing and Reporting Obligations:

Some of the mandatory listings and reporting that businesses need to include:

- ***ESG Framework:*** The term 'Environment, Social, and Corporate Governance (ESG)' has gained a lot of popularity across the globe in recent years. It is not new, and has evolved over 20 years from its predecessor, the 'triple bottom line'. This is increasingly happening in India as well, with SEBI notifying guidelines that apply to the thousand largest listed companies. Social sustainability is more complex, especially in India. SEBI's 2020 guidelines have included factors like the provision of child care, health insurance, skill level, including that of disabled employees, gender diversity, etc. From a stakeholder perspective, articulating a holistic story of how a company creates value for the stakeholders society, and the environment and sharing the progress of this journey is a strength. For investors, it offers a proxy for management quality; for customers, it allows responsible choice and enhances brand loyalty; for governments, it highlights where to partner for global action; and for communities, it allows a company to maintain its social licence to operate.

- ***Legal Prerequisite:*** Improvements in Indian CSR can be traced back to 2007 when the Reserve Bank of India issued a circular highlighting the role of financial institutions in sustainable development. In 2014, India became one of the first countries to impose the legal prerequisite that corporations set aside 2% of their profits for social development projects. Since then, there has been considerable focus on CSR spending, with an increasing amount of corporate earnings being directed towards education and public health initiatives[7].

---

7   Sustainability Governance Scorecard: India Report, Argudan Governance Academy

- ***National Voluntary Guidelines:*** The government of India also released the National Voluntary Guidelines on Social, Environmental, and Economic Responsibilities of Business (NVGs), which provide a robust framework for companies to voluntarily adopt and address the interests of various stakeholders, including employees, customers, and investors. This principles-based approach sets guidelines for companies to create a positive impact on their communities and the environment while remaining profitable. Furthermore, the SEBI mandated in November 2011 that the 100 top-listed entities submit Business Responsibility reports, as part of their annual reports. The requirement was then expanded to the 500 largest companies in SEBI's Disclosure Requirements Regulations in 2015[8].

- ***Business Responsibility Reporting (BRR):*** As per SEBI Circular ref. CIR/CFD/CMD/10/2015 dated, November 04, 2015; the annual report of all listed companies shall contain a business responsibility report describing the initiatives taken by the listed entity from an ESG perspective, in the format as specified by the Board[9]. The BRR requirement is a key section in the sustainability reporting of corporations in India. This section may refer to several necessary ESG-related data even if they are omitted in other sections.

- ***Global Reporting Initiative (GRI):*** There is also evidence of uptake in adherence to GRI Guidelines. Indian companies use the GRI framework to measure and report ESG data. A possible reason for this broader uptake is that the standards can also be used to comply with the BRR requirements mandated by the SEBI.

- ***UN's 17 Sustainable Development Goals (SDG):*** During the 2014 UN Sustainable Development Summit, members from 193 countries of the United Nations collaboratively committed

---

8   SEBI Circular on BRR

9   Reimagining the Balanced Scorecard for the ESG Era by Robert Kaplan and David McMillan, Harvard Business Review, 2nd Feb 2021

to adopting 17 Sustainable Development Goals. The countries also committed themselves to meeting the 2030 agenda for sustainable development. The 17 SDGs and 169 interlinked targets within them addressed a variety of issues, from ending poverty to stemming climate change and providing a pathway to a sustainable and more prosperous world. Since the SDG must be implemented by 2030, it requires immense effort not only from governments but also from businesses.

Adapting Balanced Scorecard for Triple Bottom Line and ESG

Traditional accounting and control systems fall short of meeting the requirements of reporting on social and environmental aspects of the Triple Bottom Line and Environment, Social, and Corporate Governance (ESG) framework. However, the Balanced Scorecard system overcomes the limitations by introducing two principles: the scorecard itself, which offers a framework for adding non-financial performance matrices, and the strategy map, which enables a visual representation of a company's multiple and linked strategic objectives across various stakeholders.

Some companies adapted their scorecard to reflect their interest in pursuing Triple Bottom Line strategies, including societal and environmental performance.

Amanco, a Latin American producer and installer of plastic pipes for water treatment solutions, built its strategy map to include environmental and societal objectives in parallel with financial ones and added a new perspective (social and environmental) to highlight processes that drove environmental and social progress. The financial perspective now has a Triple Bottom Line perspective superimposed on top of it. Exhibit 21.1 shows Amanco's Triple Bottom Line strategy map.

Managers at every level are held accountable for performance along the Triple Bottom Line metrics. Putting the new objectives on the strategy map did not make them easy to achieve; it means that any proposed investment or initiative would be assessed by its environmental and societal impact as well as its financial payback.

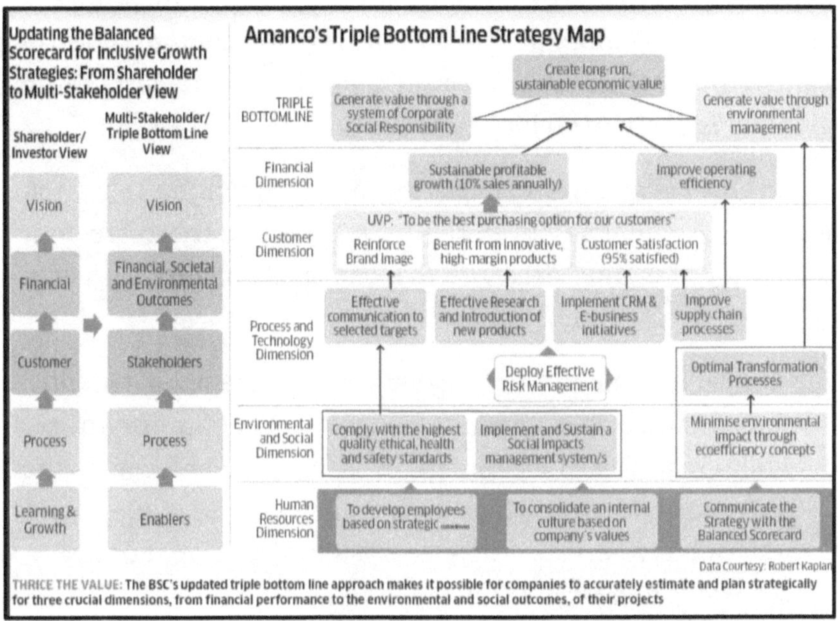

Exhibit-21.1

Creating a New Ecosystem for Inclusive Growth

Supply chains are critical links that connect an organization's inputs to its outputs. Many companies' greatest sustainability risks and opportunities are in the supply chain. However, the sustainability efforts of many companies are limited to measuring the sustainability of their own business operations and do not extend these efforts to their suppliers and customers. Encouraging companies to measure and report more details about suppliers can lead to improved performance.

Leading companies in sustainability accept responsibility throughout their value chains and work with their suppliers to implement sustainability initiatives on a wider playing field. This may involve utilizing its purchasing power to encourage, audit, collaborate with, and provide benchmarking and learning opportunities to its suppliers on key sustainability issues.

Scalable and profitable strategies for inclusive growth require companies to create a new ecosystem that replaces economically and socially inefficient supply chains with ones that are more profitable and capable of bringing more people into the formal economy. One thing is certain: Without the involvement of a profit-seeking corporation, no programme is likely to go far.

According to Palladium's experience of implementing more than 35 projects in 25 countries over the past 15 years, there are four key principles for designing strategies that can create inclusive, sustainable, and profit-generating ecosystems[10]:

- Companies need to search for systematic, multisector opportunities that generate economic benefits for themselves while creating socioeconomic gains for all other actors in the new ecosystem. The aim is not to incrementally upgrade an existing system but to create a new ecosystem that is economically self-sustaining and organically growing.
- Companies must mobilize complementary partners, as they certainly cannot create a transformational ecosystem on their own. It needs to partner with a catalyst organization to engage actors from multiple sectors in collaborative relationships and strategies for economic and social value creation. The catalyst can be an NGO or a consulting company committed to such a cause. Catalysts are usually better placed than companies to spot such opportunities.
- Companies are required to provide seed and scale-up financing, as they would seem to be the prime beneficiary when projects succeed and they have the resources to invest in projects that have positive net present values. However, this can be challenging, as corporate funds favour safe projects with short payback periods over projects designed to create new, socially inclusive business models and ecosystems. Another option can be Impact Investment Funds, which currently manage about $80 billion in assets worldwide and are growing rapidly.

However, a corporation must be an engaged partner because a significant corporate presence is critical to funders' decision to invest.

- In addition, companies must conceptualize and implement a new measurement and governance system to build commitment, monitor progress, and sustain alignment among the key players involved in creating the new ecosystem. The new ecosystem requires collaboration among unrelated actors from multiple sectors—corporate, NGOs, and the public. And these multiple stakeholders need to be aligned around the new strategy.

Adapting Strategy Map and Balanced Scorecard for the New Ecosystem

Traditionally, a strategy map is used as part of Balanced Scorecard implementation to create organizational alignment around the strategy. A co-created strategy map helps partners align around common goals and how to achieve them. The strategy map provides a pictorial view of the organization's overall objectives and how they relate to one another. It also represents how an organization's capabilities—tangible and intangible—and resources are used to create value for customers. The scorecard measures the progress against the strategy. The strategy map and the scorecard provide the common language for the strategic intent and direction. Wider participation in developing the scorecard also increases acceptance.

Since the new ecosystem would benefit all participants, it is reasonable to assume that potential partners would collaborate, possibly under the leadership of the catalyst for developing the strategy map and scorecard. The strategy map would show how the multiple stakeholders are aligned and how each one of them will contribute to the new strategy. The shared matrices of the scorecard would provide accountability and the basis for measuring performance and governance. Specific actions will be planned for the achievement of the objectives and planned performance. Monitoring and governance will occur during periodic meetings where all participants discuss performance, identify the root causes of any shortfall, and develop remedial action plans.

Building on the original Balanced Scorecard and adding all the stakeholders in the value chain to it, the new Balanced Scorecard would look like the one shown in exhibit 21.2.

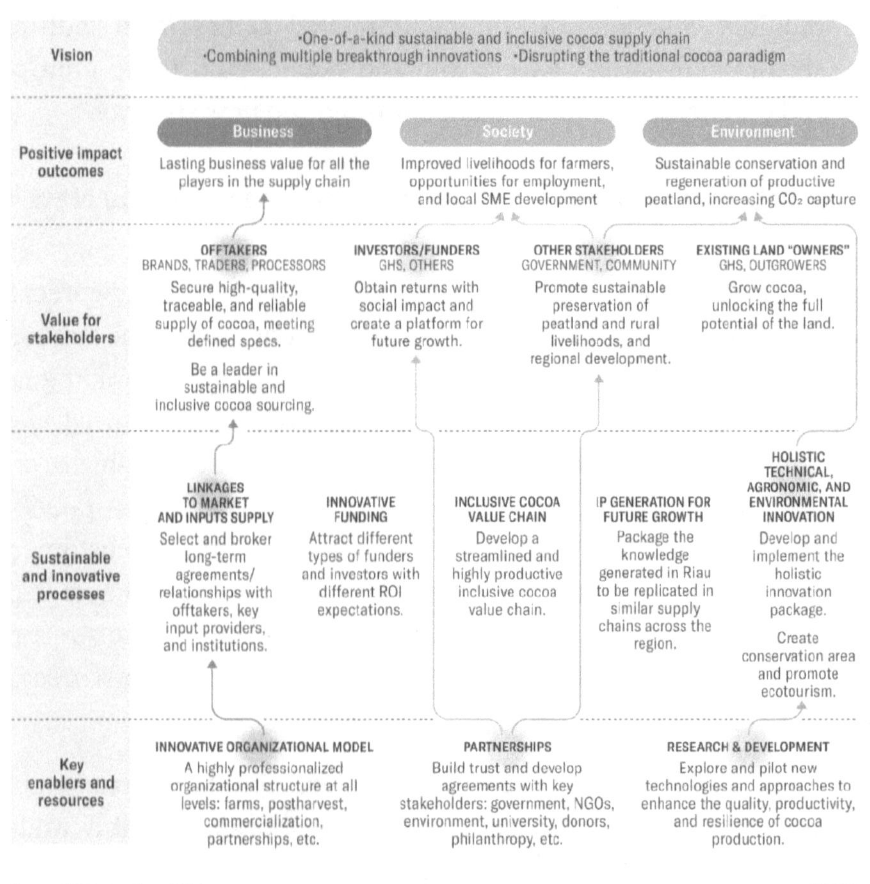

Exhibit-21.2

Playing the True Role of Trusteeship

CSR is extremely important for the sustainable development of all stakeholders (all the people on whom the business has an impact, including society at large). CSR under the Companies Act, 2013 enables companies to play the role of trustees, engage in social welfare activities, and take part in the development of society.

Proponents of CSR argue that companies make more long-term profits by operating with a perspective, while critics argue that CSR distracts from the economic role of businesses. Nevertheless, the importance of CSR cannot be undermined, and a Balanced Scorecard offers an opportunity for businesses to aim for inclusive growth for all stakeholders, including society.

According to an article by Apresh Mishra, Editor, India, CSR Network (www.indiacsr.in), India's policies and programs are output-driven and neglect outcomes and impact. India was the first country to legally mandate CSR. Over the past seven years (up to 2021), India Inc. has spent more than Rs 1 lac crore on CSR, but the outcomes have largely been invisible.

Apart from infusing money into the development sector, the intention of CSR was the involvement of companies in the hope that they would bring diverse expertise and fresh insight into solving the myriad social problems. However, the only visible outcome of the new legislation has been the magnitude of the amount spent by India's corporate.

To address this issue, the newly notified amendment in the Companies (Corporate Social Responsibility) Act mandates that every company that is obligated to spend a minimum CSR amount of Rs 10 crore and above should undertake an impact assessment (through an independent agency) for those CSR projects that have outlays of Rs 1 crore and above.

Collaborative action holds the key to the impact of such CSR projects. For example, the EdelGive Foundation has built, curated, and nurtured various collaboratives that consist of stakeholders, funders, and NGOs. It has created two collaboratives, namely Collaborators for Transforming Education and the Coalition for Women Empowerment.

Another Success story is ACT Grants, a nonprofit alliance of more than 100 volunteers from startups and VCs. The grant was launched in March 2020 with INR 100 crore to help tech-driven companies that could fight against COVID-19 connect with companies which had relevant products and solutions for the governments and the NGOs in fighting the pandemic. It helped grantees increase their reach by bringing together networks, startups, and additional grants as a force multiplier. With this approach and the collective support of the startup community, ACT in phase one was able to fund 54 startups and 100+ projects, impacting 49 million lives across 27 states.

These collaboratives are successful because they are purpose-driven and have a cascading effect on programs with a pool of resources (both financial and human) from multiple organizations.

A Balanced Scorecard has been successfully used to develop and implement such collaborative projects in several parts of the world to achieve inclusive growth for various stakeholders.

Accordingly, businesses can use Balanced Scorecard at two levels:

1. As a framework for implementing business strategy and, also incorporating the requirements of Triple Bottom Line and ESG reporting; and
2. As a tool for implementing strategy and adapting it to address the needs of the new ecosystem by including a wider range of stakeholders in its value chain.

Author's Note: This chapter is based on the author's research paper/ dissertation submitted to the Institute of Directors, India, as part of the requirements of the Masterclass of Directors (Batch No. 270) leading to Certified Corporate Directorship.

PART – 5

Case Study

Chapter – 22

Implementing a Strategy Map and Balanced Scorecard in a Commercial Organization

Building an organization's first strategy map and Balanced Scorecard can be accomplished through a systematic process that builds consensus and clarity about how to translate its mission and strategy into operational objectives and measures.

It is always a good practice to revisit an organization's mission, vision, and values if these are more than five years old.

The Company

ABC Group was a well-diversified group with interests in electromechanical projects, manufacturing, and trading. After starting from a very humble beginning as a small trading company, today, the group has a turnover of more than $150 million. The group had 11 companies under its umbrella with centralized support services (HR, IT, procurement, and legal). Each of the businesses was headed by a Business Unit Head and the group was headed by a group CEO, supported by senior directors for marketing and projects. The group embarked on an ambitious journey to create synergies among the business units and create unified systems and processes for similar businesses. All business units cater to one single industry: Building and Construction Industry. The group CEO felt that the group had the potential to become more efficient and improve revenues by synergizing and cross-selling. The CEO was also looking at developing a strategy and a performance management system that would serve the group for the next ten years. The key objectives of this exercise were:

- Amidst the expansion, management seemed to have lost focus on the overall objectives of the group and felt that some units were not adding value to the portfolio.
- The primary focus was on tracking and reporting financial performance, and the business units were mostly reactive and operated in firefighting mode.
- The group wanted to harness synergies among various units and increase focus on quality management, design, value engineering, production planning, inventory management, strategic relationships with key customers, and cross-selling to add more value.
- It wanted to develop a second line of leadership and management bandwidth to reduce dependence on a few individuals.
- The group wanted to reduce the extent of firefighting, ad hoc actions, unnecessary meetings, and ambiguities and focus on the strategic agenda.
- The group also wanted to revisit its mission, vision, and values; have a streamlined process for strategy planning; and was keen on implementing an enterprise-wide performance management system at all levels.

The Solution

After initial discussions with the management, the scope of the engagement and a tentative schedule were finalized (exhibit 22.1).

Activities	1	2	3	4	5	6	7	8	9	10	11	12	13	14	15	16
Ph. 1 - Project Planning	■															
Ph. 1- BSC Training	■															
Ph. 1 - Business Assesssessment: Formats & Templates		■														
Ph. 1 - Business Assessessment Review - BU1		■														
Ph. 1 - Business Assessessment Review - BU2		■														
Ph. 2 - Finalizing Corporate MVV			■													
Ph. 2 - Decomposing Vision			■													
Ph. 2 - Develop Corporate Strategy, Map, SO, KPIs				■												
Ph. 2 - Develop Strategy, Map, SO, KPIs - BU1					■											
Ph. 2 - Develop Strategy, Map, SO, KPIs - BU2						■										
Ph. 3 - Develop Initiatives for Corporate							■									
Ph. 3 - Develop Corporate BSC & MDM							■									
Ph. 3 - Develop Initiatives for BU1								■								
Ph. 3 - Develop BSC & MDM for BU1								■								
Ph. 3 - Develop Initiatives for BU2									■							
Ph. 3 - Develop BSC & MDM for BU2									■							
Ph. 3 - Develop Strategy, BSC & MDM for HR										■						
Ph. 3 - Develop Strategy, BSC & MDM for Business Dev.											■					
Ph. 3 - Develop Strategy, BSC & MDM for Procurement												■				
Ph. 3 - Develop Strategy, BSC & MDM for IT													■			
Ph. 4 - Business Risk Management														■		
Ph. 4 - Strategic Performance Review Architecture															■	
Ph. 4 - Project Closure																■

Exhibit-22.1

The Scope

Broadly speaking, the scope included:

Strategy Development:

- Initial diagnostic study to understand corporate structure, expectations, and current challenges
- Developing mission, vision, and values at the corporate level
- Decomposition of vision at the cluster and individual business-unit (BU) levels
- Developing a corporate-level strategy and high-level objectives
- Developing business unit-level strategy and high-level objectives
- Developing strategy and high-level objectives for support functions – HR, Procurement, and IT

Strategy Deployment using a Balanced Scorecard:

- Design of corporate and business units' strategy maps and balanced scorecards
- Design of strategy maps and balanced scorecards for the support functions

- Setting targets and finalizing initiatives for business units and support functions
- Implementing a review architecture

Strategy Development

Developing Vision, Mission, and Values (VMV)

A one-day training was organized for the leadership team, covering the purpose of VMV and the methodology for developing VMV. Subsequently, three separate workshops (one each for mission, vision, and values) were organized to develop mission, vision, and values at the corporate level, attended by the CEO, Deputy CEO, business unit heads, and functional heads. The group was first given time to articulate individual versions. All the inputs were then consolidated, and the three best options were discussed in the group and arrived at a consensus.

While working on identifying the organizational values, participants were also asked to identify their own personal values. Individuals were asked to choose five organizational and personal values each from a list of more than 50 values. The final values were arrived at through consensus. Individual values were used to check if anyone had any personal value that was in contradiction with the finalized organizational values. Fortunately, we did not find any such instance.

By the end of three days, we had finalized the mission and vision statements and values.

The next step was to decompose the vision at cluster and individual Business Unit levels.

Decomposition of Vision

The decomposition of the vision involved looking at the historical performance, market potential, and capacity of each of the business units. The nine business units were grouped into three clusters (contracting, manufacturing, and trading) based on the industry they operated in. Based on the current performance and market potential, high-level objectives were set for each of the clusters and business units.

All strategic analyses were done at the corporate level to develop the corporate strategy. This included assessing market growth and its potential up to 2030, carrying out PESTEL and SWOT analysis, analyzing customers' requirements, competition, key stakeholders' expectations, SBUs portfolio analysis, SBUs synergy analysis, articulating strategic advantage and challenges, CSFs, etc. Strategy development also involved segmentation, targeting, positioning, and a value proposition.

Developing a Corporate-level Strategy and High-level Objectives

Based on SWOT and TOWS matrices and other analyses, key strategies were derived at the corporate level. The clustering of these strategies led to the three strategic themes, which were termed 3Es – Expansion, Enhancement, and Excellence. Expansion involved new products, business lines, and new geographies. Enhancement meant selling more of existing products and services within existing territories through cross-selling and penetration. Excellence was supposed to improve value chain efficiency and effectiveness by implementing best-in-class systems, processes, and infrastructure. Incidentally, these three strategic themes were also repeated at the cluster level.

Developing Business Unit-level Strategy and High-level Objectives

Based on SWOT and TOWS matrices and other analyses for individual business units, key strategies were also developed for all the business units. The process was similar to the one used for developing corporate strategy. Each business unit looked at the external and internal environments specific to its own business to develop its key strategies.

Developing Strategy and High-level Objectives for Support Functions

Based on the corporate and Business Unit's strategies and objectives, strategies and objectives were developed for the support functions—

HR, Procurement, and IT. HR had three strategic themes: talent acquisition, talent development, and talent engagement. A diagnostic study was done to check the current state of the HR function, and the availability of required systems/processes, resources, and people for realizing the vision. Based on the data and providing weightage to various elements, an HR Readiness Index was developed to track the progress of the HR function.

The strategy and objectives of the IT function were derived based on the premise that IT was supposed to be the key enabler for realizing the vision. Like HR, an IT Readiness Index was developed, which included existing systems and infrastructure and the new requirements for the realization of the corporate vision with appropriate emphasis. This was then converted into a 'Readiness Index' that was tracked and reviewed periodically.

A similar exercise was done for the central procurement function.

Strategy Deployment

Design of corporate and Business Units' Strategy Maps and Balanced Scorecards

Prior to adopting a Balanced Scorecard and Strategy Maps for strategy management, the company had a serious problem regarding communicating the strategy across all business units (especially due to dispersed locations). For this reason, 80% of the employees did not know what the company's strategy was or what it was trying to achieve.

Once the corporate objectives and KPIs were finalized as part of strategy development, the next step was to develop a strategy map. The company viewed the Balanced Scorecard as a tool to implement and communicate its strategy and monitor the progress of its broader strategy and vision. The overarching financial objective was to 'drive shareholder value'. This primary objective was supported by four others: accelerating organic growth, improving asset utilization, driving cash flow generation, and lowering the cost base.

The customer perspective described how the company differentiated itself from its competitors by focusing on providing the best products, services, and solutions, and becoming a partner of choice and one-stop shop for its targeted customers.

The internal perspective had strategic objectives around three themes: Expansion, Enhancement, and Excellence. For example, the expansion theme included objectives for exploring export markets, building strategic partnerships, and developing new business lines. Enhancements included leveraging cross-SBU synergies and cross-selling while the excellence theme focused on implementing best-in-class systems and processes and improving overall value chain efficiency.

Most of these themes and objectives were cascaded to the business units, keeping in mind the industry-specific performance parameters. There were not many changes in objectives from financial, customer, and learning & growth perspectives. The changes were mostly from an internal process perspective. For example, for project business, the internal perspective included objectives related to cost (project budget), time (project duration), and quality (of construction).

The learning & growth perspective included objectives related to strengthening IT and HR functions, knowledge management, and organizational culture.

Design of Strategy Maps and Balanced Scorecards for the Support Functions

Support units create value by aligning their strategies with the corporate and business units' strategies and determining the set of strategic services to be offered. The process started with a clear understanding of the corporate and Business Unit strategies. Each of the support functions then identified a portfolio of strategic services that would have the greatest impact on the implementation of corporate/Business Unit strategies.

The HR strategic services portfolio involved:

- ***Strategic Competency Development Programs***: Developing personal competencies that are important to the success of the organization. This involved identifying strategic job families, developing competency frameworks, analyzing the gaps, and finally developing training programs for employees to close the gap.

- ***Leadership Development***: These programs were aimed at developing leaders, promoting teamwork, fostering an appropriate culture, and creating a culture of cooperation and support. The HR strategy map included these elements from an internal process perspective. The HR Readiness Index tracked the progress of these critical elements of the HR strategy.

Like HR, IT capabilities also had three components: IT infrastructure, Transaction processing and business analytics, and decision support. The gaps were identified between the desired state and the current state of the IT services, and action plans were developed to bridge the gaps. Like the HR Readiness Index, the IT Readiness Index was developed to track progress.

Along similar lines, a finance portfolio of strategic services was also developed. The three components were: transaction control and processing, planning and decision support, and external compliance and communication.

Once the strategic services were established for the support units, a strategy, a strategy map, and a Balanced Scorecard were developed for each of the support units. A support unit, like the business unit, has a mission, customers, services, and employees. But support units do not exist to make profits; their purpose is to support business units to generate revenue and profits. Also, support units' customers are always internal.

The financial perspective of the support unit's strategy map had two components: efficiency and effectiveness. The efficiency part covered the cost of service delivered, and effectiveness described the impact that the support unit had on the enterprise strategy. The customer perspective included Business Unit managers and employees who received the services directly or indirectly. The internal process perspective included objectives related to the support function's objectives for operational excellence, relationships with its internal customers, and strategic support of the business (effectiveness). The learning & growth perspective included the support function's own developmental requirements in terms of resources and systems.

Finally, SLAs were developed for all three support functions within the business units.

Setting Targets and Finalizing Initiatives for Business Units and Support Functions

Targets were set for all the business units and support functions based on the corporate's objectives and targets during the strategy planning phase. These were revisited and finalized in discussion with each business unit and support function in one-on-one meetings.

Initiatives were developed while finalizing the targets for each business unit. Each business unit came with its own list of initiatives. These initiatives were discussed in detail, along with the budgets. Rationalization and prioritization matrices were used to arrive at a finalized and prioritized list of initiatives for each business unit. Duplicating and overlapping initiatives were dealt with separately.

Implementing a Review Architecture

The Review architecture contained a list of recommended meetings that each of the business units and corporates were required to conduct to review their progress. These included:

- Strategy review meetings
- Operational review meetings
- Functional review meetings (HR, IT, Finance, and Procurement)
- Internal coordination meetings (within the business unit)

For each of the meetings, the purpose, attendees, agenda, and frequency, were also agreed upon. The business unit/support function was required to come prepared with all the data and reports in the prescribed format.

For this assignment, we worked as an in-house resource and transferred all the knowledge, documents, and templates that were used for completing the scope. We also trained the trainers, who could train the existing and new employees to ensure the continued use of our work.

The project helped the client build in-house capabilities in strategy management and the use of a Balanced Scorecard.

Author's Note: Some of the strategy maps and Balanced Scorecards associated with this case study are included in the appendices.

PART – 6

Appendices

Appendix – A

Standard Templates

Sl. No.	Template Name	Page Number
01	Mission Statement Worksheet	199
02	Vision Statement Worksheet	201
03	Value Statement Worksheet	205
04	Initial Core Competency Identification	207
05	Evaluation & Finalization of Core Competencies	208
06	Initial SWOT Matrix	209
07	SWOT Analysis Matrix	210
08	Final SWOT Matrix	211
09	TOWS Matrix	212
10	Strategic Advantages	213
11	Strategic Challenges	214
12	Critical Success Factors	215
13	Segment vs Customer Needs	216
14	Market Attractive Matrix	217
15	Objective Matrix Corporate-Business Unit	218
16	Measurement Detailing Matrix (MDM)	219
17	Action Plan Template	220
18	Action Rationalization Matrix	221
19	Action Prioritization Matrix	222

20	Service Level Agreement (SLA)	223
21	HR Readiness Matrix	224
22	IT Readiness Matrix	225
23	Review Meeting Template	226
24	Strategic Review Meeting Agenda	227

Mission Statement Worksheet

PART I

What is the problem(s) that (our organization) exists to solve? What need(s) does this organization exist to resolve?

- Who is affected by the problem?
- How would our customers be better off if our efforts were successful in solving the problem or responding to their needs?

____

____

____

PART II

What is the purpose of (our organization)?

- Why does it exist?
- What is the ultimate outcome or result you are hoping to achieve?

____

____

____

PART III

What business are you in? What do you do to fulfill your purpose? What is the broadest way in which you could state your work?

____

____

____

PART IV

For whom do we do this work? Who is our target population, customers & market?

____

____

____

PART V

Where do we do our work? What are our geographic boundaries?

____

____

____

PART VI

What values (or guiding principles) we are going to use to guide our actions (in parts I to 5 above)?

(1)________________(2)________________(3)________________

<u>Your Mission Statement</u>

Vision Statement Worksheet

PART I

In each of these important business areas, state your mental picture of your current business situation & your preferred future state:

Business Area	Now	Preferred Future
Business Products & Services		
Production Practices		
Business Size & Scope		
Markets & Linkages		
Management Structure		
Social Responsibilities		
Workforce (nos., Skills & Environment		
Customers		

PART II

Take a moment & write an article that you would love to see published about your organization 15 years from now. Include the name(s) of the publication(s) in which you would like to see it appear (not more than 100-120 words).

PART III

Transform the three to five most exciting snippets from your article into vivid description that brings the envisioned future life.

1. ____

2. ____

3. ____

4. ____

5. ____

PART IV

Test the vivid description against these test questions:

Yes	No	Does the Vivid Description conjure up pictures and images of what it will be like to achieve your vision? **IF THE VIVID DESCRIPTION DOES NOT CREATE A CLEAR PICTURE IN YOUR MIND'S EYE, THEN IT IS NOT VIVID ENOUGH.**
Yes	No	Does it use specific, concrete examples and analogies to bring the vision to life, rather than bland & tired expression?
Yes	No	Does it express passion, intensity, and emotion?
Yes	No	When reading the vivid description, do you think, "Wow, it would be really fantastic to make all this happen. I would really want to be a part of that, and I'm willing to put out significant effort to realize this vision!"?

PART V

As a group, select or create 10- to 20-year BHAG for the organization that encapsulates the vivid description and that is linked somehow back to the core purpose (Mission):

____

____

____

____

PART VI

Test the BHAG against the following questions:

Yes	No	Do you find this BHAG exciting?
Yes	No	Is the BHAG clear, compelling, and easy to grasp?
Yes	No	Does this BHAG somehow connect to the core purpose?
Yes	No	Will this BHAG be exciting to a broad base of people in the organization, not just those with executive responsibility?
Yes	No	Is it undeniably a Big Hairy Audacious Goal, not a verbose, hard to understand, convoluted, impossible to remember mission or vision "statement"? In other words, does it pass the "Mount Everest Standard"?
Yes	No	Do you believe the organization has less than 100% chance of achieving the BHAG (50% to 70% chance is ideal) yet at the same time believe the organization can achieve the BHAG if fully committed?
Yes	No	Will achieving the BHAG require a quantum step in the capabilities and characteristics of the organization?
Yes	No	In 25 years, would you be able to tell if you have achieved the BHAG?

PART VII

Putting all it together:

Now develop a compelling Vision Statement aligned with Mission, Value, BHAG & Envisioned Future.

<u>**Your Vision Statement**</u>

<u>Value Statement Worksheet</u>

STEP I – Your Personal Values – That reflect your character & you are not willing to compromise on

- Write your five most important values from the list (add if it is not in the list).
- Prioritize these values & write number, 1,2,3,4 or 5 against these values, 1 for most important or dear to you... 5 for the least.

_____________________ (   )   _____________________ (   )

_____________________ (   )   _____________________ (   )

_____________________ (   )

STEP II – Your Organizational Values – That reflect on your organization's character and you believe are non-negotiable

- Write your five most important values from the list (add if it is not in the list). These are based on: 1) how your organization operates (e.g. its activities, standards, quality, etc); 2) how your organization is perceived externally (i.e. in the eyes of the public or other external stakeholders); and 3) how staff carry out your organization's services and activities?
- Prioritize these values & write number, 1,2,3,4 or 5 against these values, 1 for most important or dear to you... 5 for the least.

_____________________ (   )   _____________________ (   )

_____________________ (   )   _____________________ (   )

_____________________ (   )

<u>List of Values</u>

Acceptance	Accomplishment	Accountability	Achievement	Alignment
Authenticity	Charity	Coach	Collaboration	Compassion
Competitiveness	Consideration	Constancy	Contentment	Contribution
Cooperation	Courage	Creativity	Credibility	Dedication
Dependability	Dignity	Discipline	Diversity	Efficiency
Effectiveness	Emotional Wellbeing	Empathy	Empowerment	Encouragement
Equality	Ethics/Ethical	Excellence	Expertise	Fairness
Flexibility	Freedom	Friendliness	Fun	Generosity
Gratitude	Guidance	Happiness	Harmony	Helpfulness
Honesty	Honor	Humility	Imagination	Improvement
Independence	Individuality	Innovativeness	Inspiration	Integrity
Intelligence	Involvement	Justice	Kindness	Knowledge
Learning	Love	Loyalty	Mastery	Nobility
Originality	Optimism	Persistence	Personal development	Positive attitude
Power	Proficiency	Quality	Recognition	Relationships
Reliability	Resourcefulness	Respect	Responsibility	Responsiveness
Risk	Safety	Self-awareness	Self- respect	Service
Simplicity	Stability	Strength	Success	Support
Teamwork	Trust	Truthfulness	Understanding	Wisdom

Preliminary Listing of Core Competencies
Individual Exercise

Your Name:

Function:

Location:

Date:

Guidelines:

1. In this very preliminary exercise, individual participant to merely identify 4 "Core Competencies", that are of utmost importance to the company according to him/her.

2. Rank identified core competencies on the sale of 1to 4 (1 being MOST RELEVANT and 4 being LEAST RELEVANT).

Core Competency	Value statement (Substantiate with examples, validation & supporting documents)	Rank

Evaluation and Finalization of Core Competencies & Process Linkages

Short-listed Core Competencies	Is it?		Mandatory Characteristics					Supporting Facts			
Group Exercise											
Group ID											
Location											
Group Participants											
	Advantage	Expertise	Unique	Inimitable	challening to imitate	Sustainable	Adding value	Creating differentiator	Accepted by competitors	Perceived by the customer	Validated through external agency

Put "√" if answer to the questions is yes.

Note: If a short-listed core competency is your strategic advantage, it is **NOT** a core competency

LINKAGE BETWEEN CORE COMPETENCIES AND WORK PROCESSES GROUP EXTERCISE		
Group ID		
Location		
Group Participants		
Short-listed Core Competencies	Work Processes	Supporting Processes

Note: If a short-listed core competency is your strategic advantage, it is **NOT** a core competency

Initial Strengths-Weaknesses-Opportunities-Threats	
INTERNAL FACTORS	**EXTERNAL FACTORS**
STRENGTH	**OPPORTUNITY**
S1	O1
S2	O2
S3	O3
S4	O4
S5	O5
S6	O6
S7	O7
S8	O8
S9	O9
S10	O10
S11	O11
S12	O12
WEAKNESS	**THREAT**
W1	T1
W2	T2
W3	T3
W4	T4
W5	T5
W6	T6
W7	T7
W8	T8
W9	T9
W10	T10
W11	T11
W12	T12

<u>Strengths-Weaknesses-Opportunities-Threat Analysis</u>

Strength and Weakness are internal to an Organization. These come from an analysis of internal processes.
Opportunities and Threats are imposed by the External Environment.

Sr. No.	Strengths	Reasons for Add, Delete, Modify	Modification	Why do we call it a Strength? What benefits can we derive from this Strength?
S1				
S2				
S3				
S4				
S5				
S6				
S7				
S8				
S9				
S10				
S11				
S12				
S13				
S14				
S15				

Sr. No.	Weaknesses	Reasons for Add, Delete, Modify	Weaknesses	Why do we call it a Weakness? How does it impact us?
W1				
W2				
W3				
W4				
W5				
W6				
W7				
W8				
W9				
W10				
W11				
W12				
W13				
W14				
W15				

Sr. No.	Opportunities	Reasons for Add, Delete, Modify	Opportunities	How does this translate into a business opportunity for us?
O1				
O2				
O3				
O4				
O5				
O6				
O7				
O8				
O9				
O10				
O11				
O12				
O13				
O14				
O15				

Sr. No.	Threats	Reasons for Add, Delete, Modify	Threats	Do these really threaten to dislodge us from our current position?
T1				
T2				
T3				
T4				
T5				
T6				
T7				
T8				
T9				
T10				
T11				
T12				
T13				
T14				
T15				

Final Strengths-Weaknesses-Opportunities-Threats	
INTERNAL FACTORS	**EXTERNAL FACTORS**
STRENGTH	**OPPORTUNITY**
S1	O1
S2	O2
S3	O3
S4	O4
S5	O5
S6	O6
S7	O7
S8	O8
S9	O9
S10	O10
S11	O11
S12	O12
WEAKNESS	**THREAT**
W1	T1
W2	T2
W3	T3
W4	T4
W5	T5
W6	T6
W7	T7
W8	T8
W9	T9
W10	T10
W11	T11
W12	T12

<table>
<tr><td colspan="9"><u>TOWS Matrix: Development of Strategic Alternatives / Initiatives</u></td></tr>
<tr><td rowspan="2"></td><td rowspan="2"></td><td colspan="3">OPPORTUNITY</td><td colspan="3">THREAT</td></tr>
<tr></tr>
<tr><td></td><td></td><td colspan="3">O1</td><td colspan="3">T1</td></tr>
<tr><td></td><td></td><td colspan="3">O2</td><td colspan="3">T2</td></tr>
<tr><td></td><td></td><td colspan="3">O3</td><td colspan="3">T3</td></tr>
<tr><td></td><td></td><td colspan="3">O4</td><td colspan="3">T4</td></tr>
<tr><td></td><td></td><td colspan="3">O5</td><td colspan="3">T5</td></tr>
<tr><td></td><td></td><td colspan="3">O6</td><td colspan="3">T6</td></tr>
<tr><td></td><td></td><td colspan="3">O7</td><td colspan="3">T7</td></tr>
<tr><td></td><td></td><td colspan="2">SO Strategies / Initiatives</td><td>Comb</td><td colspan="2">ST Strategies / Initiatives</td><td>Comb</td></tr>
<tr><td rowspan="7">STRENGTH</td><td>S1</td><td>SO1</td><td></td><td></td><td>ST1</td><td></td><td></td></tr>
<tr><td>S2</td><td>SO2</td><td rowspan="3">Use interal STRENGTHS to exploit external OPPORTUNITIES</td><td></td><td>ST2</td><td rowspan="3">Use internal STRENGTHS to minimize the impact of external THREATS</td><td></td></tr>
<tr><td>S3</td><td>SO3</td><td></td><td>ST3</td><td></td></tr>
<tr><td>S4</td><td>SO4</td><td></td><td>ST4</td><td></td></tr>
<tr><td>S5</td><td>SO5</td><td></td><td></td><td>ST5</td><td></td><td></td></tr>
<tr><td>S6</td><td>SO6</td><td></td><td></td><td>ST6</td><td></td><td></td></tr>
<tr><td>S7</td><td>SO7</td><td></td><td></td><td>ST7</td><td></td><td></td></tr>
<tr><td></td><td></td><td colspan="2">WO Strategies / Initiatives</td><td>Comb</td><td colspan="2">WT Strategies / Initiatives</td><td>Comb</td></tr>
<tr><td rowspan="7">WEAKNESS</td><td>W1</td><td>WO1</td><td></td><td></td><td colspan="2" rowspan="7">Avoid as far as possible to preserve resources and assets</td><td></td></tr>
<tr><td>W2</td><td>WO2</td><td rowspan="3">Overcome internal WEAKNESSES to exploit external OPPORTUNITIES</td><td></td><td></td></tr>
<tr><td>W3</td><td>WO3</td><td></td><td></td></tr>
<tr><td>W4</td><td>WO4</td><td></td><td></td></tr>
<tr><td>W5</td><td>WO5</td><td></td><td></td><td></td></tr>
<tr><td>W6</td><td>WO6</td><td></td><td></td><td></td></tr>
<tr><td>W7</td><td>WO7</td><td></td><td></td><td></td></tr>
</table>

Strategic Advantages

<u>**Direction:**</u>

Strategic Advantages are generally derived from Company's Strengths and help an organization to make use of the Opportunities as well as deal with the Threats

OPPORTUNITY
O1
O2
O3
O4
O5
O6
O7
O8
O9
O10
O11
O12
O13
O14
O15

STRENGTHS		STRATEGIC ADVANTAGES	Combination
	S1	SA1	e.g. S1-O1
	S2	SA2	
	S3	SA3	
	S4	SA4	
	S5	SA5	
	S6	SA6	
	S7	SA7	
	S8	SA8	
	S9	SA9	
	S10	SA10	
	S11	SA11	
	S12	SA12	
	S13	SA13	
	S14	SA14	
	S15	SA15	

Strategic Challenges

Direction:

Strategic Challenges can generally be derived from Threats and Weaknesses in view of the available opportunities. Otganizations need to work of their weaknesses in view of the threats.

THREATS
T1
T2
T3
T4
T5
T6
T7
T8
T9
T10
T11
T12
T13
T14
T15

WEAKNESSES	STRATEGIC CHALLENGES	Combination
W1	SC1	e.g. W1-T1
W2	SC2	
W3	SC3	
W4	SC4	
W5	SC5	
W6	SC6	
W7	SC7	
W8	SC8	
W9	SC9	
W10	SC10	
W11	SC11	
W12	SC12	
W13	SC13	
W14	SC14	
W15	SC15	

<u>Critical Success Factors</u>

<u>**Direction:**</u>

What are those factors that our Company must manage well in order to achieve its Strategic Vision? These factors must be seen in the light of existing and potential competitors

Strategic Challenges
SC1
SC2
SC3
SC4
SC5
SC6
SC7
SC8
SC9
SC10
SC11
SC12
SC13
SC14
SC15

		CRITICAL SUCCESS FACTORS	Combination
Strategic Advantages	SA1	CSF1	e.g. SA1-SC1
	SA2	CSF2	
	SA3	CSF3	
	SA4	CSF4	
	SA5	CSF5	
	SA6	CSF6	
	SA7	CSF7	
	SA8	CSF8	
	SA9	CSF9	
	SA10	CSF10	
	SA11	CSF11	
	SA12	CSF12	
	SA13	CSF13	
	SA14	CSF14	
	SA15	CSF15	

	Key Customer Requirements vs. Market Segments				
Sl. No.	Key Customer Requirements	Segment 1	Segment 2	Segment 3	Segment 4
1	Brand Image				
2	Product Quality				
3	Customer Relationship				
4	Price Competitiveness				
5	etc.				
6					
7					
8					
9					
10					

A. Market Attractiveness Matrix (MAM) - Based on Customer Requirements				
Indicators -Market Attractiveness	Segment 1	Segment 2	Segment 3	Segment 4
Market Size				
Indicative Segment growth				
Trends				
Competitive Structure				
Barriers to entry				
Industry profitability				
Technology				
Regulations				
Workforce Intensive				
Size of the opportunity				
Present status				

B. Market Attractiveness Matrix (MAM) - Based on Geogprahical Location				
Indicators -Market Attractiveness	Geography 1	Geography 2	Geography 3	Geography 4
Market Size				
Market Growth rate				
Competitive Structure				
Barriers to entry				
Industry profitability				
Technology				
Regulations				
Workforce Availability				
Size of the opportunity				
Present status				

Objective Matrix (Corporate-Business Unit Alignment)

	Corporate BSC Objectives	Identical	Contributory	New	N/A	Business Unit BSC Objectives
Financial						
Customer						
Internal						
Learning & Growth						

Measure:		BSC Measure Code:
Strategic Objective: Measurement Intent:		Frequency of Update: Unit of Measurement:

Measure Type:	Data / Formula
Measurement Definition/Formula:	

Formula Element (cover each element of the formula)	Data Source (for tracking the Formula Element)	Responsibility of Update	Reviewed At

Assumptions/ Remarks	

Drill-downs	

Actual 2013	Target 2014	Phasing of 2014 Target (as per Frequency of Update, identified above)											
		Jan'14	Feb'14	Mar'14	Apr'14	May'14	Jun'14	Jul'14	Aug'14	Sep'14	Oct'14	Nov'14	Dec'14

Action Plan Template

Action Plan No.: [ ] **Start Date:** [ ]

Action Plan Title: [ ] **End Date:** [ ]

Action Owner: [ ] **Frequency of Review:** [ ]

Department Goal Linkage: [ ]

Strategic Objective Linkage: [ ]

Strategic Challenge Linkage: [ ]

Strategic Advantage Linkage: [ ]

Brief Action Plan Description: [ ]

Team Details:

S. No.	Name	Department	Role	Other Resources
1				
2				
3				
4				
5				

Activity Planning Chart:

Sr No.	Sub-activity	Responsibility	Start	End	Remarks	Weights
1						
2						
3						
4						
5						
6						
						0

STRATEGIC INITIATIVES - Rationalization Matrix														
Strategic Themes / Strategic Objectives	**Initiative Portfolio**													
	Initiative 1	*Initiative 2*	*Initiative 3*	*Initiative 4*	*Initiative 5*	*Initiative 6*	*Initiative 7*	*Initiative 8*	*Initiative 9*	*Initiative 10*	*Initiative 11*	*Initiative 12*	*Initiative 13*	*Initiative 14*
Strategic Objective 1														
Strategic Objective 2														
Strategic Objective 3														
Strategic Objective 4														
Strategic Objective 5														
Strategic Objective 6														
Strategic Objective 7														
Strategic Objective 8														
Strategic Objective 9														
Strategic Objective 10														

STRATEGIC INITIATIVES - PRIORITIZATION MATRIX

SL. No.	Strategic Initiatives	Evaluation Criteria							Total Weighted Score	Priority No.
		Strategic Fit	Value Provided	Total Cost to Implement	Time to Implement	Availability of Project Team / Skills	Risks	Depth & Breadth of Change		
	Criterion's Weight:	2	2	1	1	1	1	1		
1	Initiative 1								0	
2	Initiative 2								0	
3	Initiative 3								0	
4	Initiative 4								0	
5	Initiative 5								0	
6	Initiative 6								0	
7	Initiative 7								0	
8	Initiative 8								0	
9	Initiative 9								0	
10	Initiative 10								0	

Note: (To be customized / Validated):

Overall score scale - 1 to 9	
Strategic Fit:	1. Low; 5 - Medium; 9 - High
Value Provided:	1 - Low to Modest (<10% impact on closing performance gap); 5 - Significant Value (11-25% impact on closing performance gap); 9 - Breakthrough Results (>25% impact on closing performance gaps)
Total Cost to Implement:	1 - > 1000K; 3 - 500-1000K; 5 - 200-500K; 7 - 50-200K; 9 - <50K
Time to Implement:	1 - >24 months, 3 - 18-24 months, 5 - 12-18 months; 7 - 6-12 months; 9 - <6 months
Availability of Project Team / Skills:	1 - Insufficient staff / skills available in-house; 5 - Sufficient staff / skills available in-house, but difficult to allocate; 9 - Sufficient staff / skills available in-house for allocation
Risks:	1 - High risks; 5 - Medium risks; 9 - Low risks
Depth & Breadth of Change:	1 - High degree of org. change required; 5 - Moderate Change; 9 - Little Change.

| Sr No | | WHAT & WHY | WHO | | | | ALERT | | WHEN | ACTIVITY RELATES TO |
| | | | | | Name of the Person | | Alert Type (phone, email, system etc.) | | | |
		Activity	Originator	Recipient	Originator	Recipient	Originator	Recipient	When (Frequency)	Location
1		Sales Order Receipt and Order Transmittal								
	1.1	Sales Order Receipt								
	1.2	Sales Order Verification								
	1.3	Order Transmittal – Factory								
2		Order Acceptance and Execution								
	2.1	Order Acceptance by – Factory								
	2.2	Change Order Notification								
	2.3	Order Readiness by Factory								
3		Sample Requirement								
	3.1	Sample Request								
4		Customer Complaints / Service Request								
	4.1	Customer complaint handling								
5		LC Documentation and Payment Collection follow up								
	5.1	LC Documentation								
	5.2	Debt (Payment) collection & follow up								

STRATEGIC HUMAN RESOURCE READINESS INDEX 2015-16

Strategic Themes		Theme-1			Theme-2			Theme-3		
Strategic Processes		SP-1	SP-2	SP-3	SP-4	SP-5	SP-6	SP-7	SP-8	SP-9
Strategic Job Families / Actions										
Nos. Required	Existing Geographies	0	0	0	0	0	0	0	0	0
	New Geographies	0	0	0	0	0	0	0	0	0
	Existing Verticals	0	0	0	0	0	0	0	0	0
	New Verticals	0	0	0	0	0	0	0	0	0
	Total	0	0	0	0	0	0	0	0	0
Nos. Avaliable	Existing Geographies	0	0	0	0	0	0	0	0	0
	New Geographies	0	0	0	0	0	0	0	0	0
	Existing Verticals	0	0	0	0	0	0	0	0	0
	New Verticals	0	0	0	0	0	0	0	0	0
	Total	0	0	0	0	0	0	0	0	0
HR Readiness (%)		#DIV/0!	#DIV/0!	#DIV/0!	#DIV/0!	#DIV/0!	#DIV/0!	#DIV/0!	#DIV/0!	#DIV/0!
Relative Weightage		10	15	10	15	15	15	7	7	6
Weighted Readiness		#DIV/0!	#DIV/0!	#DIV/0!	#DIV/0!	#DIV/0!	#DIV/0!	#DIV/0!	#DIV/0!	#DIV/0!

Organization's Overall Human Readiness Index: #DIV/0!

| IT Readiness -Target FY 2021-22 - prep on 15th Mar 2022 | | FY 21-22 | | |
	Business Process	Desired System	Score	Weightage	Weighted Score
1	Transaction Processing	SAP ERP	95	15%	14
2	Project Monitoring	Primavera 6 Online & Contract Manager	90	15%	14
3	Communication	Lotus / Open / Cloud Computing Mail	85	10%	9
4	Design & Drawing	AutoCAD & 3D Tools	85	10%	9
5	HCM & Payroll	SAP HCM	90	10%	9
6	Documentation	DMS / ACONEX / P6 CM / Email	75	8%	6
7	Tendering & Estimation	CANDY / Online System	65	8%	5
8	Contract Management	P6 Contract Manager	85	7%	6
9	Employee Engagement	SAP ESS / MSS / Intranet Portal	95	7%	7
10	Sourcing	MS Office / Mail / E-Sourcing	75	3%	2
11	Compliance Management	Active Directory / Software License Mgt	60	2%	1
12	KPI Monitoring	Dashboards / System Reports	70	5%	4
	Total			100%	85

Meeting:	Meeting Code:
Meeting Name: Meeting Intent:	Frequency of Meeting: Location:

Participants:	1. 2. 3. 4.	5. 6. 7. 8.

Agenda for the Meeting	1. 2. 3. 4. 5.	6. 7.

Key Performance Data to be Reviewed	1. 2. 3. 4. 5. 6. 7. 8.	9. 10. 11. 12.

Key MIS Reports to be Prepared / Reviewed	1. 2. 3. 4.

Recommended Meetings

1. Strategy Review Meeting:

Purpose:

- To review the strategy for its relevance & adequacy
- To focus on whether strategy implementation is on track
- Hold leaders accountable for strategic initiatives
- To deeply investigate the status of key strategic initiatives
- To track performance against key strategic objectives

Attendees:

- Senior Management Team
- Business Unit/Functional Heads
- Strategic Initiative Owners
- Strategy Manager

Preparation & Reports:

- Strategy Map & Updated Balanced Scorecard
- Objectives & Targets: Color coded by status and actual performance against targets
- Commentaries/short explanation for performance gap & action plan for strategic objectives and initiatives
- Report should be circulated in advance, read by all attendees and be ready for discussion

Meeting Agenda:

- Status Review
- Strategy Overview: CEO presents a review of strategy map, offering perspective on the business
  - Review Strategy Map
  - Highlight key issues
  - Review Strategic Initiatives
  - Review Key Performance Indicators
  - Accomplishments

- Action Log: Review status of actions from previous meeting and new actions & responsibilities
- Initiative Audit: Focus on one (or maximum two) strategic initiative(s) in each department
- Initiative Assessment: Quick overview from Initiative Owners of each strategic initiative
- Hot Topic: Allow for one operational or strategic 'Hot Topic' outside the initiatives
- Meeting Review: CEO summarizes the results of the meeting

2. Operational Review Meeting:

Purpose:

- To review business operations including revenue, turnover, costs, cash flow etc.
- To focus on whether operations are on track as per operational plans
- To track in operational expenses are as per budget/OPEX
- To investigate reasons for over-/under-performance

Attendees:

- Senior Management Team
- Business Unit Heads
- Functional Heads

Preparation & Reports:

- Financial reports with regard to revenue, expenses, cash flow
- Payables & Receivables
- Commentaries/short explanation for performance gap & action plans
- Report should be circulated in advance, read by all attendees and be ready for discussion

Meeting Agenda:

- Overall Business Performance Review

- Revenue & profitability based on geographies, segments, key customers for the last quarter/month
- New projects/customers/orders expected in next quarter
- Expected performance in next quarter
- Cash flow, payables & receivables
- Customer complaints/compliments
- Major hiccup/constraints in achieving performance
- Hot Topic: Allow for one operational topic outside the current operations
- Action Log: Review status of actions from previous meeting and new actions & responsibilities
- Any other topic

3. Functional Review Meeting:

(For independent functions – e.g. Procurement, HR, IT, Finance, Engineering)

Purpose:

- To review performance of a function
- To focus on whether function is contributing to business success
- To track expense & ensure expenses are within allocated budget
- To investigate reasons for over-/under-performance

Attendees:

- Functional Head
- Key employees from Function
- Business Unit Heads (desirable)
- Other Functions' Head

Preparation & Reports:

- Functional Performance based on KPIs/BSC
- Performance against Service Level Agreement (SLA) with business and/or other functions
- Expenses against Budget

- Key obstacles, hindrance, areas of corporate support
- Commentaries/short explanation for performance gap & action plans
- Report should be circulated in advance, read by all attendees and be ready for discussion

Meeting Agenda:

- Overall Functional Performance Review
- Performance against SLA
- Key improvement actions completed during last period
- Key improvement actions planned during next period
- Internal Customer Complaints
- Resource requirements
- Customer complaints/compliments
- Major hiccups/constraints in achieving performance
- Hot Topic: Allow for one functional topic outside the current review
- Action Log: Review status of actions from previous meeting and new actions & responsibilities

4. Coordination Meeting:

(For two interdependent functions within single business unit; for example, manufacturing & sales; manufacturing & procurement etc.)

Purpose:

- To improve coordination with focus on external Customer satisfaction
- To resolve coordination issues
- To investigate reasons for over-/under-performance

Attendees:

- Functional Heads
- Key employees from each Function
- Business Unit Heads (desirable)

Preparation & Reports:

- Functional Performance based on KPIs/BSC for each function
- Performance against Service Level Agreement (SLA), if exists
- External Customer complaints/feedback; business performance against customer requirements
- Key obstacles, hindrance, areas requiring attention
- Report should be circulated in advance, read by all attendees and be ready for discussion

Meeting Agenda:

- Overall Functional Performance Review for each function
- Performance against SLA
- External customer feedback, complaints
- Key areas requiring attention
- Key improvement actions planned during next period
- Resource requirements
- Hot Topic: Allow for one coordination are to be discussed in detail
- Action Log: Review status of actions from previous meeting and new actions & responsibilities

Appendix – B

Sample Strategy Maps

Template No.	Strategy Map for	Page Number
01	Corporate	234
02	Construction Industry	235
03	Educational Institution	236
04	Hotel Industry	237
05	Real Estate Industry	238
06	Institutional Sales	239
07	Retail Sales	240
08	Manufacturing Industry	241
09	Human Resource Function	242
10	IT Function	243
11	Procurement Function	244

Corporate Strategy Map

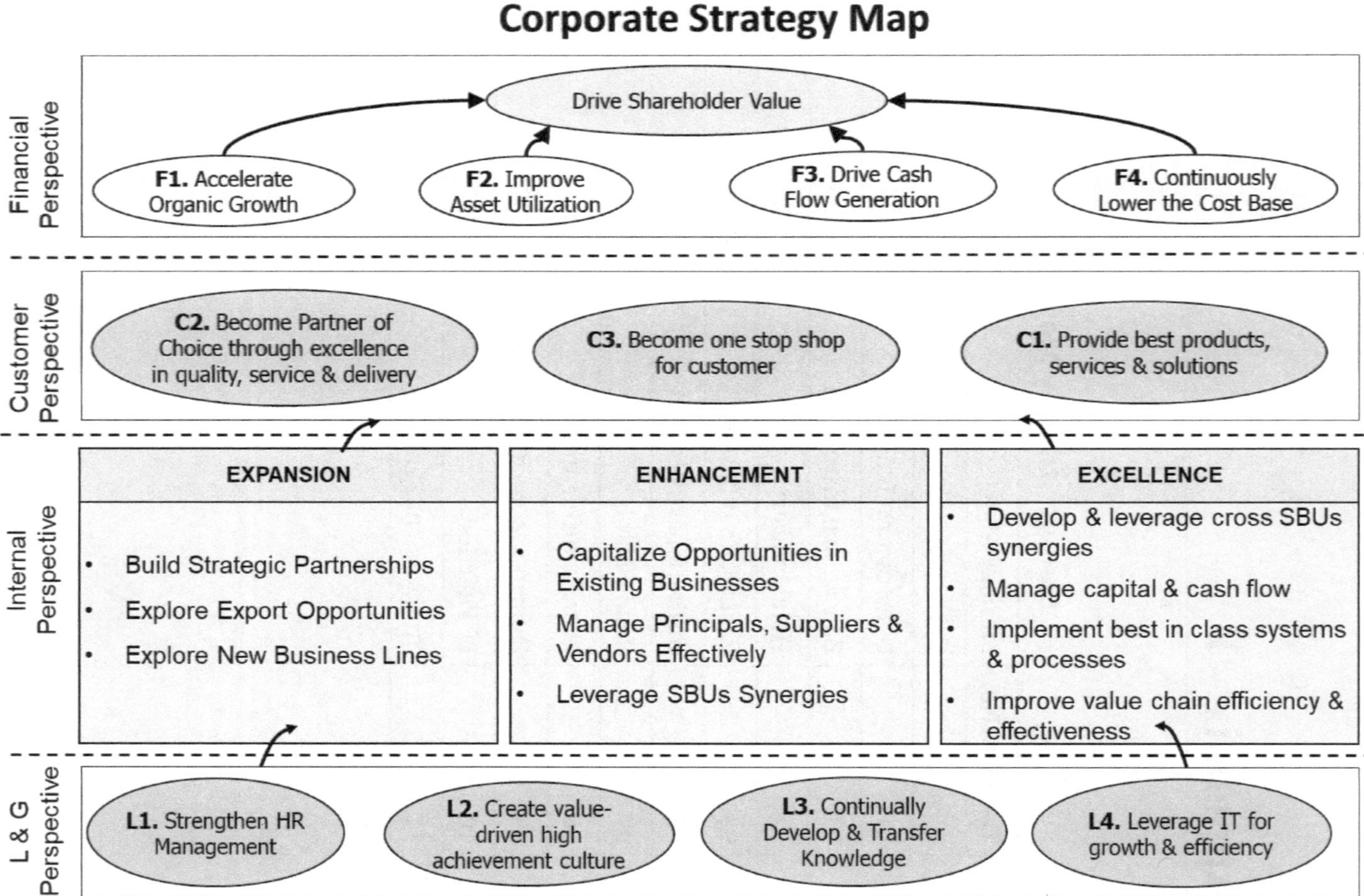

Construction Industry Strategy Map

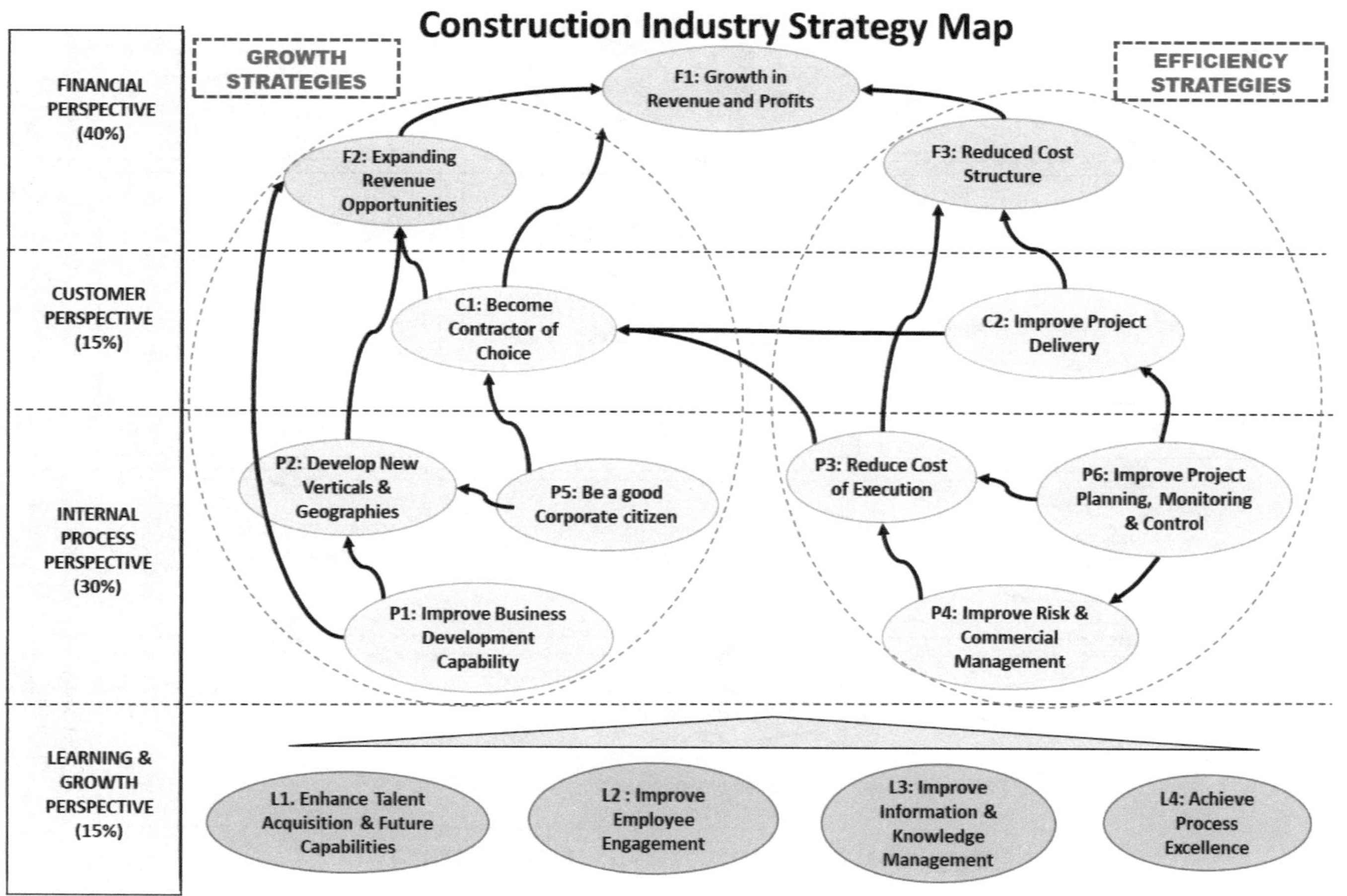

Educational Institution Strategy Map

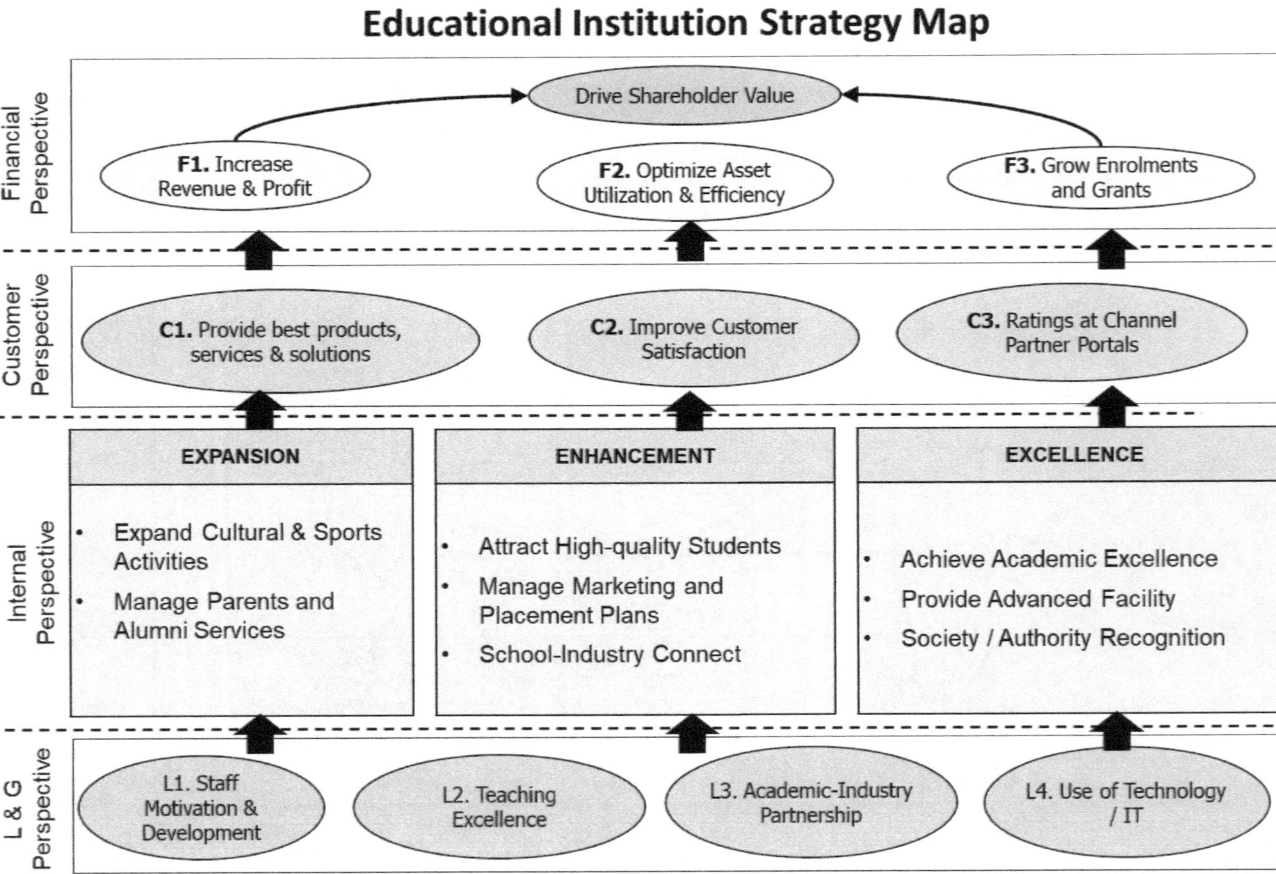

Hotel Industry Strategy Map

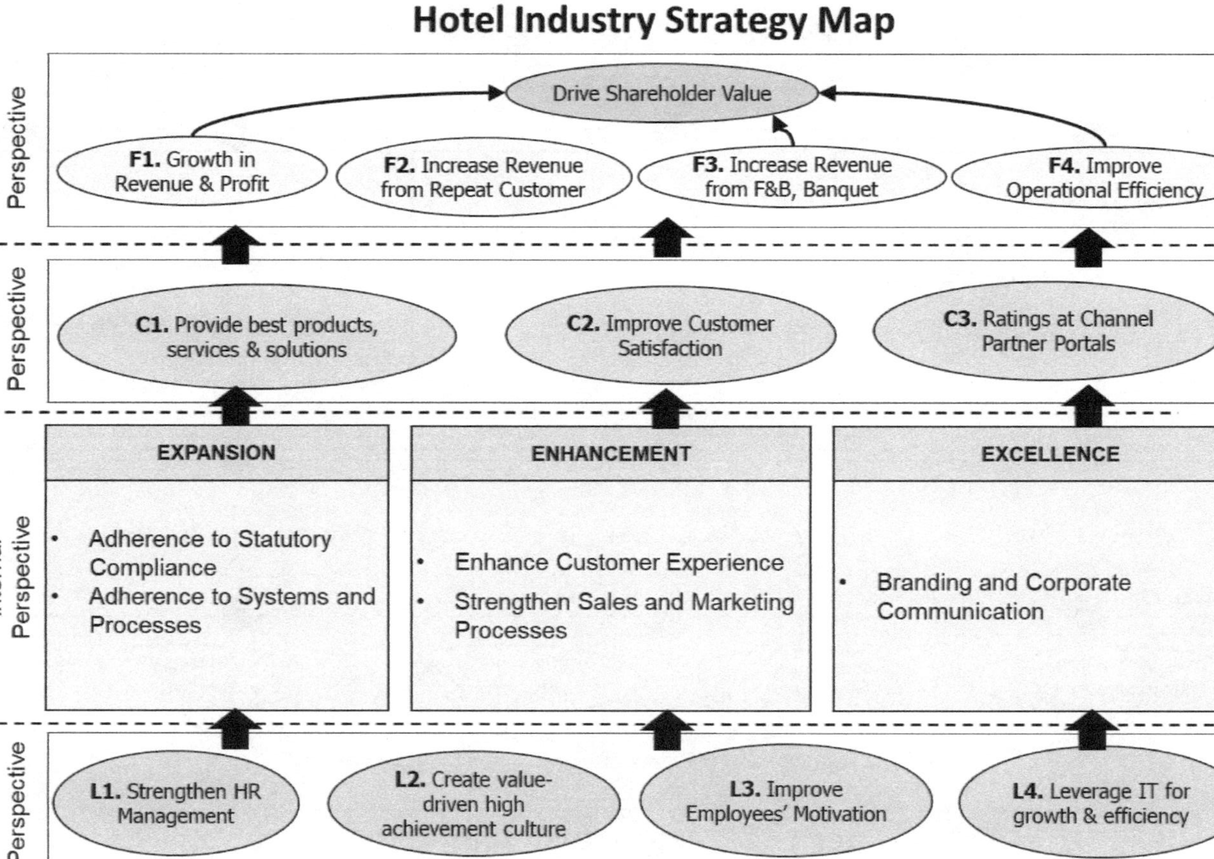

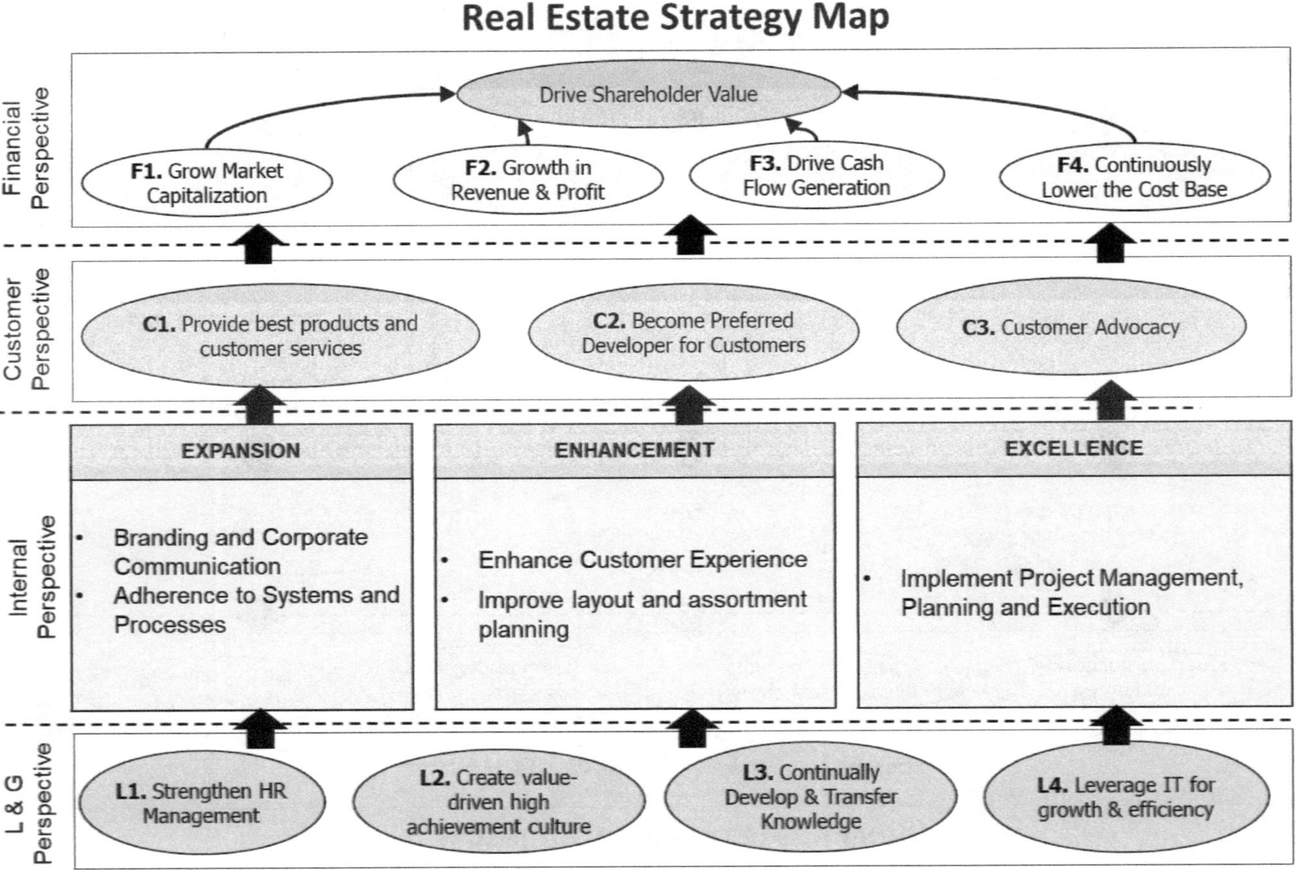

Real Estate Strategy Map

Financial Perspective
Drive Shareholder Value
F1. Grow Market Capitalization
F2. Growth in Revenue & Profit
F3. Drive Cash Flow Generation
F4. Continuously Lower the Cost Base

Customer Perspective
C1. Provide best products and customer services
C2. Become Preferred Developer for Customers
C3. Customer Advocacy

Internal Perspective
EXPANSION
Branding and Corporate Communication
Adherence to Systems and Processes
ENHANCEMENT
Enhance Customer Experience
Improve layout and assortment planning
EXCELLENCE
Implement Project Management, Planning and Execution

L & G Perspective
L1. Strengthen HR Management
L2. Create value-driven high achievement culture
L3. Continually Develop & Transfer Knowledge
L4. Leverage IT for growth & efficiency

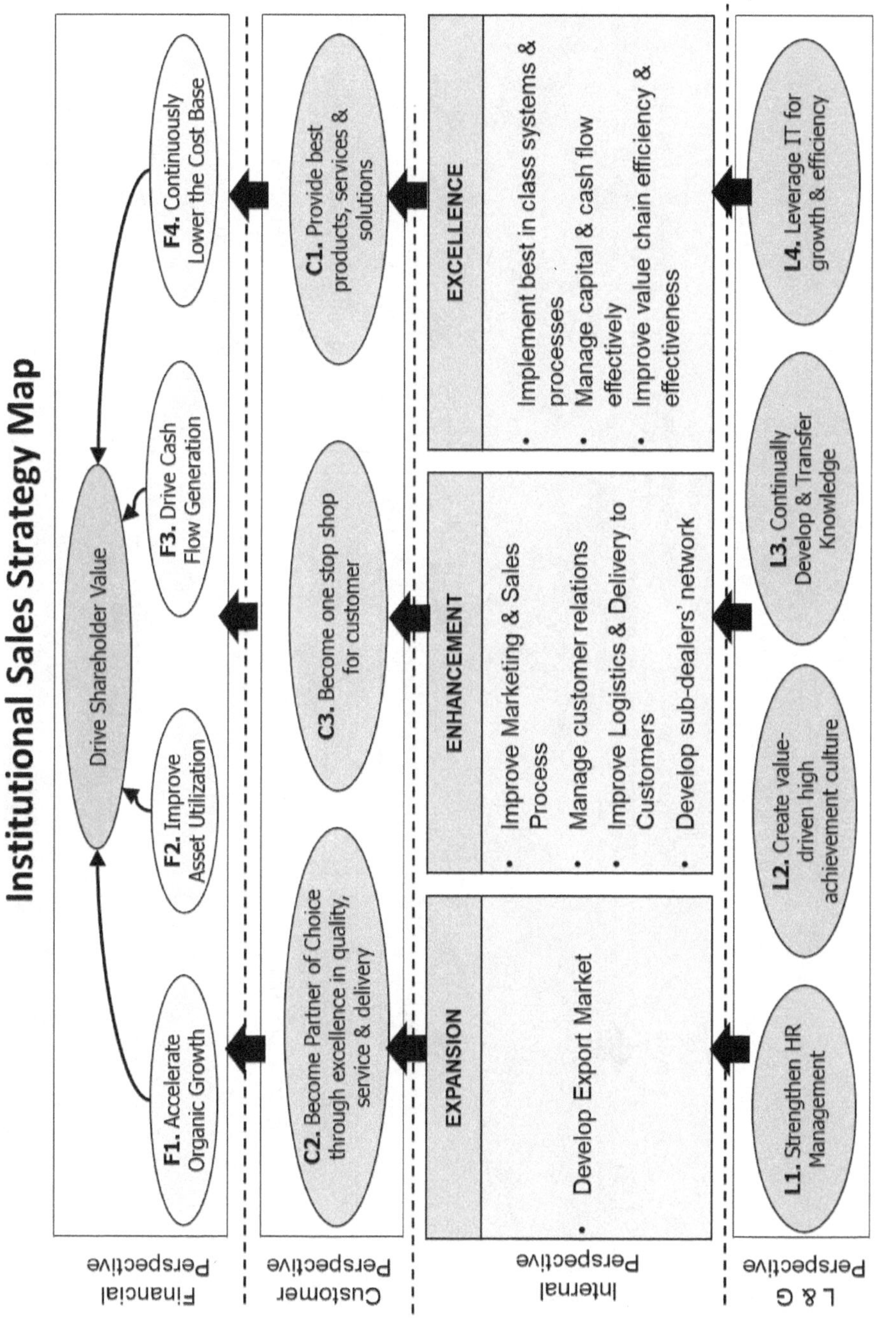

Institutional Sales Strategy Map

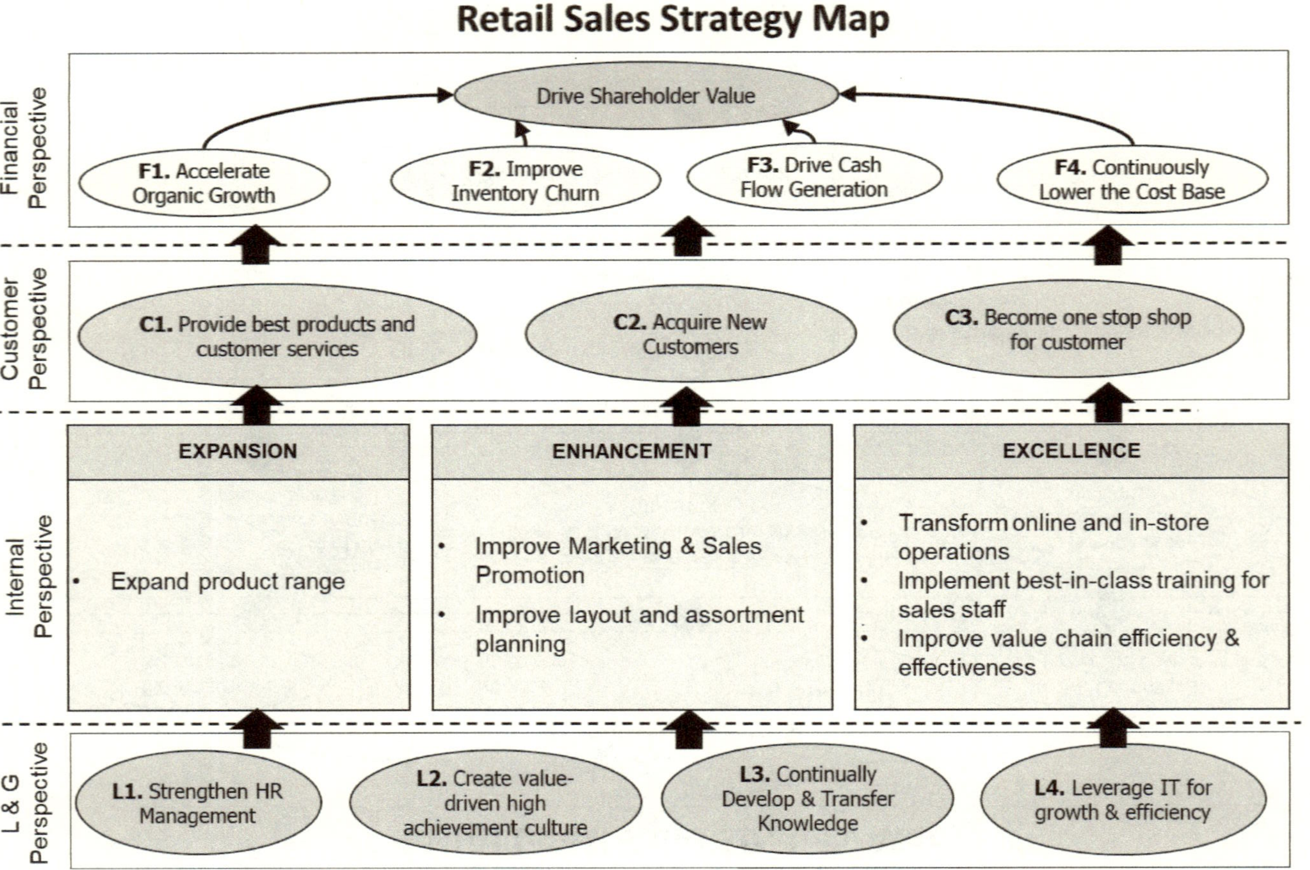

Retail Sales Strategy Map

Financial Perspective
Drive Shareholder Value
F1. Accelerate Organic Growth
F2. Improve Inventory Churn
F3. Drive Cash Flow Generation
F4. Continuously Lower the Cost Base

Customer Perspective
C1. Provide best products and customer services
C2. Acquire New Customers
C3. Become one stop shop for customer

Internal Perspective
EXPANSION
Expand product range
ENHANCEMENT
Improve Marketing & Sales Promotion
Improve layout and assortment planning
EXCELLENCE
Transform online and in-store operations
Implement best-in-class training for sales staff
Improve value chain efficiency & effectiveness

L & G Perspective
L1. Strengthen HR Management
L2. Create value-driven high achievement culture
L3. Continually Develop & Transfer Knowledge
L4. Leverage IT for growth & efficiency

Manufacturing Industry Strategy Map

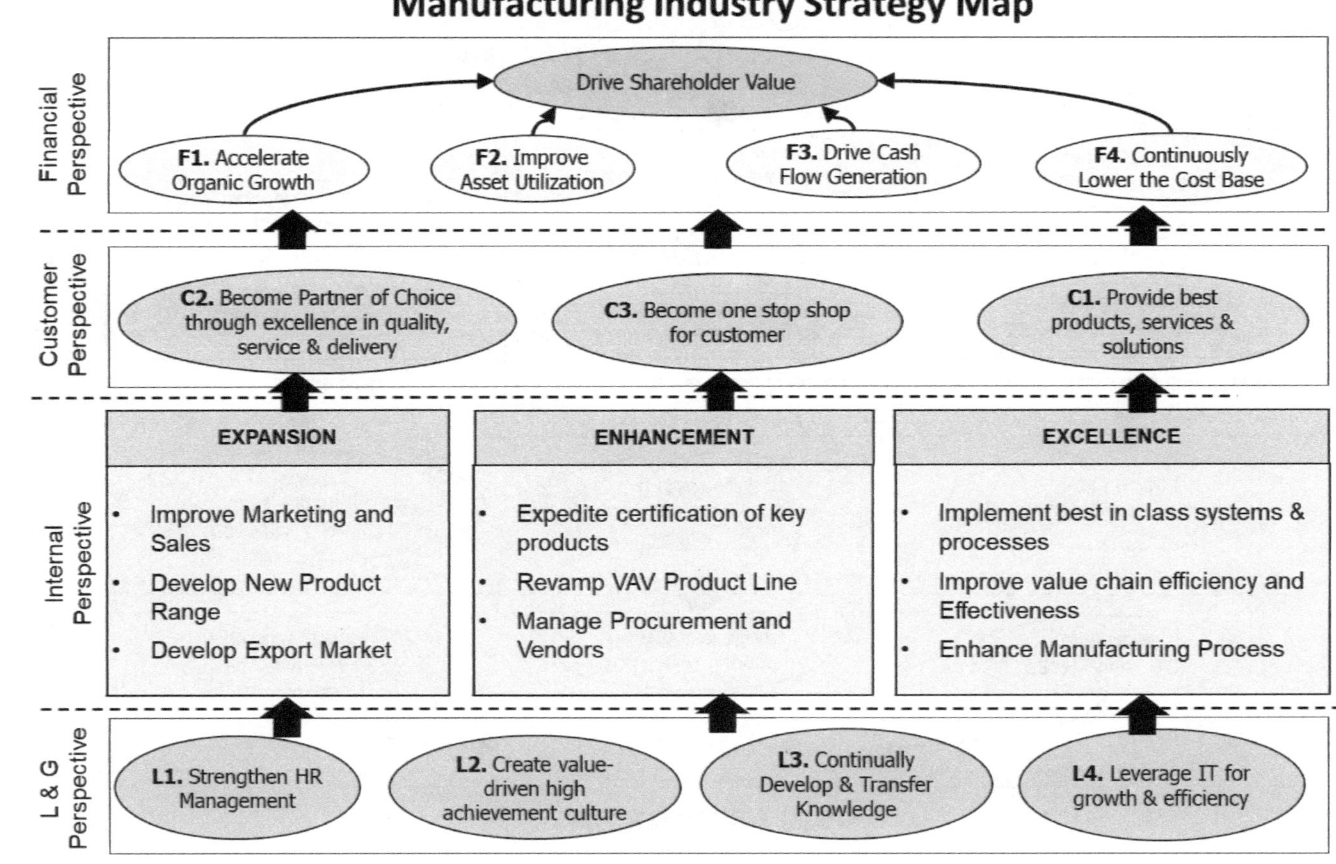

HR Strategy Map

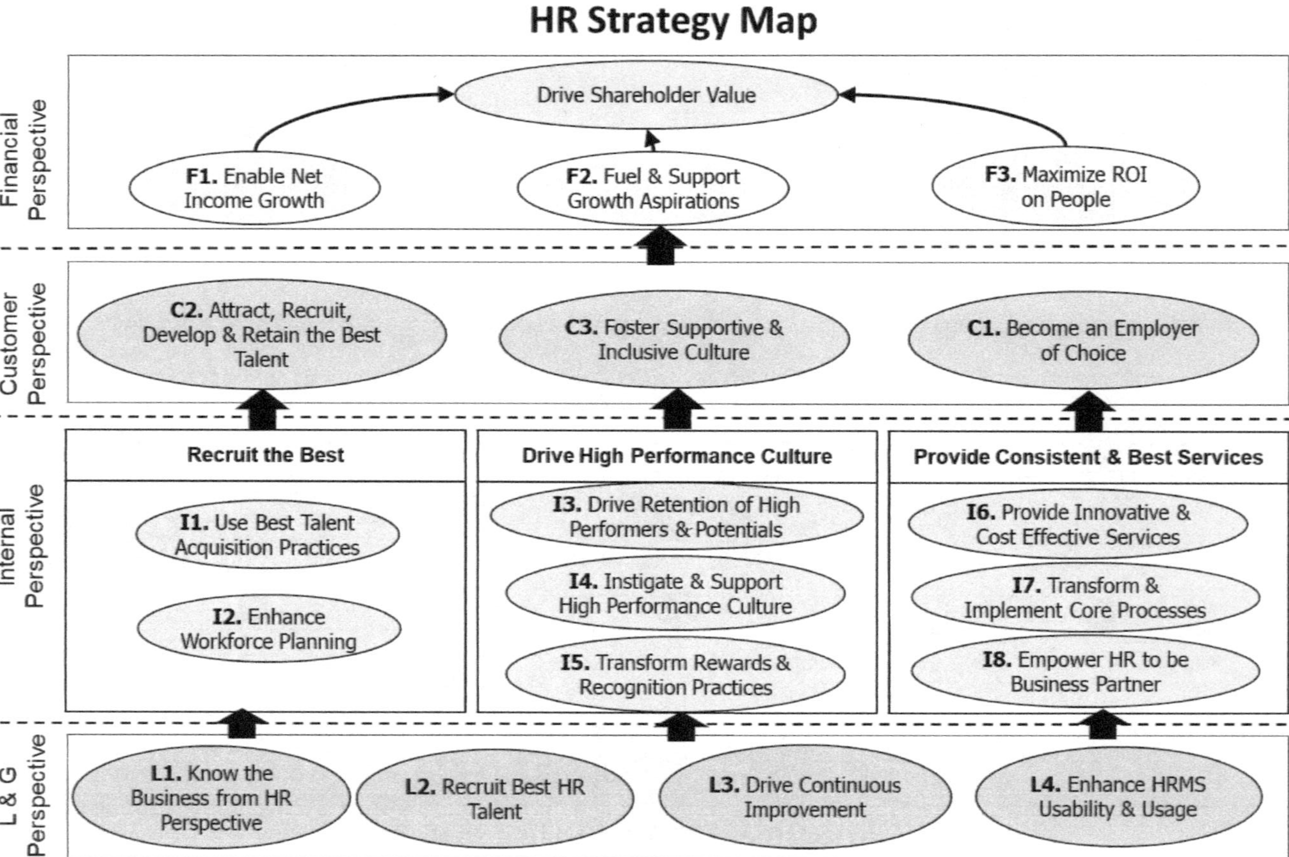

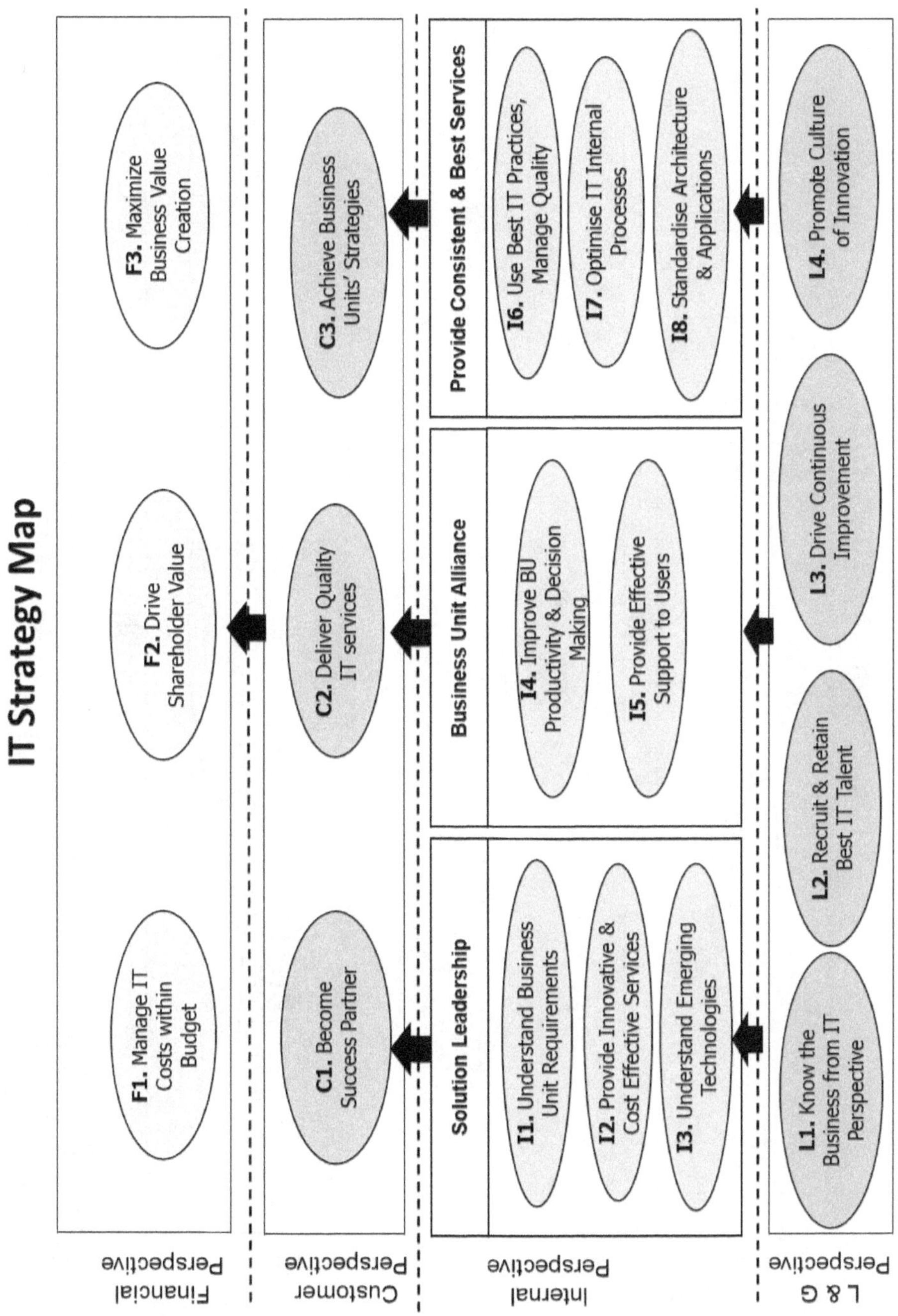
IT Strategy Map
Financial Perspective
Customer Perspective
Internal Perspective
L & G Perspective
F1. Manage IT Costs within Budget
F2. Drive Shareholder Value
F3. Maximize Business Value Creation
C1. Become Success Partner
C2. Deliver Quality IT services
C3. Achieve Business Units' Strategies
Solution Leadership
I1. Understand Business Unit Requirements
I2. Provide Innovative & Cost Effective Services
I3. Understand Emerging Technologies
Business Unit Alliance
I4. Improve BU Productivity & Decision Making
I5. Provide Effective Support to Users
Provide Consistent & Best Services
I6. Use Best IT Practices, Manage Quality
I7. Optimise IT Internal Processes
I8. Standardise Architecture & Applications
L1. Know the Business from IT Perspective
L2. Recruit & Retain Best IT Talent
L3. Drive Continuous Improvement
L4. Promote Culture of Innovation

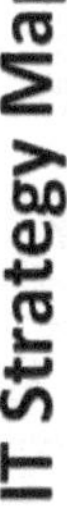

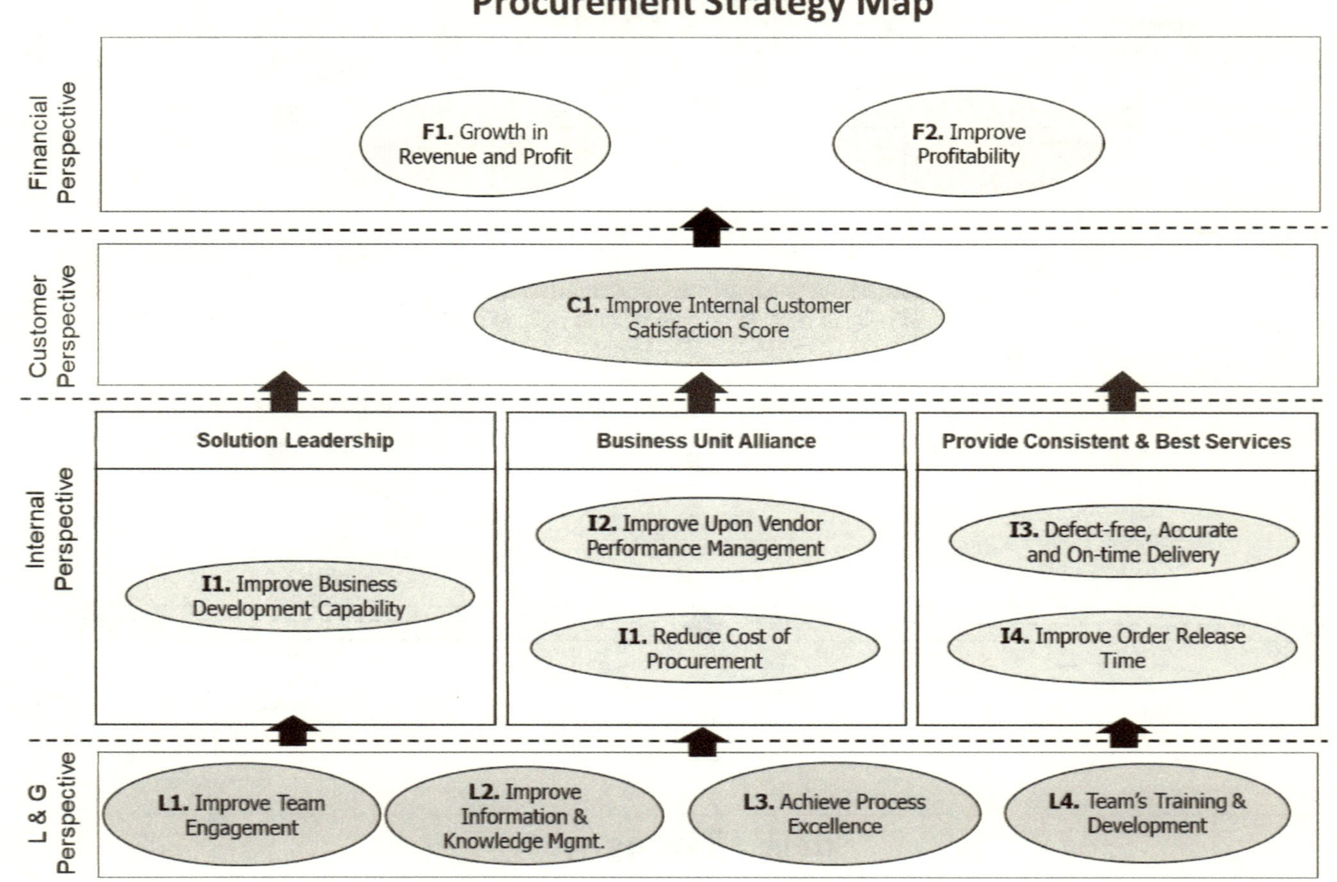

Procurement Strategy Map
Financial Perspective
F1. Growth in Revenue and Profit
F2. Improve Profitability
Customer Perspective
C1. Improve Internal Customer Satisfaction Score
Internal Perspective
Solution Leadership
I1. Improve Business Development Capability
Business Unit Alliance
I2. Improve Upon Vendor Performance Management
I1. Reduce Cost of Procurement
Provide Consistent & Best Services
I3. Defect-free, Accurate and On-time Delivery
I4. Improve Order Release Time
L & G Perspective
L1. Improve Team Engagement
L2. Improve Information & Knowledge Mgmt.
L3. Achieve Process Excellence
L4. Team's Training & Development

Appendix – C

Sample Balanced Scorecards

Template No.	Balanced Scorecard for	Page Number
01	Corporate	246
02	Construction Industry	247
03	Hotel Industry	248
04	Educational Institution	249
05	Retail Sales	250
06	Institutional Sales	251
07	Real Estate Industry	252
08	Manufacturing Industry	253
09	Human Resource Function	254
10	IT Function	255
11	Procurement Function	256

Corporate Balanced Scorecard											
Obj. Code	STRATEGIC OBJECTIVES	Wt.	Measures Code	Measure	Wt.	Unit	Final Wt.	Freq.	Target 2022	Actual 2022	Target 2030
25%	FINANCIAL PERSPECTIVE (25%)										
F1	Accelerate Organic Growth	30%	F1M1	Revenue from existing areas	70%	Rs 'Cr'	5.3%	Q			
			F1M2	Revenue from new areas (Geographies & Products)	30%	Rs 'Cr'	2.3%	Q			
F2	Improve Asset Utilization	20%	F2M1	Asset Turnover Ratio	30%	Ratio	1.5%	Q			
			F2M2	Return on Equity (%)	40%	%	2.0%	Q			
			F2M3	Inventory Turnover Ratio	30%	Ratio	1.5%	Q			
F3	Drive Cash Flow Generation	25%	F3M1	Cash Conversion Cycle	30%	Days	1.9%	Q			
			F3M2	Cash Generated from Operations	40%	Rs 'Cr'	2.5%	Q			
			F3M3	EBITDA Margin	30%	%	1.9%	Q			
F4	Continuously Lower the Cost Base	25%	F4M1	Gross Margin	30%	%	1.9%	Q			
			F4M2	Net Margin	40%	%	2.5%	Q			
			F4M3	HO Overheads as % of Revenue	30%	%	1.9%	A			
15%	CUSTOMER PERSPECTIVE (15%)										
C1	Provide Best Products, Services & Solutions	35%	C1M1	Customer Satisfaction Level	60%	Score	3.2%	H			
			C1M2	Customer Retention	40%	%	2.1%	H			
C2	Become Partner of Choice	30%	C2M1	Share of wallet from key customers	20%	%	0.9%	H			
			C2M2	Achievement of quality, service & delivery requirement	80%	%	3.6%	Q			
C3	Become one stop shop for customer	35%	C3M1	Avg. no. of SBUs successful per project	30%	Nos.	1.6%	H			
			C3M2	% revenue from cross selling (common customer)	40%	%	2.1%	Q			
			C3M3	Value of order received as % of total addressable Value through cross selling	30%	%	1.6%	Q			
40%	INTERNAL PROCESS PERSPECTIVE (40%)										
P1	Build Strategic Partnerships	10%	P1M1	No. of new strategic partnerships developed	60%	Nos.	2.4%	H			
			P1M2	% of revenues from new strategic partnerships	40%	%	1.6%	H			
P2	Manage Principals, Suppliers & Vendors effectively	10%	P2M1	Partners' Satisfaction Score	70%	Score	2.8%	H			
			P2M2	No. of partnerships lost	30%	Nos.	1.2%	H			
P3	Capitalize opportunities in existing business	10%	P3M1	Revenue from Existing areas	50%	Rs 'Cr'	2.0%	Q			
			P3M2	% of market share from estimated existing market	50%	%	2.0%	Q			
P4	Explore Export Opportunities	7%	P5M1	% revenue from export	70%	%	2.0%	Q			
			P5M2	No. of products exported	30%	Nos.	0.8%	Q			
P5	Explore New Business Lines	8%	P6M1	No. of new business lines identified & actioned	100%	Nos.	3.2%	H			
P6	Implement best in class systems & processes	20%	P7M1	Level of Systems/Process Implementation	30%	%	2.4%	Q			
			P7M2	No.of Processes reviewed & improved from total	20%	%	1.6%	Q			
			P7M3	Strategy & BSC Created & aligned to Corporate Strategy (%)	30%	%	2.4%	Q			
			P7M4	Lost work days	20%	Days	1.6%	Q			
P7	Manage capital & cash flow effectively	15%	P8M1	Net interest expenses as % of revenue	50%	%	3.0%	Q			
			P8M2	% of bank debt overdue	50%	%	3.0%	Q			
P8	Improve value chain efficiency	20%	P9M1	Direct Material Costs as % of total revenue	40%	%	3.2%	Q			
			P9M2	Direct Labor Costs as % of total revenue	40%	%	3.2%	Q			
			P9M3	Marketing & Sales costs as % of total revenue	20%	%	1.6%	Q			
20%	LEARNING & GROWTH PERSPECTIVE (20%)										
L1	Strengthen HR management	25%	L1M1	Talent acquisition as per plan	40%	%	2.00%	Q			
			L1M2	Attrition rate	20%	%	1.00%	Q			
			L1M3	Employee Satisfaction score	40%	Score	2.00%	A			
L2	Create value-driven high-achievement culture	30%	L2M1	% of employees multi-tasking	25%	%	1.50%	H			
			L2M2	% of employees having goals aligned to strategy	40%	%	2.40%	H			
			L2M3	% of employees who are high-achiever	35%	%	2.10%	H			
L3	Continually develop & transfer knowledge	25%	L3M1	No. of Knowledge documents generated	25%	Nos.	1.25%	Q			
			L3M2	No. of in-house training programs	35%	Nos.	1.75%	Q			
			L3M3	Total in-house training/best practice sharing hours	40%	Nos.	2.00%	Q			
L4	Leverage IT for Growth & Efficiency	20%	L4M1	% achievement of IT roadmap	80%	%	3.20%	H			
			L4M2	% reports that are system-generated	20%	%	0.80%	H			

	Balanced Scorecard for Electro-mechanical Contracting Company								
Obj. Code	Strategic Objective	Wt.	Measure Code	Measure	Wt.	Unit	Final Wt.	Freq.	Target	Actual
40%	FINANCIAL PERSPECTIVE (40%)									
F1	Growth in Revenue and Profits	60%	F1M1	Turnover	40%	Rs 'Cr'	9.6%	M		
			F1M2	Divisional Contribution	30%	Rs 'Cr'	7.2%	Q		
			F1M3	Cash generation from operations	30%	Rs 'Cr'	7.2%	Q		
F2	Expanding Revenue Opportunities	20%	F2M1	Order Booking from Existing Business Areas	50%	Rs 'Cr'	4.0%	M		
			F2M2	Order Booking from New Business Areas	50%	Rs 'Cr'	4.0%	M		
F3	Reduced Cost Structure	20%	F3M1	Overheads to Turnover Ratio	55%	%	4.4%	Q		
			F3M2	Staff (except labour) Cost to Turnover Ratio	45%	%	3.6%	Q		
15%	CUSTOMER PERSPECTIVE (15%)									
C1	Become Contractor of Choice	35%	C1M1	Share from Key Accounts' MEP contract awards (value)	50%	%	2.6%	Q		
			C1M2	Customer Satisfaction Index - Execution stage	50%	Index	2.6%	A		
C2	Improve Project Delivery	65%	C2M1	% of Project Work certified vs. planned (cummulative as on date)	60%	%	5.9%	M		
			C2M2	% of total manpower resources mobilized as per schedule	40%	%	3.9%	M		
30%	INTERNAL PROCESS PERSPECTIVE (30%)									
P1	Improve Business Development Capability	10%	P1M1	Order Hit Ratio (Based on value) for existing Business Areas	100%	%	3.0%	Q		
P2	Develop New Verticals & Geographies	15%	P2M1	Order Hit Ratio (Based on value) for New Geographies	50%	%	2.3%	Q		
			P2M2	Order Hit Ratio (Based on value) for New Verticals	50%	%	2.3%	Q		
P3	Reduce Cost of Execution	40%	P3M1	Actual Manhours as a percentage of budgeted manhours	40%	%	4.8%	M		
			P3M2	Actual Material Cost as a percentage of budgeted Material Cost	30%	%	3.6%	M		
			P3M3	Surplus Material Value for completed projects (at PAC) as % of Total Material Cost of the Project	15%	%	1.8%	A		
			P3M4	Savings on design & engineering costs for existing projects on account of Centralized Team	15%	%	1.8%	Q		
P4	Improve Risk & Commercial Management	20%	P4M1	Percentage of Variation (in value) considered for realisation which has been approved or	45%	%	2.7%	Q		
			P4M2	Percentage of outstanding claims & variations (i.e. realisable value) certified between PAC & six months beyond expiry of Defect Liability Period	15%	%	0.9%	Q		
			P4M3	Certified payments contractually due, outstanding for over 3 months	20%	Rs 'Cr'	1.2%	Q		
			P4M4	Difference Between Revenue Recognized in C&P Statement and Actual Payments Certified	20%	Rs 'Cr'	1.2%	Q		
P5	Be a Good Corporate Citizen	8%	P5M1	Safety Performance Index	50%	%	1.2%	Q		
			P5M2	Achievement of Sustainability Scorecard	50%	%	1.2%	Q		
P6	Improve Project Planning, Monitoring & Control	7%	P6M1	% of Projects using Primavera with More than 60% utility	100%	%	2.1%	Q		
15%	LEARNING & GROWTH PERSPECTIVE (15%)									
L1	Enhance Talent Acquisition & capabilities	50%	L1M1	HR Readiness Index	50%	%	3.8%	Q		
			L1M2	Attrition Rate	20%	%	1.5%	Q		
			L1M2	Achievement of Succession Plans	30%	%	2.3%	Q		
L2	Improve Employee Engagement	15%	L2M1	Employee Engagement Score	100%	Score	2.3%	A		
L3	Improve Information & Knowledge Management	20%	L3M1	IT Readiness Index	50%	%	1.5%	Q		
			L3M2	Knowledge Management Index	50%	%	1.5%	Q		
L4	Achieve Process Excellence	15%	L4M1	Excellence Score in Combined Internal Assessment	100%	Score	2.3%	A		

				Hotel Industry Balanced Scorecard						
Obj. Code	Strategic Objective	Wt.	Measure Code	Measure	Wt.	Unit	Final Wt.	Freq.	Target 2022	Actual 2022
25%				*FINANCIAL PERSPECTIVE (35%)*						
F1	Growth in Revenue and Profit	30%	F1M1	Growth in Revenue	50%	%	3.8%	M		
			F1M2	Gross Margin	25%	%	1.88%	Q		
			F1M3	Net Profit	25%	%	1.88%	Q		
F2	Increase Revenue from Repeat Customers	20%	F1M1	Revenue from repeat guests	50%	Rs.	2.5%	M		
			F1M2	Revenue growth from repeat guests	50%	%	2.5%	M		
F3	Increase Revenue from F&B, conference and banquet facilities	30%	F3M1	Revenue from private functions	50%	%	3.8%	M		
			F3M2	Revenue from F&B of non-guest	50%	%	3.8%	M		
F4	Improve Operational Efficiency	20%	F4M1	Operating cost as % of total cost	50%	%	2.5%	Q		
			F4M2	Operating cost as % of total revenue	50%	%	2.5%	Q		
20%				*CUSTOMER PERSPECTIVE (15%)*						
C1	Provide best products, services & solutions	30%	C1M1	Overall Customer Satisfaction Index	50%	Index	3.0%	H		
			C1M2	No. of customer complaints	50%	Nos.	3.0%	M		
C2	Improve Customer Satisfaction	50%	C3M1	Customer Satisfaction score of guests	40%	Score	4.0%	H		
			C3M2	Customer Satisfaction score for banquet & conference facilities	30%	Score	3.0%	H		
			C3M3	Customer Satisfaction score of F&B outlets	30%	Score	3.0%	H		
C3	Ratings at Channel Partner Portals	20%	C4M1	Average rating at cahnnel partners' portal	100%	Rating	4.0%	Q		
35%				*INTERNAL PROCESS PERSPECTIVE (35%)*						
P1	Adherence to Statutory Complaince	20%	P1M1	Compliance Index	50%	Index	3.5%	Q		
			P1M2	No. of non-comliance notices	50%	Nos.	3.5%	Q		
P2	Adherence to Systems and Processes	15%	P2M1	Adherence to processes	60%	%	3.2%	Q		
			P2M2	Adherence to Health, Safety & environment requirements	40%	%	2.1%	Q		
P3	Enhance Customer Experience	25%	P3M1	Adherence to promotional & marketing plans	30%	%	2.6%	Q		
			P3M2	Units sold at desired price	30%	%	2.6%	Q		
			P3M3	Enquiry to conversion ratio	20%	%	1.8%	Q		
			P3M4	Average Occcpancy	20%	%	1.8%	Q		
P4	Branding and Corporate Communication	20%	P4M1	Participation in trade fares	40%	Nos.	2.8%	Q		
			P4M2	Corporate communication initiatives	30%	Nos.	2.1%	Q		
			P4M3	Brand building initiatives	30%	Nos.	2.1%	Q		
P5	Strengthen Sales and Marketing Processes	20%	P5M1	Revamp sales & marketing sytems	30%	%	2.1%	M		
			P5M2	Sales incentive as % of total remuneration of sales team	30%	%	2.1%	M		
			P5M3	Revenue per sales person	40%	Rs.	2.8%	M		
20%				*LEARNING & GROWTH PERSPECTIVE (15%)*						
L1	Strengthen HR Management	30%	L1M1	Employee satisfaction or engagement Index	50%	Index	3.0%	H		
			L1M2	Attrition rate	25%	Ratio	1.5%	Q		
			L1M3	Key positions vacant for more than 30 days	25%	Nos.	1.5%	M		
L2	Create Value-Driven High Performance Culture	25%	L2M1	Average training mandays / employee	50%	Mandays	2.5%	Q		
			L2M2	Traning effectiveness score	50%	Score	2.5%	Q		
L3	Improve Employee Motivation	30%	L3M1	Number of rewards and recognitions schemes implemented	40%	Nos.	2.4%	Q		
			L3M2	% of emplioyees rewarded	60%	%	3.6%	Q		
L4	Leverage IT for Growth & Efficiency	15%	L4M1	Adherence to IT roadmap	50%	%	1.5%			
			L4M2	IT Internal Satisfaction Survey Index	50%	Index	1.5%	H		

Obj. Code	Strategic Objective	Wt.	Measure Code	Measure	Wt.	Unit	Final Wt.	Freq.	Target 2022-23
				Educational Institution Balanced Scorecard					
20%				*FINANCIAL PERSPECTIVE (20%)*					
F1	Increse Revenue & Profit	30%	F1M1	Revenue	50%	Rs.	3.0%		
			F1M2	Net Profit	50%	Rs.	3.0%		
F2	Oprimize Asset Utilization and efficiency	30%	F2M1	Cost per student	50%	%	3.0%		
			F2M1	Operating Expenses as % of Revenue	50%	%	3.0%		
F3	Grow Enrolments & Grants	40%	F3M1	Revenue from new enrolments	30%	Rs.	2.4%		
			F3M2	No. of new enrolements	30%	Nos.	2.4%		
			F3M3	Annual grants and permanent endowment	40%	Nos	3.2%		
20%				*STAKEHOLDER PERSPECTIVE (20%)*					
C1	Satisfied Parents / Guardians	50%	C1M1	Parents / Guardians Satisfaction Survey Index	30%	Index	3.0%		
			C1M2	Student Satisfaction Suvey Index	30%	Index	3.0%		
			C1M3	Graduate Student Placement / Enrolement for higher studies	40%	%	4.0%		
C2	Improve Parents / Guardians Relationships	50%	C2M1	% of parents Indicated ABC School as their first choice	40%	%	4.0%		
			C2M2	Parents Advocacy Level	30%	%	3.0%		
			C2M3	Student Retention Ratio	30%	%	3.0%		
40%				*INTERNAL PROCESS PERSPECTIVE (40%)*					
P1	Achieve Academic Excellence	25%	P1M1	No. of new couses, programs & curriculum launched and implemented	25%	%	2.5%		
			P1M2	Distribution of Grades Awarded (% students in top 2)	25%	%	2.5%		
			P1M3	Exit Exam or student competency evaluation Scores	25%	Score	2.5%		
			P1M4	Number of unique programs offered	25%	Nos.	2.5%		
P2	Provide Advanced Facility	15%	P2M1	% of infrastructure facilities created vs. required	50%	%	3.0%		
			P2M2	% Facilities available for identified special needs	25%	%	1.5%		
			P2M3	Parents / Students satisfaction with facilities	25%	%	1.5%		
P3	Attract High-quality Students	10%	P3M1	% of students with 65% marks in previous class	50%	%	2.0%		
			P3M2	Average score in school admission assessment	50%	Score	2.0%		
P4	Expand Cultural & Sports Activities	10%	P4M1	No. of non-academic activites/events held	50%	Nos.	2.0%		
			P4M2	No. of sports activities offered	50%	Nos.	2.0%		
P5	Manage Parent & Alumni Services	10%	P5M1	% of Alumni tracked & database created	40%	%	1.6%		
			P5M2	No. of alumani events and connect programs	30%	Nos.	1.2%		
			P5M3	No. of parents-teacher meeting	30%	Nos.	1.2%		
P6	School-Industry Connect	15%	P6M1	No. of internships available	30%	Nos.	1.8%		
			P6M2	No. of Industry Visits	20%	Nos.	1.2%		
			P6M3	No. of industry-campus partnerships	30%	Nos.	1.8%		
			P6M4	No. of entrepreneurial initiatives	20%	Nos.	1.2%		
P7	Manage Marketing & Placement Plans	10%	P7M1	School's standing in local /international ranking table	50%	Score	2.0%		
			P7M2	Applicants vs. seats ratio	50%	Ratio	2.0%		
P8	Society / Authority Recognition	5%	P8M1	No. of External Certification / Accreditation / Recognition	100%	Nos.	2.0%		
20%				*INNOVATION, LEARNING AND GROWTH PERSPECTIVE (20%)*					
L1	Staff Motivation and Development	30%	L1M1	Staff Competency Matching Ratio	30%	%	1.8%		
			L1M2	% of budget spent on staff development	30%	%	1.8%		
			L1M3	No. of cross-trained or multi-skilled staff	20%	Nos.	1.2%		
			L1M4	Staff satisfaction or engagement index	20%	Index	1.2%		
L2	Teaching Excellence	30%	L2M1	No. of teaching workshops attended by faculty	30%	Nos.	1.8%		
			L2M2	No. of teaching innovation projects	30%	Nos.	1.8%		
			L2M3	No. of curriculums revised & new curriculums offered in last 5 years	40%	Nos.	2.4%		
L3	Academia-Industry Parnership	25%	L3M1	No. of companies involved	30%	Nos.	1.5%		
			L3M2	No. of joint activities	30%	Nos.	1.5%		
			L3M3	% of students covered / involved	40%	%	2.0%		
L4	Use of Technology / IT	15%	L4M1	No. of courses incorporating latest technology	50%	Nos.	1.5%		
			L4M2	IT Readiness Index	50%	Score	1.5%		

* This scoecard is generic and need to be customized depending on the school type and curriculum offered.

				Retail Sales Balanced Scorecard						
Obj. Code	Strategic Objective	Wt.	Measure Code	Measure	Wt.	Unit	Final Wt.	Freq.	Target 2022	Actual 2022
30%				**FINANCIAL PERSPECTIVE (35%)**						
F1	Accelerate Organic Growth	50%	F1M1	Revenue from existing areas (Geographies & Product Line)	55%	Rs.	8.3%	M		
			F1M2	Revenue from new areas (New Geographies & Product Line)	20%	Rs.	3.0%	M		
			F1M3	Same Store / Region sales growth	25%	%	3.8%	M		
F2	Improve Inventory Churn	10%	F2M1	Inventory Turnover Ratio	100%	Ratio	3.0%	Q		
F3	Drive Cash Flow Generation	20%	F3M1	Cash Conversion Cycle	55%	Ratio	3.3%	Q		
			F3M2	Cash Flow from Operations	45%	Rs.	2.7%	M		
F4	Continuously Lower the Cost Base	20%	F4M1	Gross Margin	50%	%	3.0%	Q		
			F4M2	Net Margin	50%	%	3.0%	Q		
20%				**CUSTOMER PERSPECTIVE (15%)**						
C1	Provide best products, services & solutions	30%	C1M1	Customer Satisfaction Level (scale 1-5)	100%	Index	6.0%	H		
C2	New customer acquisition	40%	C2M1	New customer acquisition	100%	%	8.0%	Q		
C3	Become one stop shop for customer	30%	C3M1	Average no. of product-range sold per customer	100%	Nos.	6.0%	Q		
35%				**INTERNAL PROCESS PERSPECTIVE (35%)**						
P1	Expand Product Range	20%	P1M1	New categories launched	50%	Nos.	3.5%	Q		
			P1M2	New brands added to same category	50%	Nos.	3.5%	Q		
P2	Improve Marketing & Promotion	10%	P2M1	Promotions effectiveness (foot fall)	60%	%	2.1%	Q		
			P2M2	Number of promotions	40%	Nos.	1.4%	Q		
P3	Improve Layout and Assortment Planning	20%	P3M1	Sales per square foot	50%	Rs.	3.5%	M		
			P3M2	Average transaction value	50%	Rs.	3.5%	M		
P4	Transform Online & In-store Operations	20%	P4M1	Conversion rate	40%	%	2.8%	Q		
			P4M2	Foot traffic	30%	Nos.	2.1%	M		
			P4M3	Digital traffic	30%	Nos.	2.1%	M		
P5	Implement Best in Class Training for sales staff	20%	P5M1	Sales per employee	50%	Rs.	3.5%	Q		
			P5M2	Customer retention rate	50%	%	3.5%	Q		
P6	Improve Value Chain Efficiency & Effectiveness	10%	P7M1	Inventory shrinkage	100%	%	3.5%	Q		
20%				**LEARNING & GROWTH PERSPECTIVE (15%)**						
L1	Strengthen HR Management	30%	L1M1	Employee satisfaction or engagement Index	50%	Index	3.0%	H		
			L1M2	Employee turnover ratio	25%	Ratio	1.5%	Q		
			L1M3	Key positions vacant for more than 30 days	25%	Nos.	1.5%	M		
L2	Create Value-Driven High Performance Culture	25%	L2M1	Employees achieving their targets	60%	%	3.0%	Q		
			L2M2	Average training mandays / employee	40%	Days	2.0%	Q		
L3	Continually Develop & Transfer Knowledge	30%	L3M1	Knowledge Documents developed and Shared	25%	Nos.	1.5%	Q		
			L3M2	Internal Training Programs Organized	30%	Nos.	1.8%	Q		
			L3M2	Cross visits between stores / regions	45%	Nos.	2.7%	Q		
L4	Leverage IT for Growth & Efficiency	15%	L4M1	IT Internal Satisfaction Survey Index	100%	Index	3.0%	H		

Obj. Code	Strategic Objective	Wt.	Measure Code	Measure	Wt.	Unit	Final Wt.	Freq.	Target 2022	Actual 2022
Institutional Sales Balanced Scorecard										
35%	*FINANCIAL PERSPECTIVE (35%)*									
F1	Accelerate Organic Growth	50%	F1M1	Revenue from existing areas (Geographies & Product Line)	60%	Rs.	10.5%	M		
			F1M2	Revenue from Export (New Geographies)	40%	Rs.	7.0%	M		
F2	Improve Asset Utilization	10%	F2M1	Inventory Turnover Ratio	100%	Ratio	3.5%	Q		
F3	Drive Cash Flow Generation	20%	F3M1	Cash Conversion Cycle	55%	Index	3.9%	Q		
			F3M2	Cash Flow from Operations	45%	Rs.	3.2%	M		
F4	Continuously Lower the Cost Base	20%	F4M1	Gross Margin	50%	%	3.5%	M		
			F4M2	Net Margin	50%	%	3.5%	M		
15%	*CUSTOMER PERSPECTIVE (15%)*									
C1	Provide best products, services & solutions	30%	C1M1	Customer Satisfaction Level (bidding) on a scale 1-5	40%	Index	1.8%	H		
			C1M2	Customer Satisfaction Level (Post-Sales) on a scale 1-5	60%	Index	2.7%	H		
C2	Become partner of choice through excellence in quality, service & delivery	40%	C2M1	Revenue from Repeat Customers	50%	%	3.0%	Q		
			C2M2	Share of wallet from Key Accounts	50%	%	3.0%	Q		
C3	Become one stop shop for customer	30%	C3M1	Average no. of product-range sold per customer	100%	Nos.	4.5%	Q		
35%	*INTERNAL PROCESS PERSPECTIVE (35%)*									
P1	Improve Marketing & Sales Process	20%	P1M1	New prequalifications obtained	15%	Nos.	1.1%	Q		
			P1M2	New Order Booking	35%	AED	2.5%	M		
			P1M3	Order Hit Ratio (order/quotation value)	35%	%	2.5%	M		
			P1M4	Quotations from Back Office	15%	%	1.1%	M		
P2	Manage Customer Relationships Effectively	10%	P2M1	Key Accounts Identified & Developed	50%	Nos.	1.8%	Q		
			P2M2	Revenue from Key Accounts	50%	%	1.8%	Q		
P3	Improve Logistics & Delivery to Customers	15%	P3M1	On-time deliveries	50%	%	2.6%	M		
			P3M2	Accurate deliveries as per order	30%	%	1.6%	M		
			P3M3	On-time take off from factory	20%	%	1.1%	M		
P4	Develop Export Market	15%	P4M1	New countries (including Distributors) developed	70%	Nos.	3.7%	Q		
			P4M2	Revenue from export market	30%	%	1.6%	M		
P5	Implement Best in Class Systems & Processes	10%	P5M1	Processes adopted & Implemented from IBEM	50%	Nos.	1.8%	Q		
			P5M2	Adherence to SLA with manufacturing	50%	%	1.8%	Q		
P6	Manage Capital & Cash Flow Effectively	20%	P6M1	Outstanding overdue from total outstanding payments	100%	%	7.0%	M		
P7	Continuously Improve Value Chain Efficiency & Effectiveness	10%	P7M1	Sales cost to revenue ratio	100%	%	3.5%	Q		
15%	*LEARNING & GROWTH PERSPECTIVE (15%)*									
L1	Strengthen HR Management	30%	L1M1	Employee Satisfaction Survey Index	100%	Index	4.5%	H		
L2	Create Value-Driven High Performance Culture	25%	L2M1	Employees achieving their targets	100%	%	3.8%	Q		
L3	Continually Develop & Transfer Knowledge	30%	L3M1	Knowledge Documents developed and Shared	25%	Nos.	1.1%	Q		
			L3M2	Internal Training Programs Organized	30%	Nos.	1.4%	Q		
			L3M2	Cross visits between factory and sales	45%	Nos.	2.0%	Q		
L4	Leverage IT for Growth & Efficiency	15%	L4M1	IT Internal Satisfaction Survey Index	100%	Index	2.3%	H		

Real Estate Balanced Scorecard										
Obj. Code	Strategic Objective	Wt.	Measure Code	Measure	Wt.	Unit	Final Wt.	Freq.	Target 2022	Actual 2022
30%	*FINANCIAL PERSPECTIVE (35%)*									
F1	Grow Market Cap	20%	F1M1	Market Cap Value	50%	Rs.	3.0%	Q		
			F1M2	Price to Equity Ratio	50%	Ratio	3.0%	Q		
F2	Growth in Revenue and Profit	30%	F2M1	Growth in Revenue	50%	Rs.	4.5%	Q		
			F2M2	Gross Margin	25%	%	2.25%	Q		
			F2M3	Net Profit	25%	Ratio	2.25%	Q		
F3	Drive Cash Flow Generation	30%	F3M1	Debt to Equity Ratio	50%	Ratio	4.5%	Q		
			F3M2	Net Cash Flow from Operations	50%	Rs.	4.5%	Q		
F4	Continuously Lower the Cost Base	20%	F4M1	OPEX as % of Revenue	50%	%	3.0%	Q		
			F4M2	Total Expense as % of Revenue	50%	%	3.0%	Q		
20%	*CUSTOMER PERSPECTIVE (15%)*									
C1	Provide best products, services & solutions	30%	C1M1	Customer Satisfaction Index	100%	Index	6.0%	H		
C3	Become Preferred Developer for customer	50%	C3M1	Adherence to project milestones	40%	%	4.0%	Q		
			C3M2	Projects completed & delivered ontime	30%	%	3.0%	Q		
			C3M3	Project quality & performance	30%	Index	3.0%	Q		
C4	Customer Advocacy	20%	C4M1	Units sold through referrals	100%	%	4.0%	Q		
35%	*INTERNAL PROCESS PERSPECTIVE (35%)*									
P1	Adherence to Statutory Complaince	20%	P1M1	Compliance Index	50%	Nos.	3.5%	Q		
			P1M2	No. of non-comliance notices	50%	Nos.	3.5%	Q		
P2	Adherence to systems and processes	15%	P2M1	Adherence to processes	60%	%	3.2%	Q		
			P2M2	Adherence to Health, Safety & environment requirements	40%	Nos.	2.1%	Q		
P3	Enhance Customer Experience	25%	P3M1	Adherence to promotional & marketing plans	30%	Rs.	2.6%	M		
			P3M2	Units sold at desired price	30%	%	2.6%	Q		
			P3M3	Enquiry conversion ratio	20%	%	1.8%	Q		
			P3M4	Units sold against target	20%	%	1.8%	Q		
P4	Branding and Corporate Communication	20%	P4M1	Participation in trade fares	40%	%	2.8%	Q		
			P4M2	Corporate communication initiatives	30%	Nos.	2.1%	M		
			P4M3	Brand building initiatives	30%	Nos.	2.1%	M		
P5	Implement Project Management, planning and execution	20%	P5M1	Adherence to project schedule	30%	%	2.1%	M		
			P5M2	Adherence to project quality requirements	30%	%	2.1%	M		
			P5M3	Adherence to project budget	40%	%	2.8%	M		
20%	*LEARNING & GROWTH PERSPECTIVE (15%)*									
L1	Strengthen HR Management	30%	L1M1	Employee satisfaction or engagement Index	50%	Index	3.0%	H		
			L1M2	Attrition rate	25%	Ratio	1.5%	Q		
			L1M3	Key positions vacant for more than 30 days	25%	Nos.	1.5%	M		
L2	Create Value-Driven High Performance Culture	25%	L2M1	Employees achieving their targets	60%	%	3.0%	Q		
			L2M2	Average training mandays / employee	40%	Days	2.0%	Q		
L3	Continually Develop & Transfer Knowledge	30%	L3M1	Knowledge Documents developed and Shared	40%	Nos.	2.4%	Q		
			L3M2	Internal Training Programs Organized	60%	Nos.	3.6%	Q		
L4	Leverage IT for Growth & Efficiency	15%	L4M1	Adherence to IT roadmap	50%	%	1.5%			
			L4M2	IT Internal Satisfaction Survey Index	50%	Index	1.5%	H		

Balanced Scorecard for Manufacturing Business										
Obj. Code	Strategic Objective	Wt.	Measure Code	Measure	Wt.	Unit	Final Wt.	Freq.	Target 2014	Actual 2014
30%	*FINANCIAL PERSPECTIVE (35%)*									
F1	Accelerate Organic Growth	50%	F1M1	Revenue from existing areas (Geographies & Product Line)	60%	QR (M)	9.0%	M		
			F1M2	Revenue from Export (New Geographies)	40%	QR (M)	6.0%	Q		
F2	Improve Asset Utilization	10%	F2M1	Asset Turnover Ratio	50%	Ratio	1.5%	Q		
			F2M2	Inventory Turnover Ratio	50%	Ratio	1.5%	Q		
F3	Drive Cash Flow Generation	20%	F3M1	Cash Conversion Cycle	55%	Days	3.3%	Q		
			F3M2	Cash Generated from Operations	45%	QR (M)	2.7%	M		
F4	Continuously Lower the Cost Base	20%	F4M1	Gross Margin	50%	%	3.0%	M		
			F4M2	Net Margin	50%	%	3.0%	M		
15%	*CUSTOMER PERSPECTIVE (15%)*									
C1	Provide best products, services & solutions	40%	C1M1	Customer Complaints with product quality & delivery accuracy	50%	Nos.	3.0%	Q		
			C1M2	Customer Satisfaction Level (Post-Sales) on a scale 1-5	50%	Index	3.0%	H		
C2	Become partner of choice through excellence in quality, service & delivery	20%	C2M1	ICSS Score on a scale 1-5	100%	Score	3.0%	H		
C3	Become one stop shop for customers	40%		No. of new products launched	50%	%	3.0%	Q		
			C3M1	Revenue from new products	50%	%	3.0%	Q		
35%	*INTERNAL PROCESS PERSPECTIVE (35%)*									
P1	Improve Marketing & Sales	10%	P1M1	Timely development & Availability of Product Catalogue, Product Information Guidelines	100%	%	3.5%	M		
P2	Revamp VAV Product Line	10%	P2M1	Adherence to schedule for development of VAV Heaters	50%	%	1.8%	M		
			P2M2	Tie up with International Manufacturer for VAV	50%	%	1.8%	M		
P3	Expedite Certification for Key Products	10%	P3M1	No. of products certified by external bodies by due date	100%	Nos.	3.5%	M		
P4	Develop New Product Range	5%	P4M1	Adherence to Product Development schedule	100%	%	1.8%	M		
P5	Enhance Manufacturing Process	5%	P5M1	Value of products manufactured for stocking	50%	QR (M)	0.9%	M		
			P5M2	Adherence to Internal Production Plan	50%	%	0.9%	M		
P6	Implement Best in Class Systems & Processes	10%	P6M1	Processes adopted & Implemented from IBEM	40%	Nos.	1.4%	H		
			P6M2	Adherence to SLA with Sales	60%	%	2.1%	Q		
P7	Managing Procurement & Vendors	25%	P7M1	New Vendors Developed	20%	%	1.8%	Q		
			P7M2	Saving on Material Average Cost through efficient procurement	50%	%	4.4%	Q		
			P7M3	Average Credit Terms	30%	Days	2.6%	Q		
P8	Continuously Improve Value Chain Efficiency & Effectiveness	25%	P4M1	Material cost to Transfer Price Ratio	50%	%	4.4%	Q		
			P4M2	Labor Cost to Transfer Price Ratio	20%	%	1.8%	Q		
			P4M3	Overheads to Transfer Price Ratio	30%	QR (M)	2.6%	Q		
20%	*LEARNING & GROWTH PERSPECTIVE (15%)*									
L1	Strengthen HR Management	50%	L1M1	Employee Satisfaction Survey Index on scale 1-5	30%	%	3.00%	H		
			L1M2	Attrition Rate	30%	%	3.00%			
			L1M3	Variable pay as % of total compensation	40%	%	4.00%			
L2	Create High Performance Culture	15%	L2M1	Employees achieving productivity targets	100%	%	3.0%	Q		
L3	Continually Develop & Transfer Knowledge	20%	L3M1	Knowledge Documents developed	50%	%	2.0%	Q		
			L3M2	Internal Training Programs Organized	50%	%	2.0%	Q		
L4	Leverage IT for Growth & Efficiency	15%	L4M1	IT Internal Satisfaction Survey Index on scale 1-5	100%	Score	3.0%	H		

	Human Resource Function Balanced Scorecard									
Obj. Code	Strategic Objective	Wt	Measure	Wt	Measure Code	Unit	Freq.	Final Wt.	Target 2022	Actual 2022
10%	**FINANCIAL PERSPECTIVE (10%)**									
F1	Growth in Revenue	100%	Adherence to the HR & Admin. Staff Budget Cost	100%	F1M1	%	M	10.0%		
20%	**CUSTOMER PERSPECTIVE (20%)**									
C1	Satisfied Internal Customers	30%	HR ICSS Score	100%	C1M1	Index	H	6.0%		
C2	Ontime Resource Mobilisation	70%	% of total manpower resources mobilized including redeployment as per schedule	40%	C2M1	%	M	5.6%		
			% of total manpower resources demobilised as per schedule	35%	C2M2	%	M	4.9%		
			In consultation with the RD, demobilize the bottom / D rated 20% employees	25%	C2M3	%	H	3.5%		
50%	**INTERNAL PROCESS PERSPECTIVE (50%)**									
P1	Provide Efficient HR Delivery	10%	Achievement of SLA between HR & Business Unit regarding Talent Planning and Acquisition	100%	P1M1	%	Q	5.0%		
P2	Career Planning & Development	20%	% of critical positions for which successors are identified and IDP's developed	40%	P2M1	%	M	4.0%		
			% of Must Keep Managers covered under career planning and IDPs developed	40%	P2M2	%	M	4.0%		
			% of workmen promoted through potential assessment tests	20%	P2M4	%	Q	2.0%		
P3	Talent Acquisition	20%	Average lead time for mobilisation of Staff	60%	P3M1	days	M	6.0%		
			Average lead time for mobilisation of workmen	40%	P3M2	days	Q	4.0%		
P4	Employee Engagement	25%	Employee Engagement Score	30%	P4M1	Score	M	3.8%		
			Attrition Rate - Must Keep Employees	15%	P4M2	%	Q	1.9%		
			% of employees covered under employee connect program	20%	P4M3	%	Q	2.5%		
			% of employees grievances responded within 48 hours	15%	P4M5	%	M	1.9%		
			% of employees issued JD in ISO format	20%	P4M7	%	M	2.5%		
P5	Training & Development	15%	No. of trainings conducted vs. planned	40%	P5M1	%	M	3.0%		
			% of nominated employees who have completed their scheduled trainings	30%	P5M2	%	Q	2.3%		
			Training mandays per staff	30%	P5M3	days	Q	2.3%		
P6	Instigate High Performance culture	10%	No. of rewards and recognition schemes implemented	30%	P6M1	Nos.	Q	1.5%		
			% of employees receiving internal rewards and recognitions	70%	P6M2	%	Q	3.5%		
20%	**LEARNING & GROWTH (20%)**									
L1	HR Preparedness	40%	HR Readiness Index	100%	L1M1	%	Q	8.0%		
L2	IT Readiness	20%	SAP HCM implementation Level	100%	L2M1	Date	Y	4.0%		
L3	Process Excellence	40%	Business Excellence Assessment Score	80%	L3M1	Score	Y	6.4%		
			No. of HR process improved and implemented	20%	L3M2	Nos.	Q	1.6%		

<table>
<tr><td colspan="11" align="center">IT Function Balanced Scorecard</td></tr>
<tr>
<td>Obj. Code</td>
<td>Strategic Objective</td>
<td>Wt</td>
<td>Measure</td>
<td>Wt</td>
<td>Measure Code</td>
<td>Unit</td>
<td>Freq.</td>
<td>Final Wt.</td>
<td>Target 2022</td>
<td>Actual 2022</td>
</tr>
<tr><td>10%</td><td colspan="10" align="center">FINANCIAL PERSPECTIVE (10%)</td></tr>
<tr><td rowspan="3">F1</td><td rowspan="3">Growth in Revenue & Profits</td><td rowspan="3">100%</td><td>IT Cost as % of Group operating expenses</td><td>30%</td><td>F1M1</td><td>%</td><td>Q</td><td>3.0%</td><td></td><td></td></tr>
<tr><td>IT cost as % of Revenue</td><td>30%</td><td>F1M2</td><td>%</td><td>Q</td><td>3.0%</td><td></td><td></td></tr>
<tr><td>Actual operating expenses as % of budget</td><td>40%</td><td>F1M3</td><td>%</td><td>Q</td><td>4.0%</td><td></td><td></td></tr>
<tr><td>20%</td><td colspan="10" align="center">CUSTOMER PERSPECTIVE (20%)</td></tr>
<tr><td>C1</td><td>Satisfied Internal Customers</td><td>30%</td><td>IT ICSS Score</td><td>100%</td><td>C1M1</td><td>Index</td><td>H</td><td>6.0%</td><td></td><td></td></tr>
<tr><td rowspan="3">C2</td><td rowspan="3">Service Quality</td><td rowspan="3">70%</td><td>Service Availability</td><td>40%</td><td>C2M1</td><td>%</td><td>M</td><td>5.6%</td><td></td><td></td></tr>
<tr><td>Resolution of problem at first contact</td><td>35%</td><td>C2M2</td><td>%</td><td>M</td><td>4.9%</td><td></td><td></td></tr>
<tr><td>Average Resolution Time</td><td>25%</td><td>C2M3</td><td>%</td><td>M</td><td>3.5%</td><td></td><td></td></tr>
<tr><td>50%</td><td colspan="10" align="center">INTERNAL PROCESS PERSPECTIVE (50%)</td></tr>
<tr><td rowspan="2">P1</td><td rowspan="2">Provide Efficient IT Services</td><td rowspan="2">20%</td><td>Achievement of SLA between IT & Business Unit</td><td>50%</td><td>P1M1</td><td>%</td><td>Q</td><td>5.0%</td><td></td><td></td></tr>
<tr><td>IT internal customer satisfaction survey index</td><td>50%</td><td>P1M2</td><td>Index</td><td>H</td><td>5.0%</td><td></td><td></td></tr>
<tr><td rowspan="3">P2</td><td rowspan="3">IT Hardware & Infrastructure</td><td rowspan="3">20%</td><td>Adherence to standardised architecture</td><td>40%</td><td>P2M1</td><td>%</td><td>M</td><td>4.0%</td><td></td><td></td></tr>
<tr><td>Adherence to IT procedures & policies</td><td>40%</td><td>P2M2</td><td>%</td><td>M</td><td>4.0%</td><td></td><td></td></tr>
<tr><td>IT Strategic Readiness Index</td><td>20%</td><td>P2M4</td><td>%</td><td>H</td><td>2.0%</td><td></td><td></td></tr>
<tr><td rowspan="2">P3</td><td rowspan="2">IT Capability Enhancement</td><td rowspan="2">20%</td><td>Projects & New Releases completed within budget</td><td>60%</td><td>P3M1</td><td>days</td><td>H</td><td>6.0%</td><td></td><td></td></tr>
<tr><td>Projects & New Releases completed on time</td><td>40%</td><td>P3M2</td><td>days</td><td>H</td><td>4.0%</td><td></td><td></td></tr>
<tr><td rowspan="5">P4</td><td rowspan="5">Cyber Security and Service Availability</td><td rowspan="5">40%</td><td>Cyber Security Rating</td><td>30%</td><td>P4M1</td><td>%</td><td>M</td><td>6.0%</td><td></td><td></td></tr>
<tr><td>Number of critical bugs</td><td>15%</td><td>P4M2</td><td>%</td><td>Q</td><td>3.00%</td><td></td><td></td></tr>
<tr><td>Number of intrusion attempt</td><td>15%</td><td>P4M3</td><td>%</td><td>Q</td><td>3.00%</td><td></td><td></td></tr>
<tr><td>Phishing test success rate</td><td>20%</td><td>P4M5</td><td>%</td><td>M</td><td>4.0%</td><td></td><td></td></tr>
<tr><td>Server Downtime</td><td>20%</td><td>P4M7</td><td>%</td><td>M</td><td>4.0%</td><td></td><td></td></tr>
<tr><td>20%</td><td colspan="10" align="center">LEARNING & GROWTH (20%)</td></tr>
<tr><td rowspan="2">L1</td><td rowspan="2">IT Preparedness</td><td rowspan="2">60%</td><td>IT Support employee per end user</td><td>50%</td><td>L1M1</td><td>%</td><td>H</td><td>6.0%</td><td></td><td></td></tr>
<tr><td>Team Attrition Rate</td><td>50%</td><td>L2M1</td><td>Date</td><td>H</td><td>6.0%</td><td></td><td></td></tr>
<tr><td rowspan="2">L2</td><td rowspan="2">Process Excellence</td><td rowspan="2">40%</td><td>Average Training mandays/employee</td><td>50%</td><td>L3M1</td><td>Score</td><td>Y</td><td>4.0%</td><td></td><td></td></tr>
<tr><td>No. of IT processes improved and implemented</td><td>50%</td><td>L3M2</td><td>Nos.</td><td>H</td><td>4.0%</td><td></td><td></td></tr>
</table>

BSC FOR PROCUREMENT FUNCTION

OBJ. CODE	STRATEGIC OBJECTIVE	Wt.	MEASURE	Wt.	UNIT	Freq.	Final Wt.	Target	Actual
35%	FINANCIAL PERSPECTIVE (40%)								
F1	Growth in Revenue & Profits	40%	Expected Gross Margin improvement due to lower input cost	100%	%	Q	14.0%		
F2	Improve Profitability	60%	Cost savings by Procurement as % against budgeted cost (Overall)	100%	%	Q	21.0%		
15%	CUSTOMER PERSPECTIVE (25%)								
C1	Improve Internal Customer Satisfaction	30%	ICSS Score	100%	Score	Y	4.5%		
40%	INTERNAL PROCESS PERSPECTIVE (25%)								
P1	Improve Business Development Capability	10%	Updating Cost folder for Costing Team on monthly basis	100%	%	M	4.0%		
P2	Reduce Cost of Procurement	15%	e-Procurement	75%	%	H	4.5%		
			No. of Live Rate Contracts (to cover 'C' Class items)	25%	Nos.	H	1.5%		
P3	Defect-free, Accurate and Ontime Delivery as per Businss Requirement	35%	'A' Class Items	30%	days	Q	4.2%		
			B' Class Items	50%	days	Q	7.0%		
			C' Class Items	20%	days	Q	2.8%		
P4	Improve Order Release Time	20%	Average PO Release Time (Repeat orders)						
			B' Class Items	60%	days	Q	4.8%		
			C' Class Items	40%	days	Q	3.2%		
P5	Improve upon Vendor Performance Management	20%	Average vendor performance/evaluation rating	50%	Score	Y	4.0%		
			Vendor Satisfaction Index	50%	Index	Y	4.0%		
10%	LEARNING & GROWTH (10%)								
L1	Improve Team Engagement	25%	Employee Engagement Score	100%	Score	Y	2.5%		
L2	Improve Information & Knowledge Management	25%	SAP Implementation & Stabilization for MM Module	100%	%	H	2.5%		
L3	Achieve Process Excellence	25%	Number of Procurement Processes Improved	50%	Nos.	Y	1.3%		
			Process Compliance	50%	%	H	1.3%		
L4	Team's Training & development	25%	Job Rotation, Country Rotation	50%	Nos.	Y	1.3%		
			Training - Functional / Behavioural / Factory Visit / Seminar	50%	days/ person	H	1.3%		

Appendix – D: Commonly Used KPIs

Measure	Perspective	Function	Definition / Formula	Unit of Measure
Debtors over 30 days / 60 days / 90 days	Financial	Financial	No. of debtors over 30 / 60 / 90 Days	Numbers
Bad debt as percentage of turnover	Financial	Financial	(Total bad debt / Turnover)X100	%
Days sales in receivables	Financial	Financial	(Accounts receivable / Total credit sales)X No. of days	Days
Debt-to-equity ratio	Financial	Financial	Total debt / Total shareholders' equity	Ratio
Revenue from new products or services	Financial	Financial	Revenue from new products or services / Total revenue	Currency
Free cash flow	Financial	Financial	Total cash generated - (OPEX + CAPEX)	Currency
Gross Profit Margin	Financial	Financial	((Revenue - COGS)/Revenue)X100	%
Operating Profit Margin	Financial	Financial	(Operating profit/Revenue)X100	%
Net Profit Margin	Financial	Financial	(Net profit/Revenues)X100	%
EBIDTA	Financial	Financial	Revenue - Expenses (excluding interest, tax, depreciation and amortisation)	Currency
Profit before tax per employee	Financial	Financial	Total profit before tax / No. of employees	Currency
Return on Investment (ROI)	Financial	Financial	((Gain from investment - cost of investment) / cost of investment)X100	%
Return on capital employed (ROCE)	Financial	Financial	(Earning before interset & tax / Total capital employed)X100	%
Return on asset (ROA)	Financial	Financial	((Net income + interest expense) /Average Asset)) X 100	%
Return on equity (ROE)	Financial	Financial	(Net income / avg. shareholder equity) X 100	%

Measure	Perspective	Function	Definition / Formula	Unit of Measure
Revenue per employee	Financial	Financial	Total revenue / Total no. of employees	Currency
Debt to equity (D/E) ratio	Financial	Financial	Total liabilities / Total equity	Ratio
Revenue / total assets	Financial	Financial	Revenue / Total assets	Ratio
Indirect expenses as % of sales	Financial	Financial	(Total indirect expenses / Total sales)X100	%
Cash Conversion Cycle (CCC)	Financial	Financial	Days inventory outstanding + Days sales outstanding - Days payable outstanding	Days
Working capital ratio	Financial	Financial	Current assets / Current liabilities	Ratio
Operating Expense Ratio (OER)	Financial	Financial	(Operating expenses / Sales revenue) X100	Ratio
CAPEX to sales ratio	Financial	Financial	(CAPEX / Net sales) X100	Ratio
Price to earning (P/E) ratio	Financial	Financial	Current price per share / Earnings per share	Ratio
Sales to selling cost ratio	Financial	Financial	Total Sales / Total expense incurred by sales department	Ratio
Customer service requests pending for more than 48 hours	Customer	Customer	(No. of service requests pending / Total no. of requests)X100	%
Complaints not resolved during the first phone call	Customer	Customer	(Complaints not resolved / Total complaints)X100	%
Average time to resolve a complaint	Customer	Customer	Total time for complaints' resolution / Total complaints	Hours or days
Customer satisfaction index	Customer	Customer	Based on survey on a scale of 1-10, 10 being the highest.	Index
Customer turnover rate	Customer	Customer	(Lost customers over a period / Total no. of customers at the end of period)X100	%

Measure	Perspective	Function	Definition / Formula	Unit of Measure
Customer engagement	Customer	Customer	Gallup's CE[11] and other surveys	Index
Average customer complaints	Customer	Customer	Total Complaints / Total number of customers	Ratio
New product development time	Internal	Innovation	Time in days or months	Days or Months
Number of registered patents	Internal	Innovation	Number of patents	Numbers
R&D expenses as % of sales	Internal	Innovation	(Total spent on R&D / Total sales)X100	%
Rework level	Internal	Manufacturing, Services	(No. of products requiring rework/No. of products inspected)X100	%
First pass yield (FPY)	Internal	Manufacturing, Service	(no. of units without defect / No. of total units passed through process)X100	%
Time to market	Internal	Manufacturing, Service	Time from design approval to availability of product/service for purchase by customer	Days or months
Process or machine downtime level	Internal	Manufacturing, Service	(Actual productive time / Planned productive time)X100	%
Percentage of successful orders or tenders	Internal	Marketing & Sales	(No. of successful orders / Total no. of offers submitted)X100	%
Average time from customer enquiry to sales team response	Internal	Marketing & Sales	Total time to respond / Total enquiries	Hours / days
Late or incomplete deliveries	Internal	Marketing & Sales	(Total late or incomplete deliveries / Total deliveries)X100	%
Market growth rate	Internal	Marketing & Sales	(Total sales this year / Total sales last year)X100	%
Market share of company	Internal	Marketing & Sales	(Company's total sales / Total size of given market)X100	%
Relative market share	Internal	Marketing & Sales	(Company's market share / Largest competitor's market share)X100	%

Measure	Perspective	Function	Definition / Formula	Unite of Measure
Page views	Internal	Marketing & Sales	Total no. of views on an internet page	Numbers
Bounce rate	Internal	Marketing & Sales	Total no. of visits viewing only one page / Total no. of visits	Ratio
Cost per lead	Internal	Marketing & Sales	Total money spent on marketing campaign / Total leads generated	Currency
Click through rate (CTR)	Internal	Marketing & Sales	(No. of Clicks / No. of Impression of an advertisement)	%
Search engine ranking	Internal	Marketing & Sales	position a particular Web page holds in the results for a specific query	Rank
Timeliness and accuracy of price quotation to key customers	Internal	Marketing & Sales	(No. of accurate & timely quotation / total quotations)X100	%
% Sales through cross selling among business units	Internal	Marketing & Sales	(Sales by other business units / Total sales of thebusiness unit)X100	%
Capacity utilisation rate	Internal	Operations	(Actual capacity / Possible capacity)X100	%
Order fulfilment cycle time (OFCT)	Internal	Operations	Average actual cycle time for order receipts to order fulfiment	Time (Hrs., days)
Inventory shrinkage rate	Internal	Operations	(Recorded inventory - Actual inventory)/ Recorded inventory	%
Project cost variance (PCV)	Internal	Operations	Scheduled project costs - Actual project costs	Currency
Project schedule variance (PSV)	Internal	Operations	Scheduled completion date - Actual completion date	Days
No. of strategic relationships with supplier with long term agreement	Internal	Procurement	No. of strategic relationships with supplier with long term agreement	Numbers
Number of stock out situation in a month for major inventory item	Internal	Procurement	No. of stock our situation	Numbers
No. of major inventory items either above maximum or below minimum level	Internal	Procurement	No. of such instances	Numbers

Measure	Perspective	Function	Definition / Formula	Unite of Measure
Equipment downtime due to failure	Internal	Production	Total downtime in a period (month)	Days or months
% Production yield	Internal	Production	(No. of product produced fit for purpose/total products produced)X100	%
Production set up, changeover time	Internal	Production	Time spent for production set up and change over	Hours or days
Unplanned vs. planned maintenance Ratio	Internal	Production	Total no. of unplanned maintenance / no. of planned maintenance	Ratio
Production cycle time	Internal	Production	Total time taken to produce / Total no. of item produced	Hours, Days
Takt Time	Internal	Production	Time available until product delivery / No. of units to be produced	Days
Lead Time	Internal	Production	Duration between the date of delivery - date of receipt of orders	Hours, Days
Order fulfilment cycle time (OFCT)	Internal	Production	Total time required for sourcing, manufacturing and delivery	Days or months
Improvement in productivity (%)	Internal	Production	((Production in current - previous period)/Production in previous period)X100	%
No. of environment voilations and complaints	Learning & Growth	CSR	Total no. of voilations and complaints	Numbers
Percentage of waste recycled	Learning & Growth	CSR	(Waste recycled / Total waste produced)X100	%
Weekly water consumption compared to weekly production	Learning & Growth	CSR	Weekly water consumption / Weekly production	Ratio
Percentage of employess involved in community activity	Learning & Growth	CSR	(No. of employees involved in community activity / Total employees)X100	%
No. of community projects in past 12 months	Learning & Growth	CSR	No. of community projects in past 12 months	Numbers
Corporate carbon footprint	Learning & Growth	Environment / CSR	Total of direct & indirect emission of green house gases (or CO_2-equivalent)	Tons

Measure	Perspective	Function	Definition / Formula	Unite of Measure
Energy consumption	Learning & Growth	Environment / CSR	Total amount of energy purchased & consumed in a period	Kilowatts
Supply chain miles	Learning & Growth	Environment / CSR	Distance between location of production and the location of final delivery	Kilometer
Waste reduction rate	Learning & Growth	Environment / CSR	(Wasted raw material in current period / wasted material in previous period)X100	%
Waste recycling rate	Learning & Growth	Environment / CSR	(Amonth of waste recycled/Total waste produced)X100	%
Product recycling rate	Learning & Growth	Environment / CSR	(Amonth of products recycled or reused/Total amounts of products sold)X100	%
No. of accidents per 100,000 hours of work	Learning & Growth	Health & Safety	No. of accidents / No. of 100K hours of work	Ratio
No. of days lost due to accident	Learning & Growth	Health & Safety	No. of lost days in a period	Numbers
No. of Lost Time Injuries in a month	Learning & Growth	Health & Safety	No. of Lost Time Injuries	Numbers
Average Response Time	Learning & Growth	Health & Safety	Total response time for all emergencies / No. of emergencies	Time (Hrs., days)
% staff trained in first aid and emergency procedures	Learning & Growth	Health & Safety	(Staff trained / Total staff)X100	%
Average Tenure of all staff	Learning & Growth	HR	Total Tenure of all employess / Total employees	Years
% employees departed within first two years of employment	Learning & Growth	HR	(No. of employees left within two years of employment / Total no. of employees)X100	%
Employee Satisfaction Score	Learning & Growth	HR	Employee Satisfaction Score	Score
% of grievances resolved on time	Learning & Growth	HR	(Grievances resolved on time / Total no. of grievances)X100	%
No. of Suggestions per employee	Learning & Growth	HR	(Total no. of suggestions / Total no. of employees)	Ratio

Measure	Perspective	Function	Definition / Formula	Unite of Measure
% of suggestions implemented	Learning & Growth	HR	(No. of suggestions implemented / Total no. of suggestions received)X100	%
No. of trained mentors	Learning & Growth	HR	No. of Mentors	Numbers
% of new employees paired with mentors	Learning & Growth	HR	(No. of new employees paired with mentees / Total new employees)X100	%
Mentoring Feedback Score	Learning & Growth	HR	Mentoring Feedback Score	Score
Employees rewards & recognition schemes	Learning & Growth	HR	No. of rewards and recognition schemes in practice	Numbers
% of employees rewarded or recognized	Learning & Growth	HR	(No. employees rewarded or recognized / Total no. of employees)X100	%
% Employees' grievances resolved ontime	Learning & Growth	HR	(Grievenaces resolved on time/Total Grievances)X100	%
Average grievance closure time	Learning & Growth	HR	Total grievance closure time / Total no. of grievances	Time (Hrs., days)
% of employees completed appraisal on time	Learning & Growth	HR	(No. of employees completed appraisal on time / Total no. of employees)X100	%
% of employees participated in satisfaction or engagement survey	Learning & Growth	HR	(No. of employees particiapted / Total no. of employees)X100	%
% of staff developed action plan within 45 days of employees survey	Learning & Growth	HR	(No. of staff developed action plan / Total no. of supervisors & managers)X100	%
Employee Attrition rate	Learning & Growth	HR	(No. of employees resigned/Total employees)X100	%
% of employees undergone compliant training	Learning & Growth	HR	(No. of new employees had compliant training / No. of new employees)X100	%
% or employees covered for training	Learning & Growth	HR	(No. of employees undergone training / Total no. of employees)X100	%
% of critical positions for which successors are identified and trained	Learning & Growth	HR	(Succession planned for no. of critical positions / No. of critical positions)X100	%

Measure	Perspective	Function	Definition / Formula	Unite of Measure
% of must-keep-managers and fast-trackers have development plan	Learning & Growth	HR	(No. of MKMs & FTs having development plan / Total no. of MKMs and FTs)X100	%
Average Training Effectiveness score from immediate supervisor	Learning & Growth	HR	Total training effectiveness score / No. of employees trained	Score
Cost of employees' training & development as % of revenue	Learning & Growth	HR	(Amount spent on training & development of employees / Company's revenue)X100	%
% training programs conducted	Learning & Growth	HR	No. of training programs conducted / No. of training programs planned	%
% of identified training needs covered in training calander	Learning & Growth	HR	No. of training needs addressed / No. of training needs identified	%
Average training quality score	Learning & Growth	HR	Total training quality score of all attendees / no. of attendees	Score
Training cost per employee	Learning & Growth	HR	Total spent on employees' training / Average no. of employees	Currency
Interviewed to shortlisted ratio	Learning & Growth	HR	No. of shortlisted candidates / No. of candidates interviewed	Ratio
Offer to acceptance ratio	Learning & Growth	HR	No. of cadidates accepted job offer / No. of candidates offered	Ratio
Offer acceptance to joined ratio	Learning & Growth	HR	No. of candidates joined / No. of candidates accepted the job offer	Ratio
First impression survey score of new joinees	Learning & Growth	HR	Survey Score	Score
Lead time of recruitment for various grades of employees / staff	Learning & Growth	HR	Time lapse (in days) between requirement identified to employees joining date	Days
Timely completion of joining formalities for new joinees	Learning & Growth	HR	(No. of new joinees whose joining formalities completed on time / Total new joinees)X100	%
% of new joinees inducted within 30 days of joining	Learning & Growth	HR	Time lapse (in days) between date of joining and date on induction	%
% of staff suggestions implemented	Learning & Growth	HR	(No. of suggestions implemented / Total no. of suggestions)X100	%

Measure	Perspective	Function	Definition / Formula	Unite of Measure
% of employees who are high performing	Learning & Growth	HR	(No. of hign performing employees / Total employees)X100	%
Induction feedback survey score	Learning & Growth	HR	Induction feedback score	Score
Number of internal promotions	Learning & Growth	HR	Numbers	Numbers
Average training days/employee	Learning & Growth	HR	Total training days / Total employees	Training days
Revenue per employee	Learning and Growth	HR	Revenue / No. of employee	Currency
Employee satisfaction Index	Learning and Growth	HR	(Total points / Total Question) X 100	Index
Employee engagement level	Learning and Growth	HR	Engaged to Disengaged Ratio	Ratio
IT expenses as percentage of total administrative expense	Learning & Growth	IT	(IT expenses / Total administrative expenses)X100	%
Number of staff innovations implemented	Learning & Growth	Innovation	No. of staff innovations implemented	Numbers

Selected Bibliography

Kaplan, Robert S. and Norton, David P. *Balanced Scorecard: Translating Strategy into Action*: Harvard Business School Press 1996.

Kaplan, Robert S. and Norton, David P. *Strategy Focused Organization: How Balanced Scorecard Companies Thrive in the New Business Environment*: Harvard Business School Press 2001.

Kaplan, Robert S. and Norton, David P. *Strategy Maps: Converting Intangible Assets into Tangible Outcomes*: Harvard Business School Press 2004.

Kaplan, Robert S. and Norton, David P. *Alignment: Using the Balanced Scorecard to Create Corporate Synergies*: Harvard Business School Press 2006.

Kaplan, Robert S. and Norton, David P. *The Execution Premium: Linking Strategy to Operations for Competitive Advantage*: Harvard Business School Press 2008.

Leinwand, P. and Mainardi, C. with Kleiner A. Strategy That Works: *How Winning Companies Close the Strategy-to-Execution Gap*: Harvard Business School Press 2016.

Porter Michael E. *Competitive Strategy: Techniques for Analyzing Industries and Competitors*: Free Press, NY 1980.

Reeves, M., Haanaes, K. and Sinha, J. *Your Strategy Needs a Strategy: How to Choose and Execute the Right Approach*: Harvard Business School Press 2015.

Lafley, A.G. and Martin, Roger L. *Playing to Win: How Strategy Really Works*: Harvard Business School Press 2013.

Morgan, M., Levitt, Raymond E. and Malek W. *Executing Your Strategy: How to break it Down & Get it Done*: Harvard Business School Press 2007.

Anand, S. *Execution Excellence: Making Strategy Work Using the Balanced Scorecard*: John Wiley & Sons 2016.

Parmenter, D. *Key Performance Indicators: Developing, Implementing and Using Winning KPIs*: John Wiley & Sons 2015.

Hoisington, Steven H. and Vaneswaran, S.A. *Implementing Strategic Change: Tools for Transforming an Organization*: Tata McGraw-Hills 2005.

Ulrich, D. and Brockbank, W. *The HR Value Proposition*: Harvard Business School Press 2005.

Becker, Brian E., Huselid, Mark A. and Ulrich D. *The HR Scorecard: Linking People, Strategy, and Performance*: Harvard Business School Press 2001.

Huselid, Mark A. Becker, Brian E., and Beatty, Richard W. *The Workforce Scorecard: Managing Human Capital to Execute Strategy*: Harvard Business School Press 2005.

Bossidy, L. and Charan, R. *Execution: The Discipline of Getting Things Done*: Crown Business Press, NY 2002

Marr, B. *Key Performance Indicators: The 75 Measures Every Manager Needs to Know*: Pearson, GB 2012

DeLong, D. and Trautman, S. *The Executive Guide to High-Impact Talent Management: Powerful Tools for Leveraging a Changing Workforce*: McGraw Hill 2011.

Conaty, B. and Charan, R. *The Talent Masters: Why Smart Leaders Put People Before Numbers*: Random House Business Books 2011.

Harrington, H. James *Streamlined Process Improvement: The Breakthrough Strategy to Reduce Costs, Improve Quality, Increase Customer Satisfaction, and Boost Profits* : McGraw-Hills 2012.

Dresner, Howard *The Performance Management Revolution: Business Results Through Insight and Action*: John Wiley & Sons 2008.

Heskett, James L., Sasser, W. Earl and Jr. Schlesinger, Leonard A. *The Service Profit Chain: How Leading Companies Link Profit and Growth to Loyalty, Satisfaction, and Value*: The Free Press 1997.

Berry, Leonard L. *Discovering the Soul of Service: The Nine Drivers of Sustainable Business Success*: The Free Press 1999.